ISBN

S0-BZT-111

DEADPOOL VS. X-FORCE. Contains material originally published in magazine form as DEADPOOL VS. X-FORCE #1-4. First printing 2014. ISBN# 978-0-7851-5437-2. Published by MARVEL WORLDWIDE, INC., a subsidiary of MARVEL ENTERTAINMENT, LLC. OFFICE OF PUBLICATION: 135 West 50th Street, New York, NY 10020. Copyright © 2014 Marvel Characters, Inc. All rights reserved. All characters featured in this issue and the distinctive names and likenesses thereof, and all related indicia are trademarks of Marvel Characters, Inc. No similarity between any of the names, characters, persons, and/or institutions in this magazine with those of any living or dead person or institution is intended, and any such similarity which may exist is purely coincidental. **Printed in Canada.** ALAN FINE, EVP - Office of the President, Marvel Worldwide, Inc. and EVP & CMO Marvel Characters B.V.; DAN BUCKLEY, Publisher & President - Print, Animation & Digital Divisions; JOE QUESADA, Chief Creative Officer; TOM BREVOORT, SVP of Publishing; DAVID BOGART, SVP of Operations & Procurement, Publishing; C.B. CEBULSKI, SVP of Creator & Content Development; DAVID GABRIEL, SVP Print, Sales & Marketing; JIM O'KEEFE, VP of Operations & Logistics; DAN CARR, Executive Director of Publishing Technology; SUSAN CRESPI, Editorial Operations Manager; ALEX MORALES, Publishing Operations Manager; STAN LEE, Chairman Emeritus. For information regarding advertising in Marvel Comics or on Marvel.com, please contact Niza Disla, Director of Marvel Partnerships, at ndisla@marvel.com. For Marvel subscription inquiries, please call 800-217-9158. **Manufactured between 9/12/2014 and 10/20/2014 by SOLISCO PRINTERS, SCOTT, QC, CANADA.**

10 9 8 7 6 5 4 3 2 1

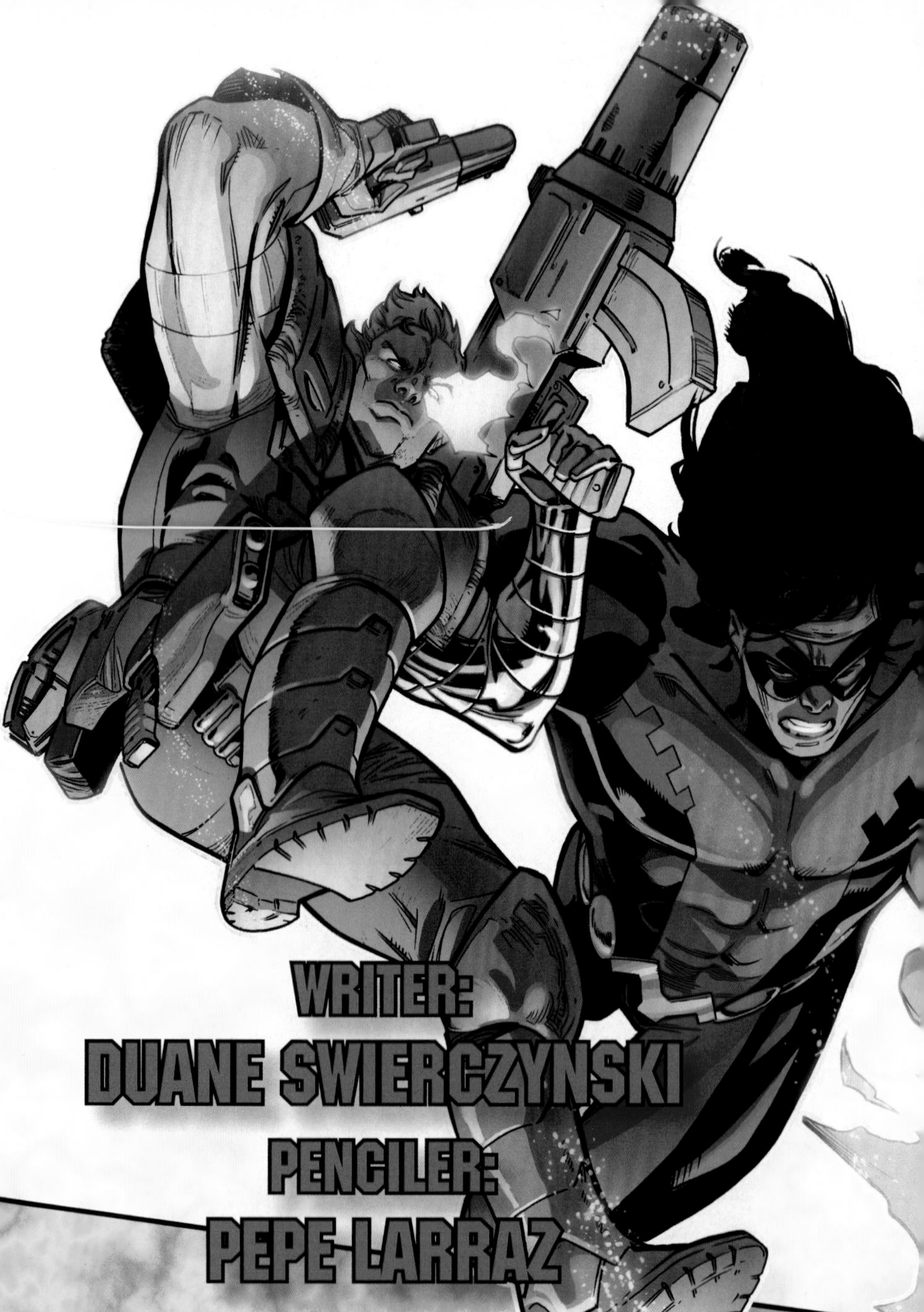

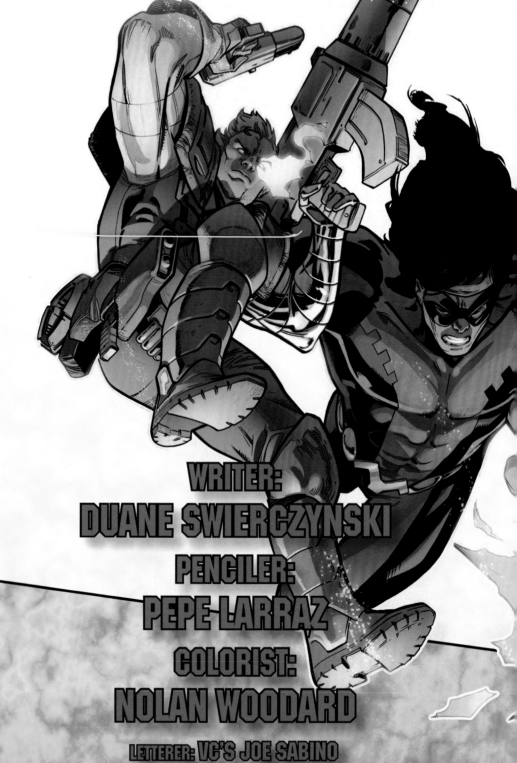

WRITER:
DUANE SWIERCZYNSKI
PENCILER:
PEPE LARRAZ
COLORIST:
NOLAN WOODARD

LETTERER: VC'S JOE SABINO
COVER ART: SHANE DAVIS & MORRY HOLLOWELL
ASSISTANT EDITORS: FRANKIE JOHNSON & XANDER JAROWEY
EDITOR: JORDAN D. WHITE
X-MEN GROUP EDITOR: MIKE MARTS

DEADPOOL CREATED BY ROB LIEFELD & FABIAN NICIEZA

DEADPOOL VS. X-FORCE

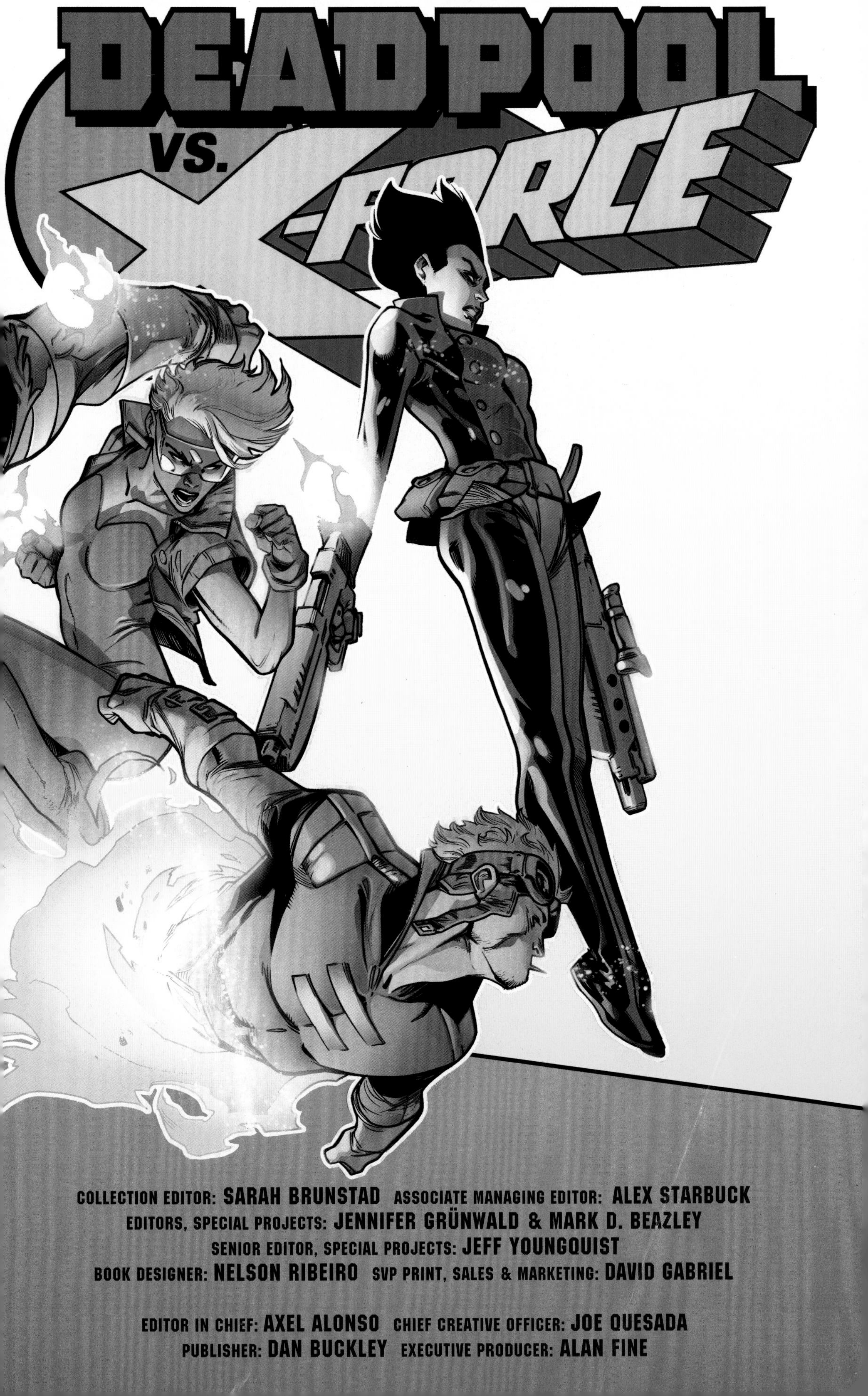

COLLECTION EDITOR: SARAH BRUNSTAD ASSOCIATE MANAGING EDITOR: ALEX STARBUCK
EDITORS, SPECIAL PROJECTS: JENNIFER GRÜNWALD & MARK D. BEAZLEY
SENIOR EDITOR, SPECIAL PROJECTS: JEFF YOUNGQUIST
BOOK DESIGNER: NELSON RIBEIRO SVP PRINT, SALES & MARKETING: DAVID GABRIEL

EDITOR IN CHIEF: AXEL ALONSO CHIEF CREATIVE OFFICER: JOE QUESADA
PUBLISHER: DAN BUCKLEY EXECUTIVE PRODUCER: ALAN FINE

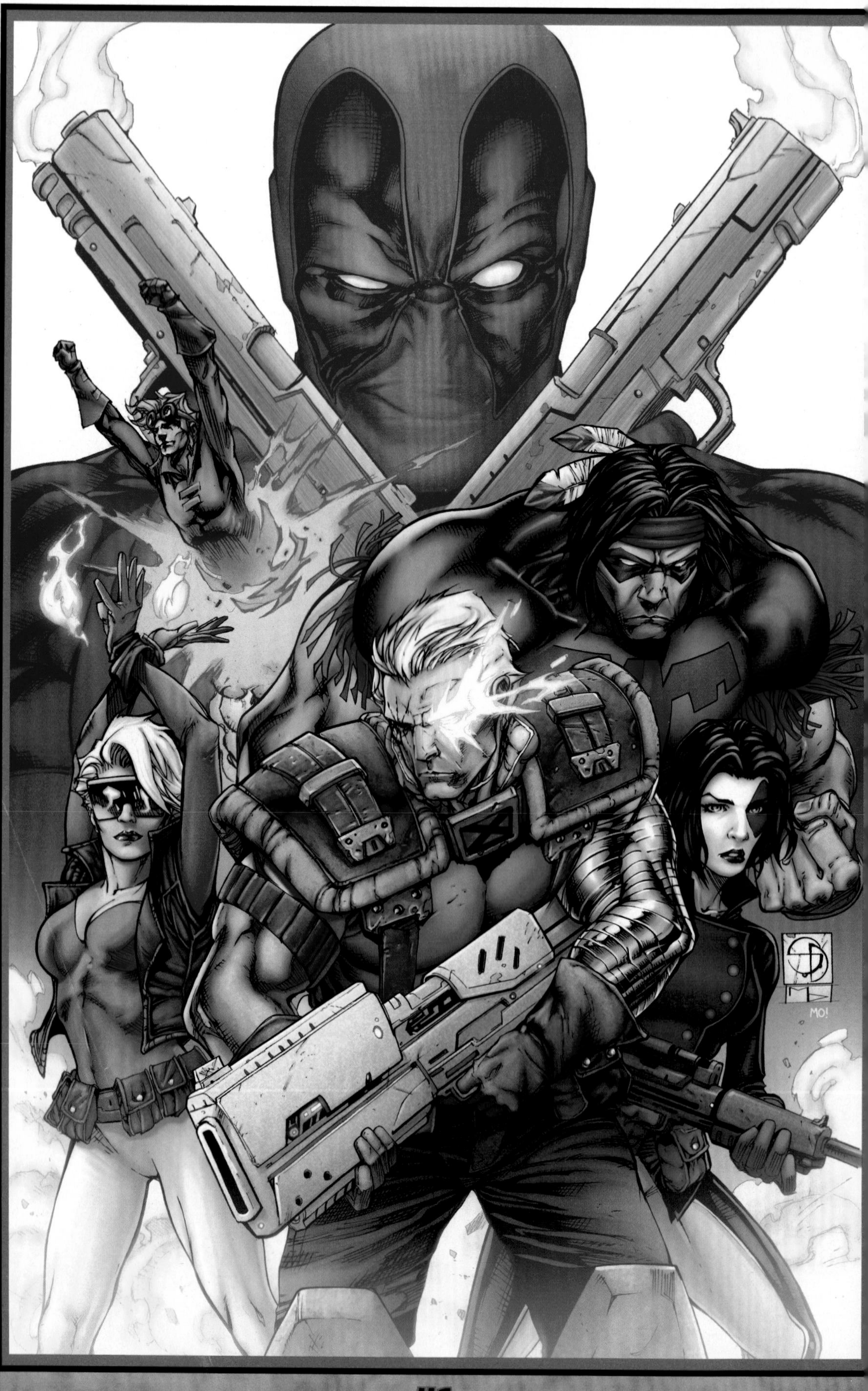
MO!

#1

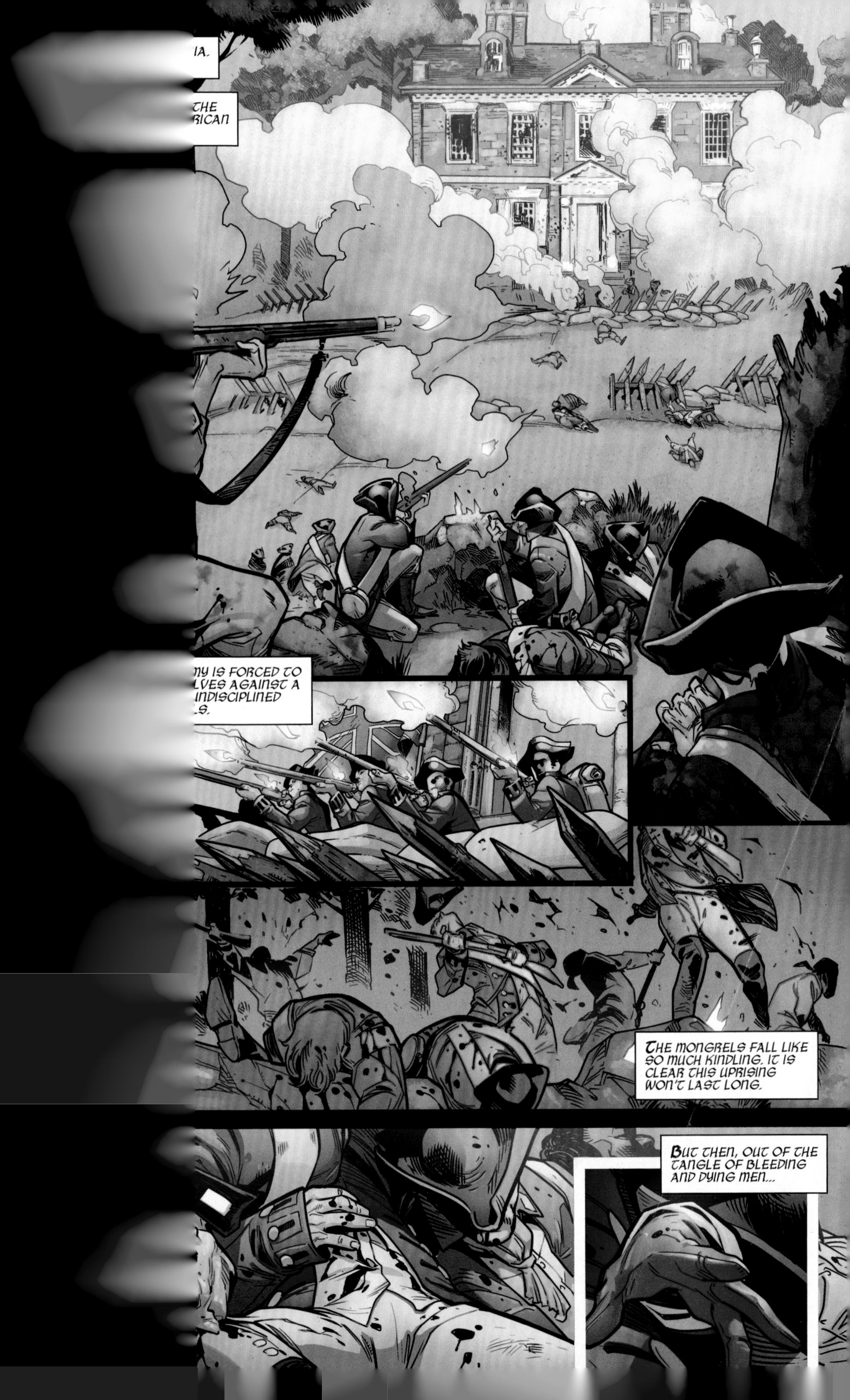
IA.
THE
RICAN
MY IS FORCED TO
LVES AGAINST A
UNDISCIPLINED
LS.
THE MONGRELS FALL LIKE SO MUCH KINDLING. IT IS CLEAR THIS UPRISING WON'T LAST LONG.
BUT THEN, OUT OF THE TANGLE OF BLEEDING AND DYING MEN...

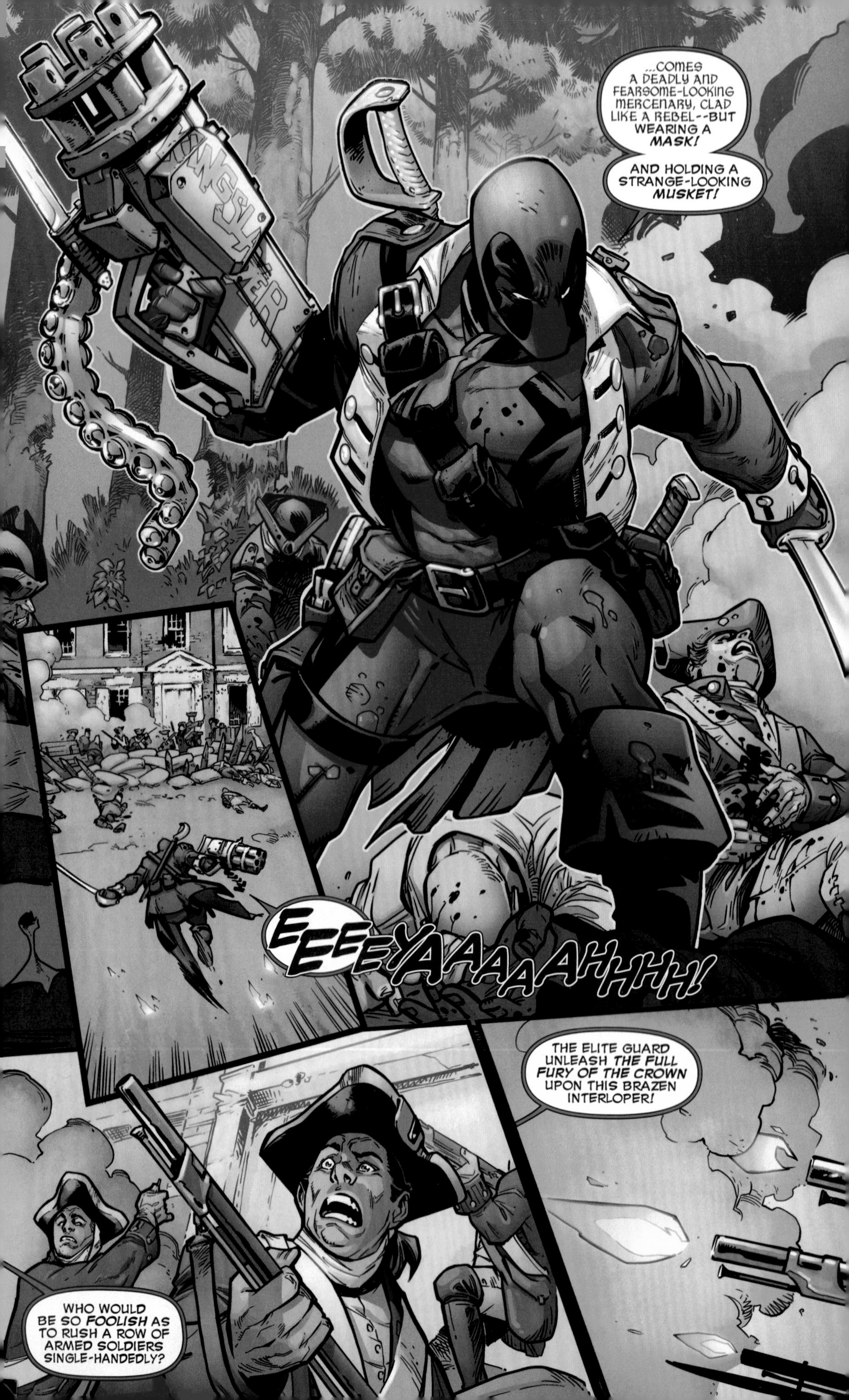
...COMES A DEADLY AND FEARSOME-LOOKING MERCENARY, CLAD LIKE A REBEL--BUT WEARING A MASK!
AND HOLDING A STRANGE-LOOKING MUSKET!
EEEEYAAAAAHHHHH!
THE ELITE GUARD UNLEASH THE FULL FURY OF THE CROWN UPON THIS BRAZEN INTERLOPER!
WHO WOULD BE SO FOOLISH AS TO RUSH A ROW OF ARMED SOLDIERS SINGLE-HANDEDLY?

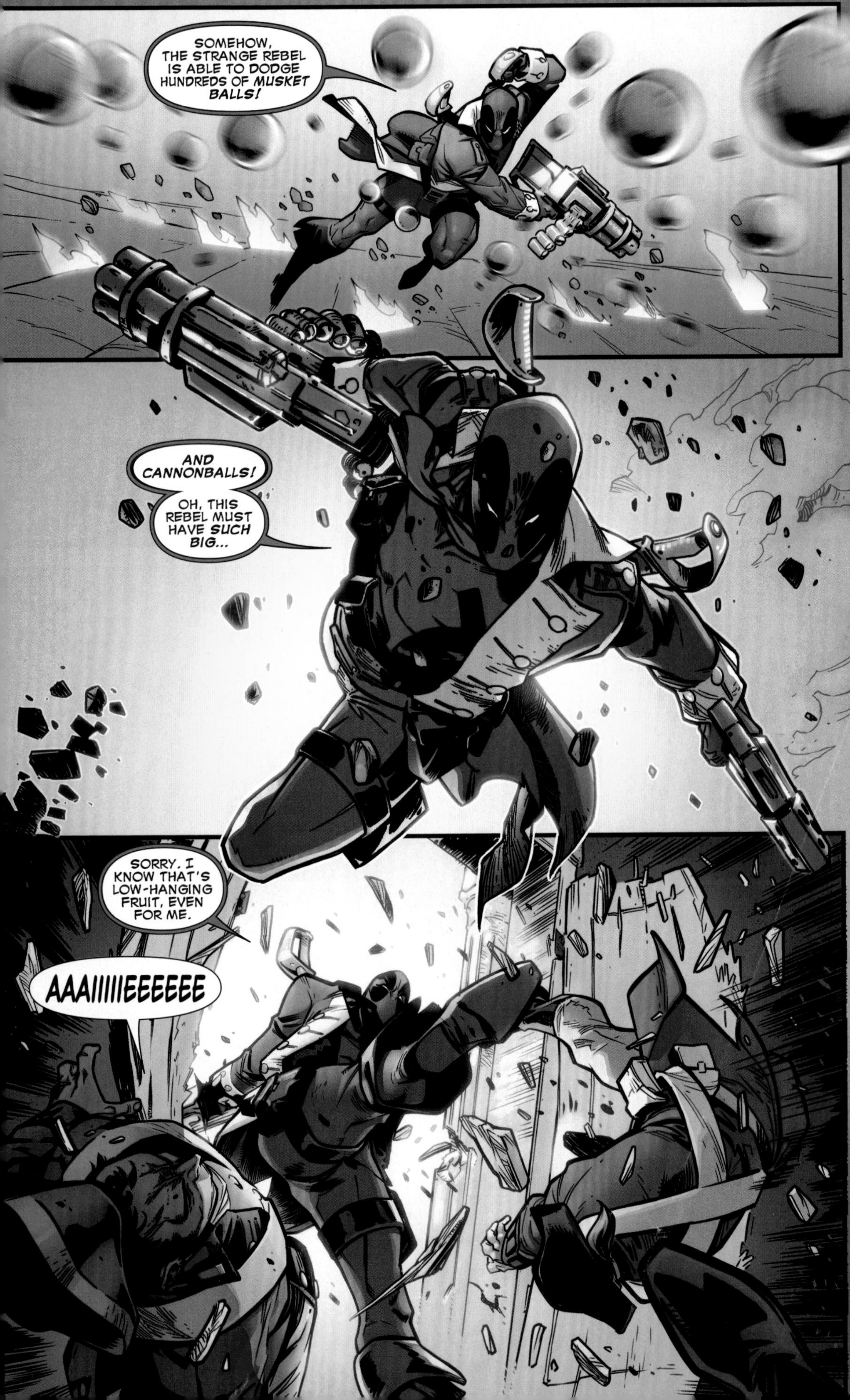
SOMEHOW, THE STRANGE REBEL IS ABLE TO DODGE HUNDREDS OF MUSKET BALLS!
AND CANNONBALLS!
OH, THIS REBEL MUST HAVE SUCH BIG...
SORRY. I KNOW THAT'S LOW-HANGING FRUIT, EVEN FOR ME.
AAAIIIIIIEEEEEE

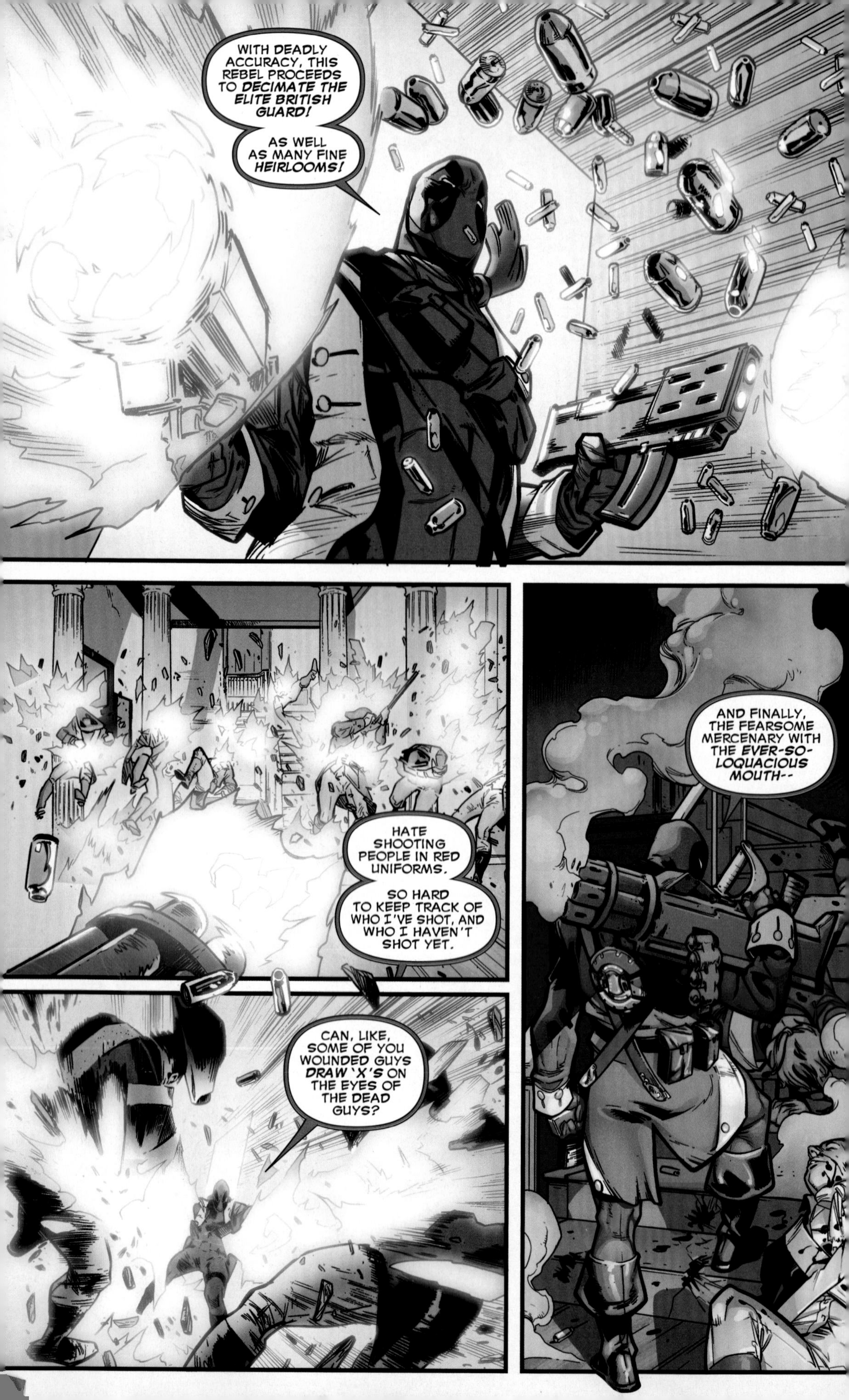

WITH DEADLY ACCURACY, THIS REBEL PROCEEDS TO DECIMATE THE ELITE BRITISH GUARD!
AS WELL AS MANY FINE HEIRLOOMS!
HATE SHOOTING PEOPLE IN RED UNIFORMS.
SO HARD TO KEEP TRACK OF WHO I'VE SHOT, AND WHO I HAVEN'T SHOT YET.
CAN, LIKE, SOME OF YOU WOUNDED GUYS DRAW 'X'S ON THE EYES OF THE DEAD GUYS?
AND FINALLY, THE FEARSOME MERCENARY WITH THE EVER-SO-LOQUACIOUS MOUTH--

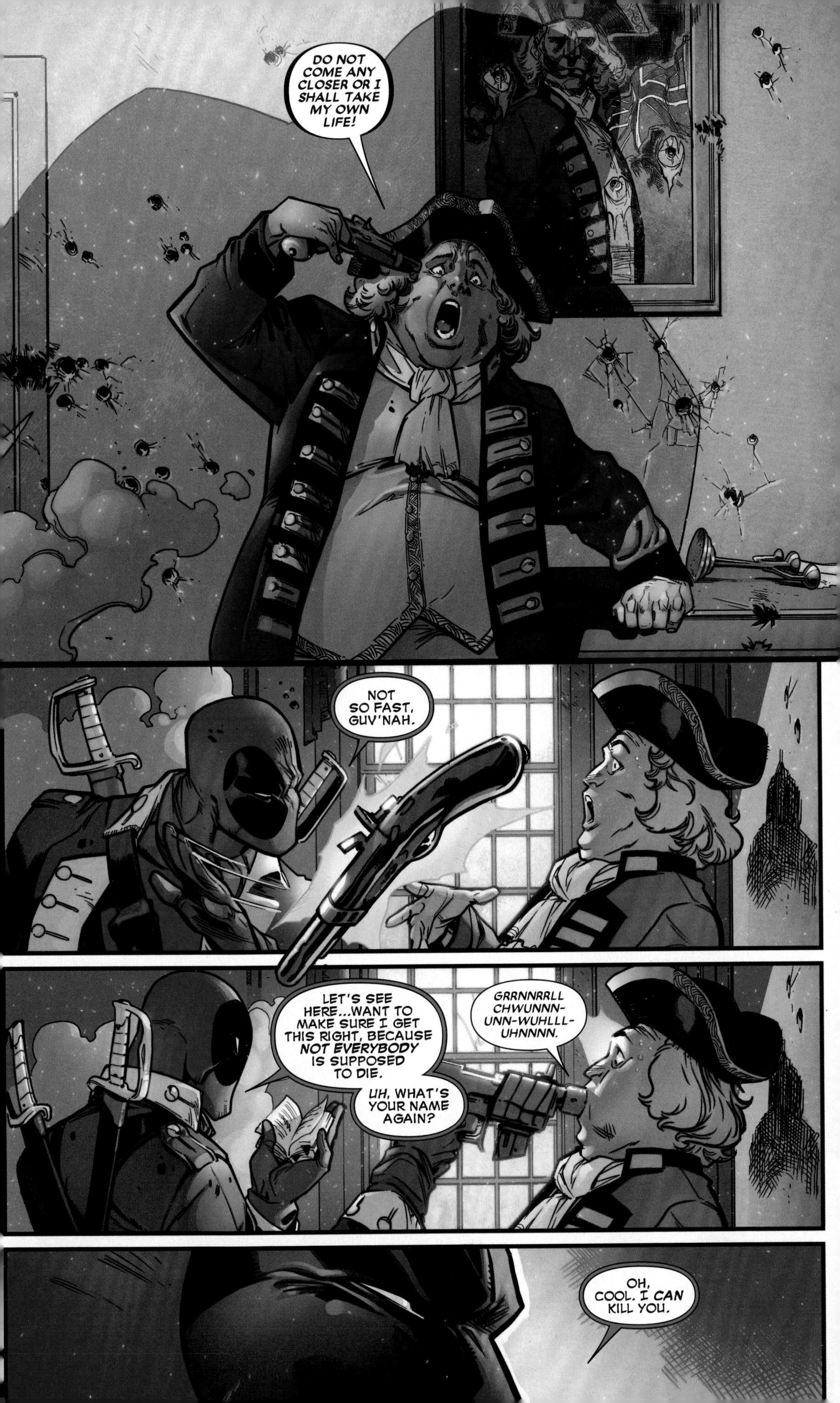

DO NOT COME ANY CLOSER OR I SHALL TAKE MY OWN LIFE!
NOT SO FAST, GUV'NAH.
LET'S SEE HERE...WANT TO MAKE SURE I GET THIS RIGHT, BECAUSE NOT EVERYBODY IS SUPPOSED TO DIE.
UH, WHAT'S YOUR NAME AGAIN?
GRRNNRRLL CHWUNNN-UNN-WUHLLL-UHNNNN.
OH, COOL. I CAN KILL YOU.

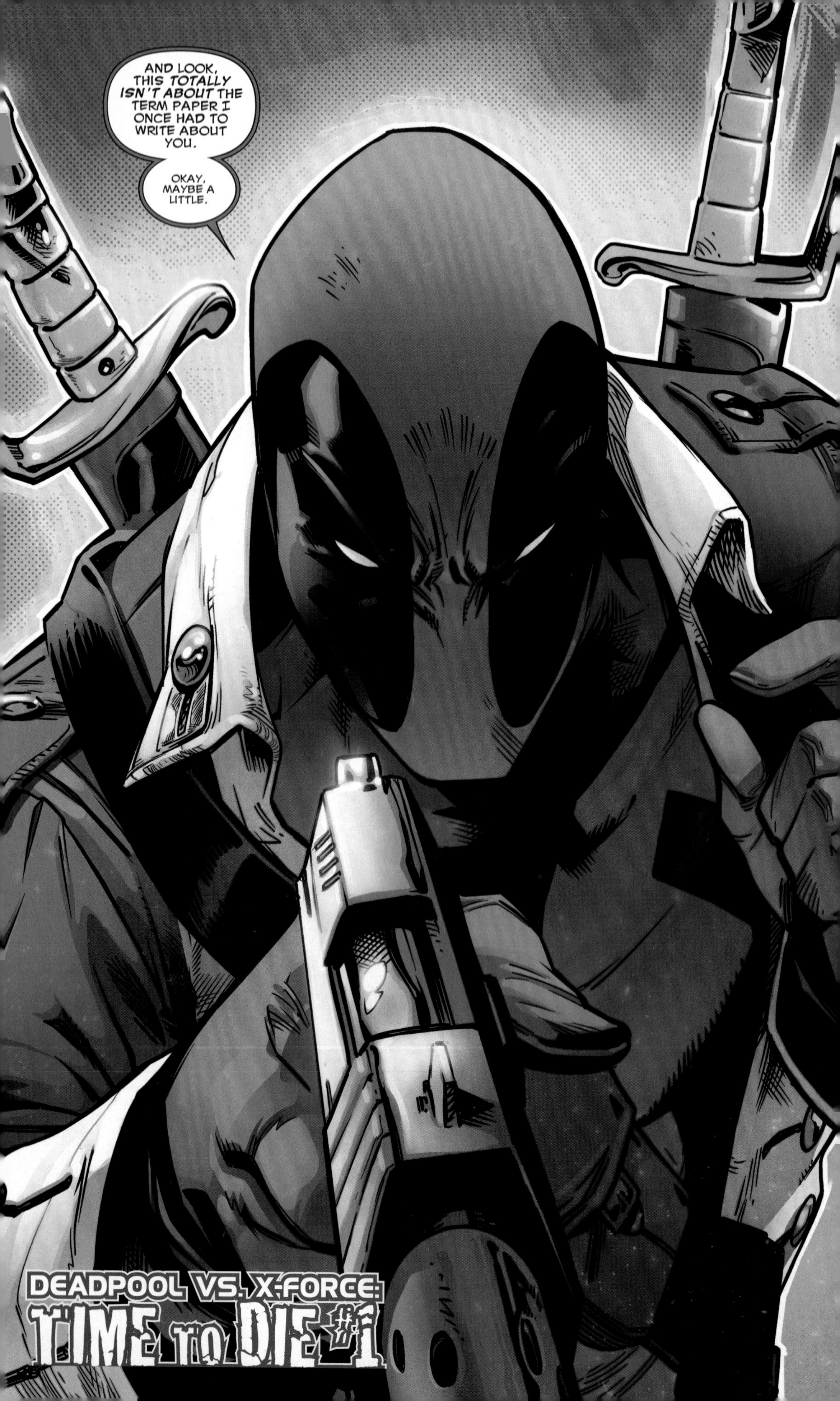

AND LOOK, THIS *TOTALLY ISN'T ABOUT* THE TERM PAPER I ONCE HAD TO WRITE ABOUT YOU.
OKAY, MAYBE A LITTLE.
DEADPOOL VS. X-FORCE:
TIME TO DIE #1

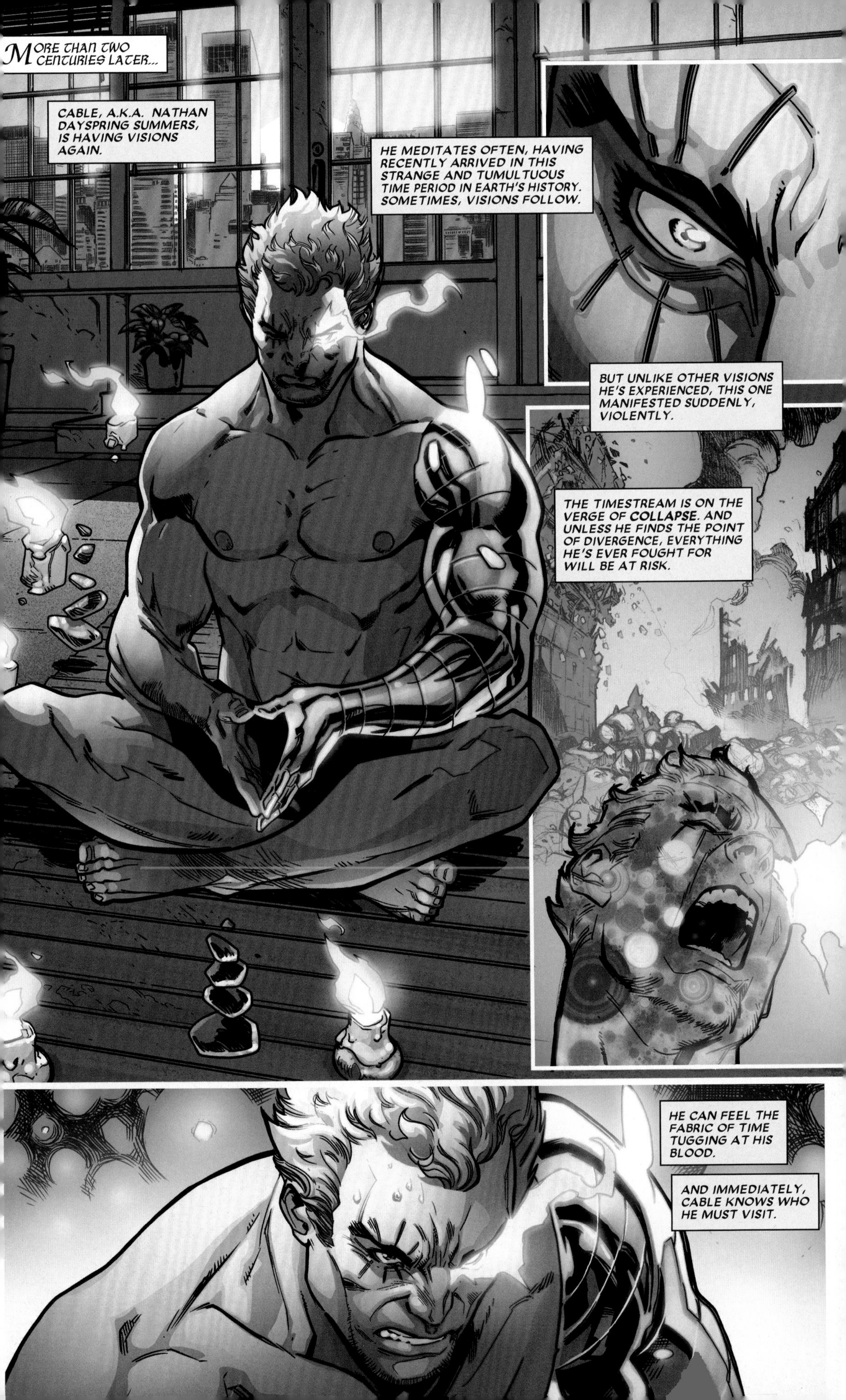
MORE THAN TWO CENTURIES LATER...
CABLE, A.K.A. NATHAN DAYSPRING SUMMERS, IS HAVING VISIONS AGAIN.
HE MEDITATES OFTEN, HAVING RECENTLY ARRIVED IN THIS STRANGE AND TUMULTUOUS TIME PERIOD IN EARTH'S HISTORY. SOMETIMES, VISIONS FOLLOW.
BUT UNLIKE OTHER VISIONS HE'S EXPERIENCED, THIS ONE MANIFESTED SUDDENLY, VIOLENTLY.
THE TIMESTREAM IS ON THE VERGE OF COLLAPSE. AND UNLESS HE FINDS THE POINT OF DIVERGENCE, EVERYTHING HE'S EVER FOUGHT FOR WILL BE AT RISK.
HE CAN FEEL THE FABRIC OF TIME TUGGING AT HIS BLOOD.
AND IMMEDIATELY, CABLE KNOWS WHO HE MUST VISIT.

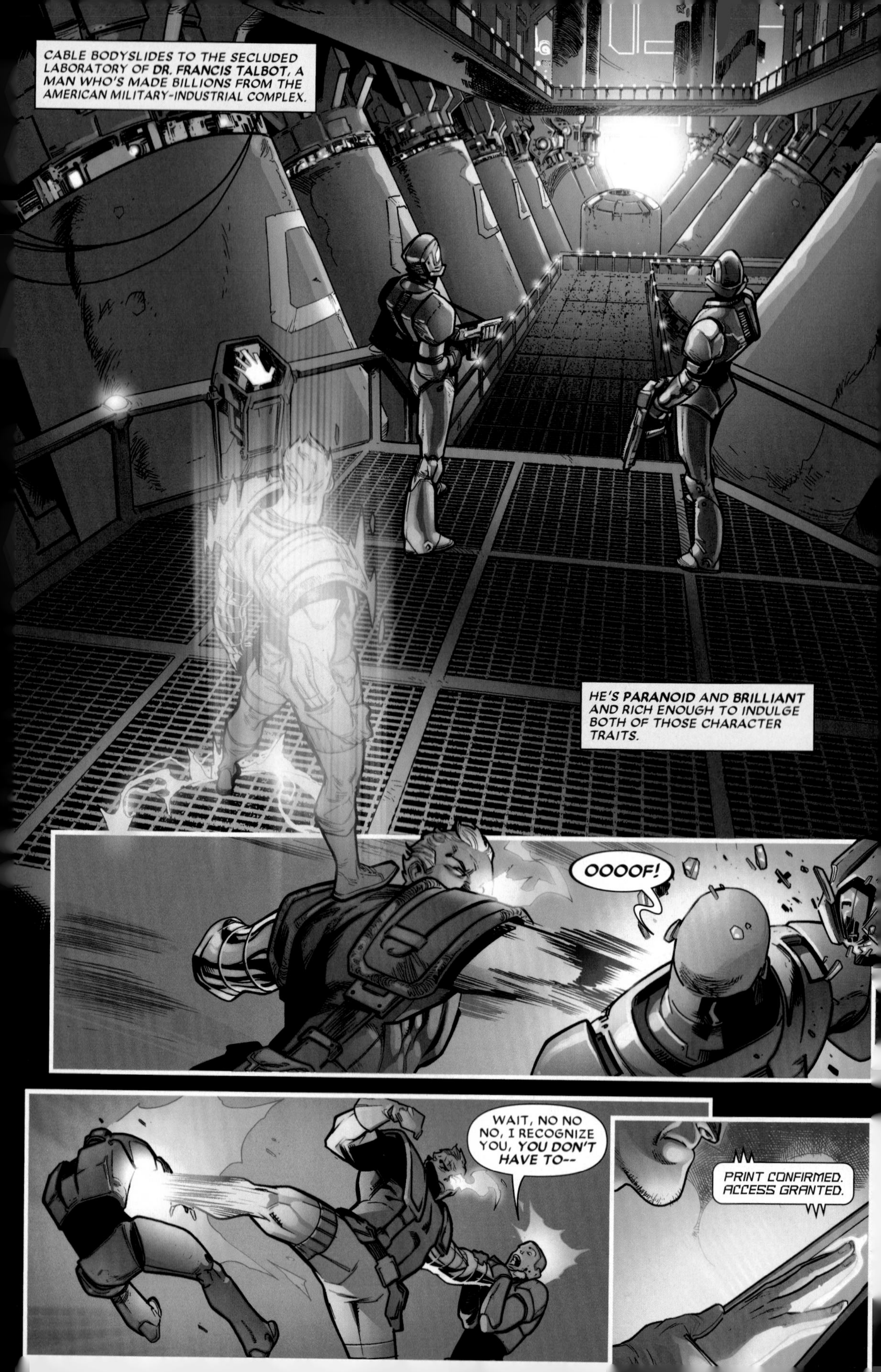
CABLE BODYSLIDES TO THE SECLUDED LABORATORY OF DR. FRANCIS TALBOT, A MAN WHO'S MADE BILLIONS FROM THE AMERICAN MILITARY-INDUSTRIAL COMPLEX.
HE'S PARANOID AND BRILLIANT AND RICH ENOUGH TO INDULGE BOTH OF THOSE CHARACTER TRAITS.
OOOOF!
WAIT, NO NO NO, I RECOGNIZE YOU, YOU DON'T HAVE TO--
PRINT CONFIRMED. ACCESS GRANTED.

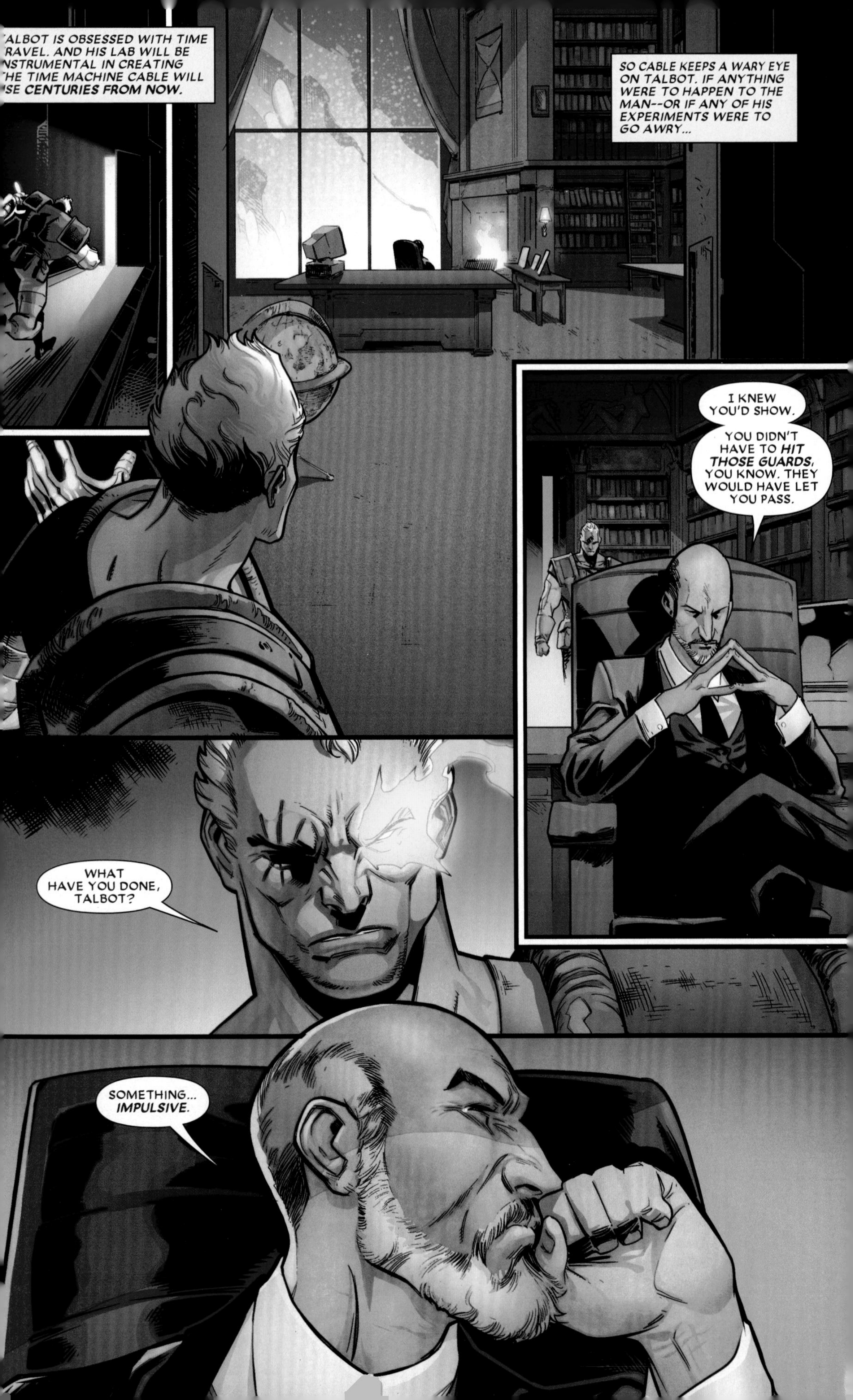

ALBOT IS OBSESSED WITH TIME RAVEL. AND HIS LAB WILL BE NSTRUMENTAL IN CREATING HE TIME MACHINE CABLE WILL SE **CENTURIES FROM NOW.**
SO CABLE KEEPS A WARY EYE ON TALBOT. IF ANYTHING WERE TO HAPPEN TO THE MAN--OR IF ANY OF HIS EXPERIMENTS WERE TO GO AWRY...
I KNEW YOU'D SHOW.
YOU DIDN'T HAVE TO ***HIT THOSE GUARDS***, YOU KNOW. THEY WOULD HAVE LET YOU PASS.
WHAT HAVE YOU DONE, TALBOT?
SOMETHING... ***IMPULSIVE***.

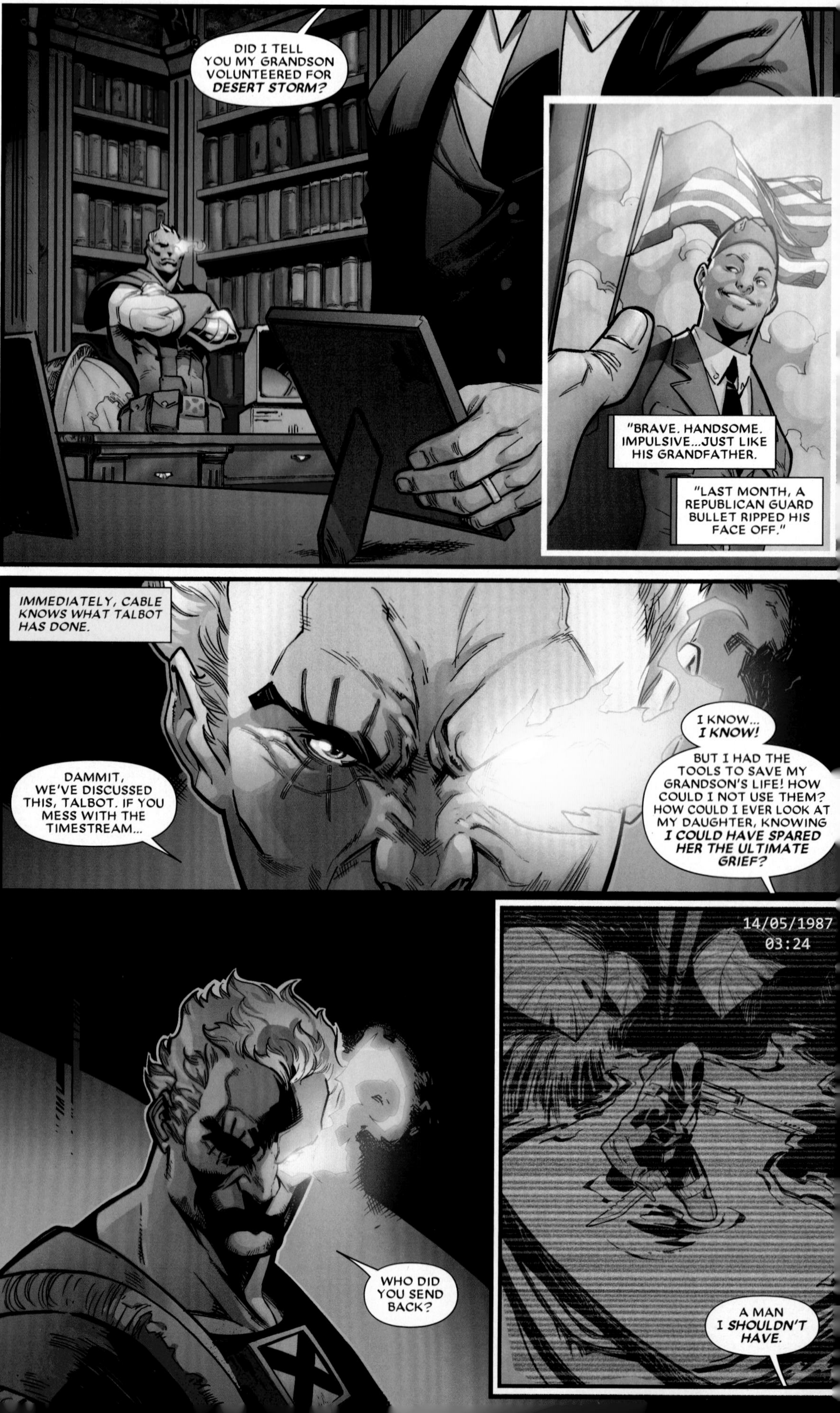
DID I TELL YOU MY GRANDSON VOLUNTEERED FOR *DESERT STORM?*
"BRAVE. HANDSOME. IMPULSIVE...JUST LIKE HIS GRANDFATHER.
"LAST MONTH, A REPUBLICAN GUARD BULLET RIPPED HIS FACE OFF."
IMMEDIATELY, CABLE KNOWS WHAT TALBOT HAS DONE.
DAMMIT, WE'VE DISCUSSED THIS, TALBOT. IF YOU MESS WITH THE TIMESTREAM...
I KNOW... ***I KNOW!***
BUT I HAD THE TOOLS TO SAVE MY GRANDSON'S LIFE! HOW COULD I NOT USE THEM? HOW COULD I EVER LOOK AT MY DAUGHTER, KNOWING ***I COULD HAVE SPARED HER THE ULTIMATE GRIEF?***
14/05/1987
03:24
WHO DID YOU SEND BACK?
A MAN I ***SHOULDN'T HAVE.***

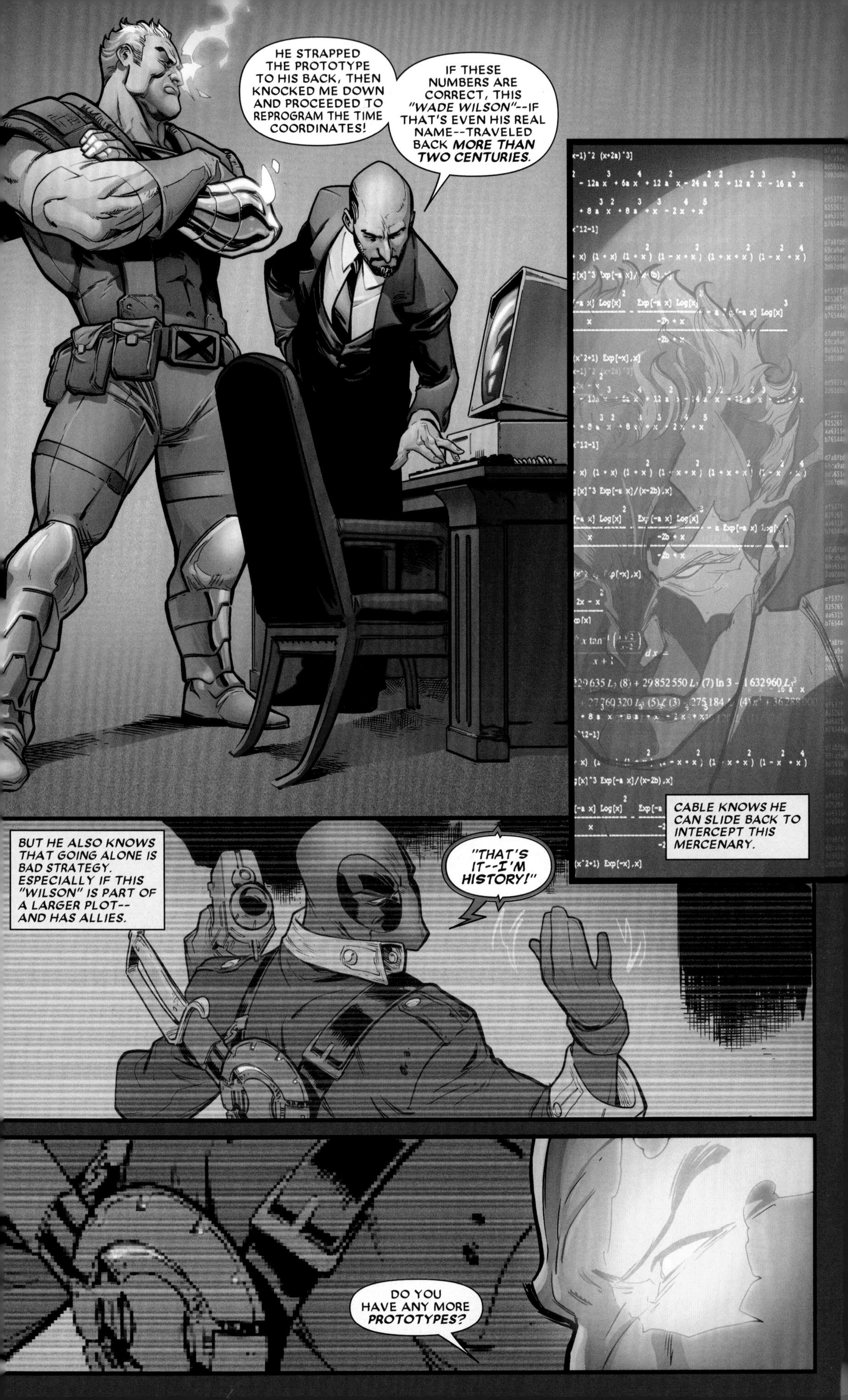
HE STRAPPED THE PROTOTYPE TO HIS BACK, THEN KNOCKED ME DOWN AND PROCEEDED TO REPROGRAM THE TIME COORDINATES!
IF THESE NUMBERS ARE CORRECT, THIS "WADE WILSON"--IF THAT'S EVEN HIS REAL NAME--TRAVELED BACK MORE THAN TWO CENTURIES.
CABLE KNOWS HE CAN SLIDE BACK TO INTERCEPT THIS MERCENARY.
BUT HE ALSO KNOWS THAT GOING ALONE IS BAD STRATEGY. ESPECIALLY IF THIS "WILSON" IS PART OF A LARGER PLOT-- AND HAS ALLIES.
"THAT'S IT--I'M HISTORY!"
DO YOU HAVE ANY MORE PROTOTYPES?

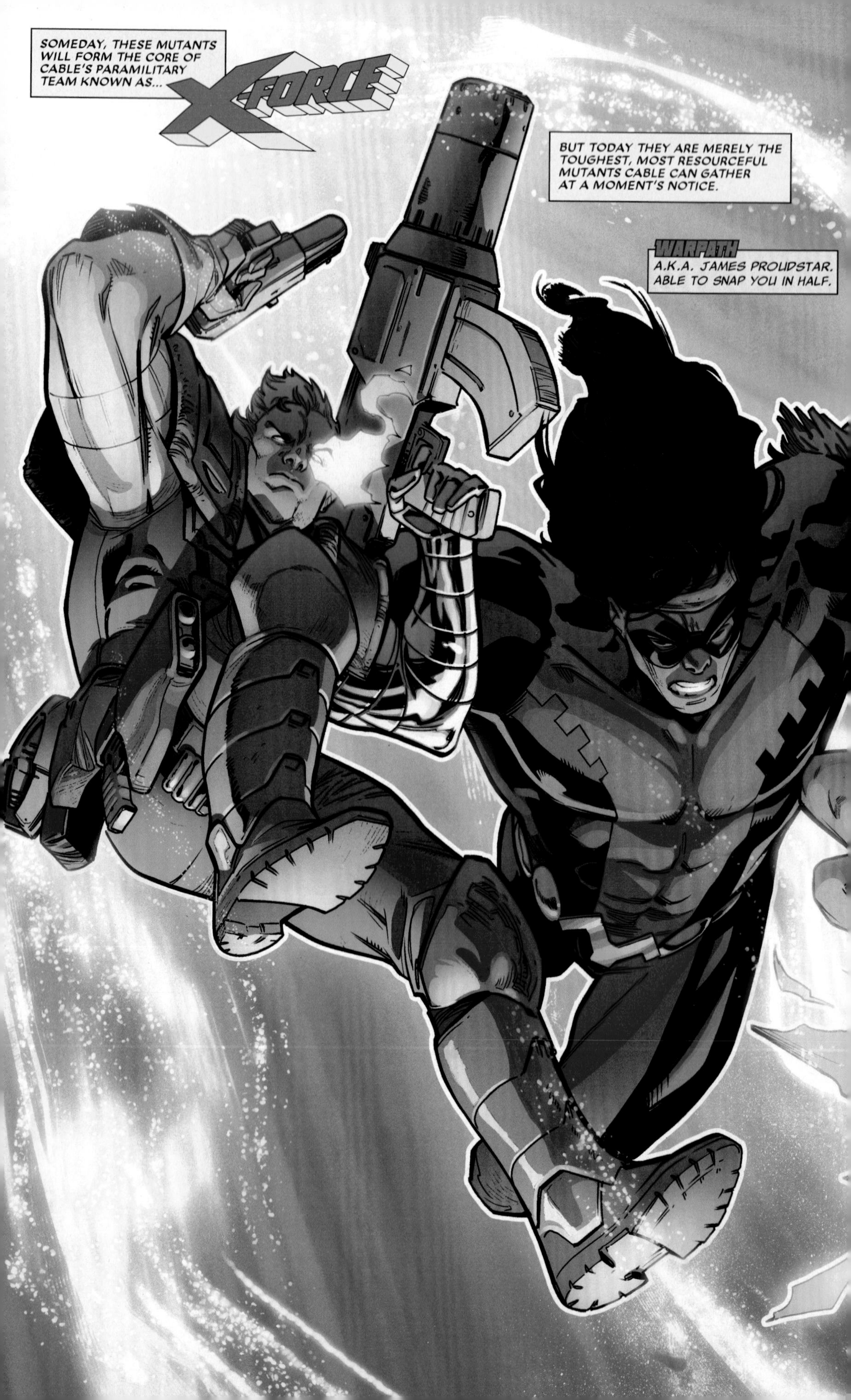
SOMEDAY, THESE MUTANTS WILL FORM THE CORE OF CABLE'S PARAMILITARY TEAM KNOWN AS...
X-FORCE
BUT TODAY THEY ARE MERELY THE TOUGHEST, MOST RESOURCEFUL MUTANTS CABLE CAN GATHER AT A MOMENT'S NOTICE.
WARPATH
A.K.A. JAMES PROUDSTAR. ABLE TO SNAP YOU IN HALF.

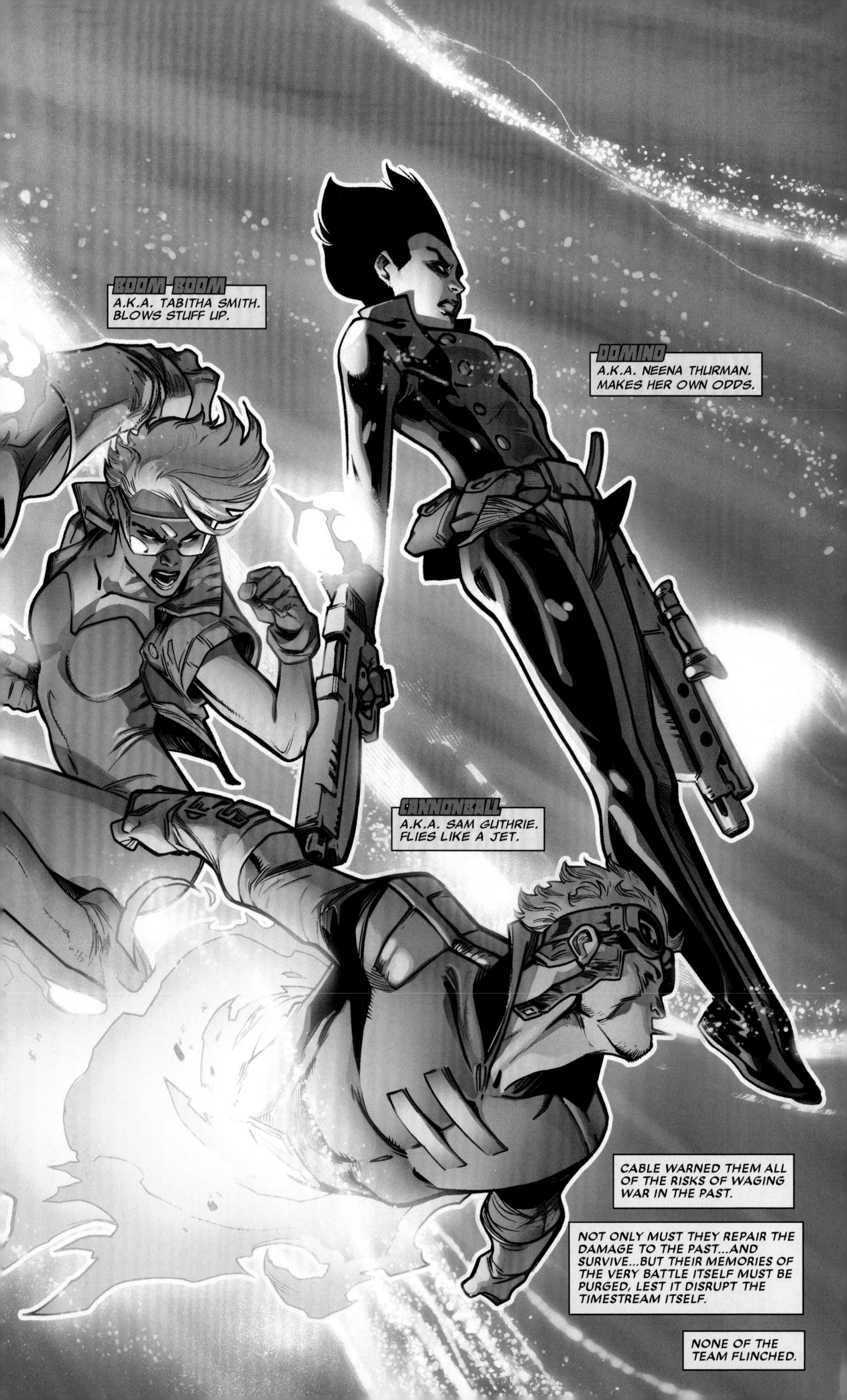
BOOM-BOOM
A.K.A. TABITHA SMITH. BLOWS STUFF UP.
DOMINO
A.K.A. NEENA THURMAN. MAKES HER OWN ODDS.
CANNONBALL
A.K.A. SAM GUTHRIE. FLIES LIKE A JET.
CABLE WARNED THEM ALL OF THE RISKS OF WAGING WAR IN THE PAST.
NOT ONLY MUST THEY REPAIR THE DAMAGE TO THE PAST...AND SURVIVE...BUT THEIR MEMORIES OF THE VERY BATTLE ITSELF MUST BE PURGED, LEST IT DISRUPT THE TIMESTREAM ITSELF.
NONE OF THE TEAM FLINCHED.

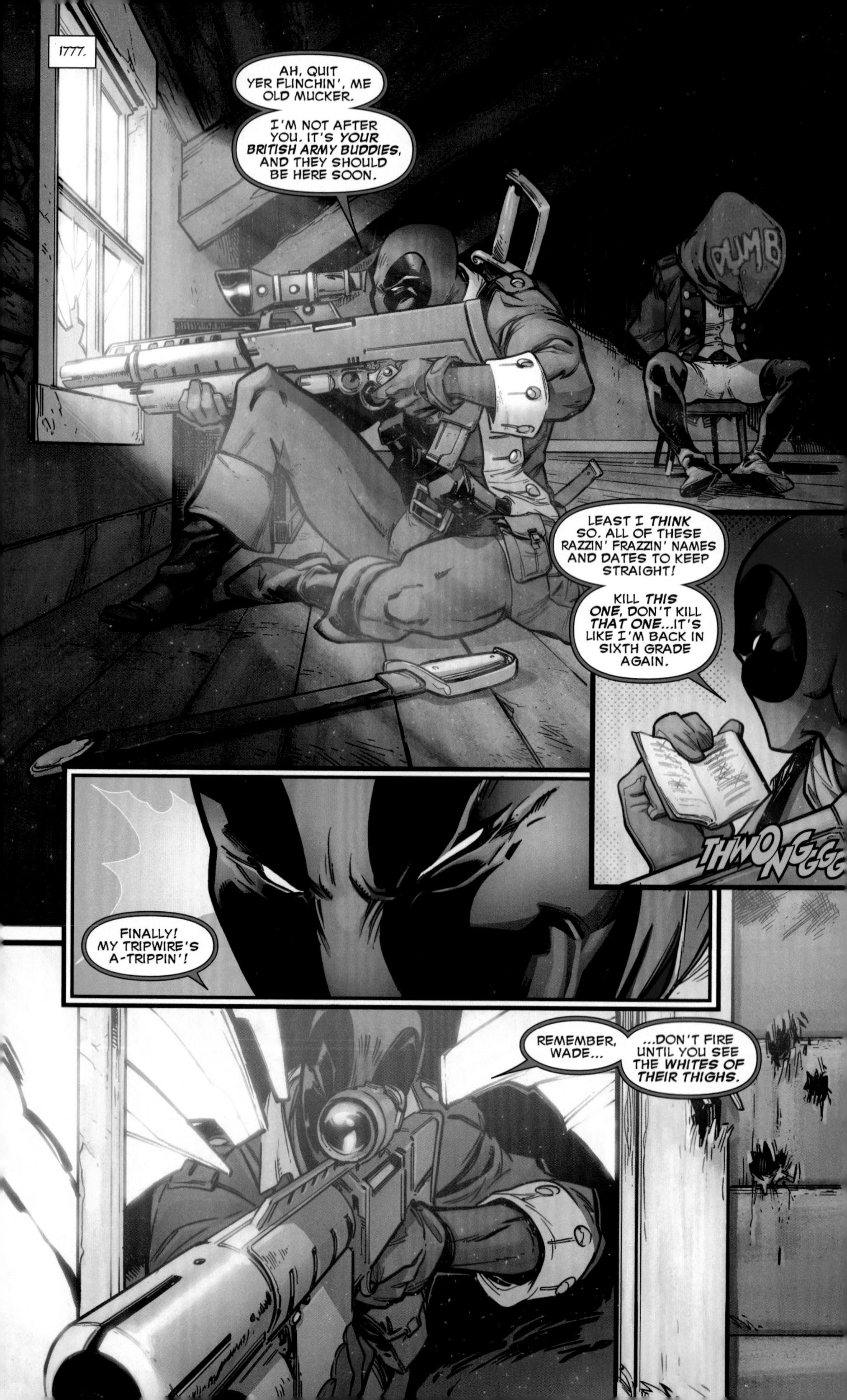
1777.
AH, QUIT YER FLINCHIN', ME OLD MUCKER.
I'M NOT AFTER YOU. IT'S YOUR BRITISH ARMY BUDDIES, AND THEY SHOULD BE HERE SOON.
DUMB
LEAST I THINK SO. ALL OF THESE RAZZIN' FRAZZIN' NAMES AND DATES TO KEEP STRAIGHT!
KILL THIS ONE, DON'T KILL THAT ONE...IT'S LIKE I'M BACK IN SIXTH GRADE AGAIN.
THWONGGG
FINALLY! MY TRIPWIRE'S A-TRIPPIN'!
REMEMBER, WADE...
...DON'T FIRE UNTIL YOU SEE THE WHITES OF THEIR THIGHS.

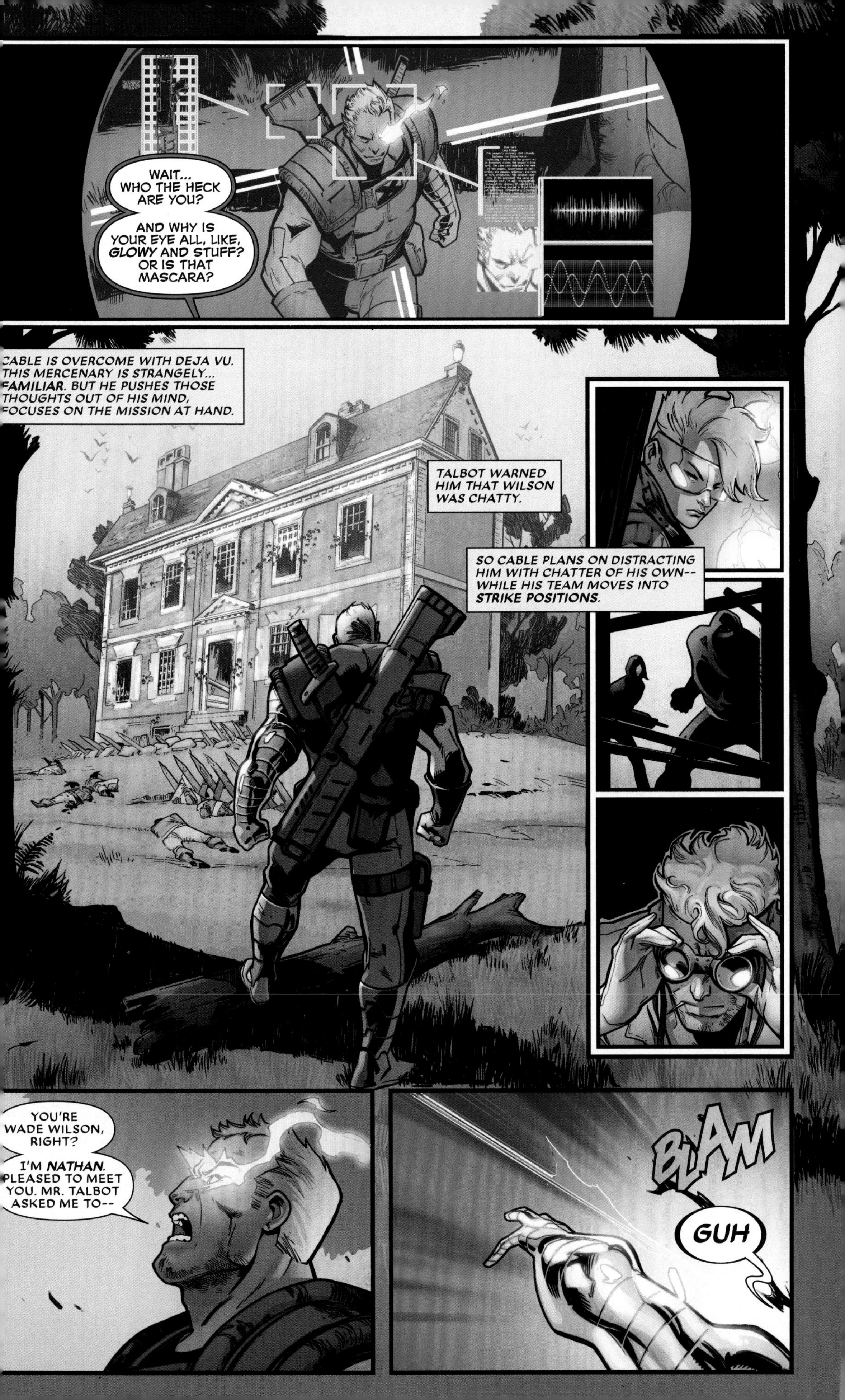

WAIT... WHO THE HECK ARE YOU?
AND WHY IS YOUR EYE ALL, LIKE, GLOWY AND STUFF? OR IS THAT MASCARA?
CABLE IS OVERCOME WITH DEJA VU. THIS MERCENARY IS STRANGELY... FAMILIAR. BUT HE PUSHES THOSE THOUGHTS OUT OF HIS MIND, FOCUSES ON THE MISSION AT HAND.
TALBOT WARNED HIM THAT WILSON WAS CHATTY.
SO CABLE PLANS ON DISTRACTING HIM WITH CHATTER OF HIS OWN-- WHILE HIS TEAM MOVES INTO STRIKE POSITIONS.
YOU'RE WADE WILSON, RIGHT?
I'M NATHAN. PLEASED TO MEET YOU. MR. TALBOT ASKED ME TO--
BLAM
GUH

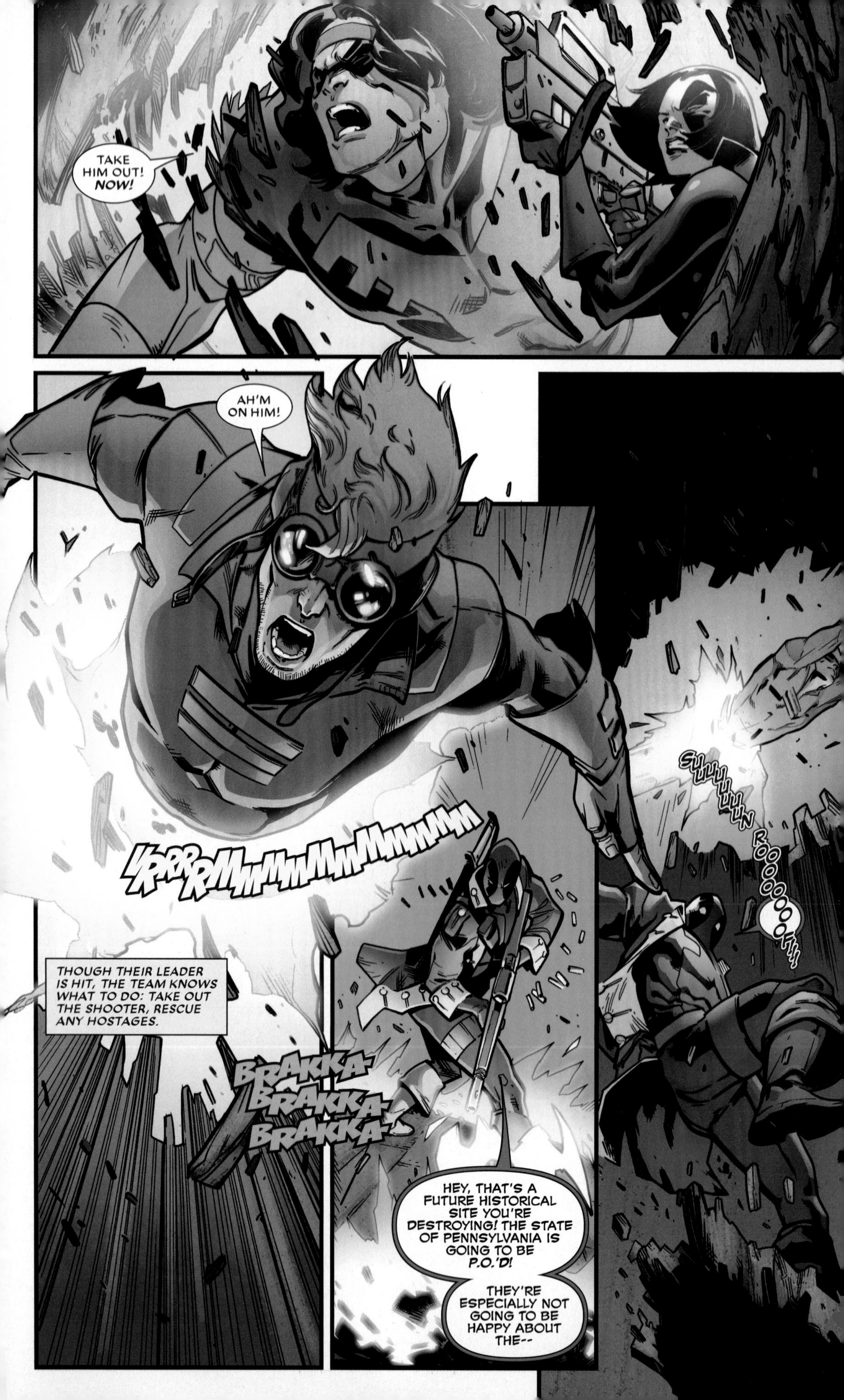

TAKE HIM OUT! NOW!
AH'M ON HIM!
VRRRRMMMMMMMMMMMMMMM
SHUUUUUUN ROOOOOOOM!!
THOUGH THEIR LEADER IS HIT, THE TEAM KNOWS WHAT TO DO: TAKE OUT THE SHOOTER, RESCUE ANY HOSTAGES.
BRAKKA-BRAKKA-BRAKKA-
HEY, THAT'S A FUTURE HISTORICAL SITE YOU'RE DESTROYING! THE STATE OF PENNSYLVANIA IS GOING TO BE P.O.'D!
THEY'RE ESPECIALLY NOT GOING TO BE HAPPY ABOUT THE--

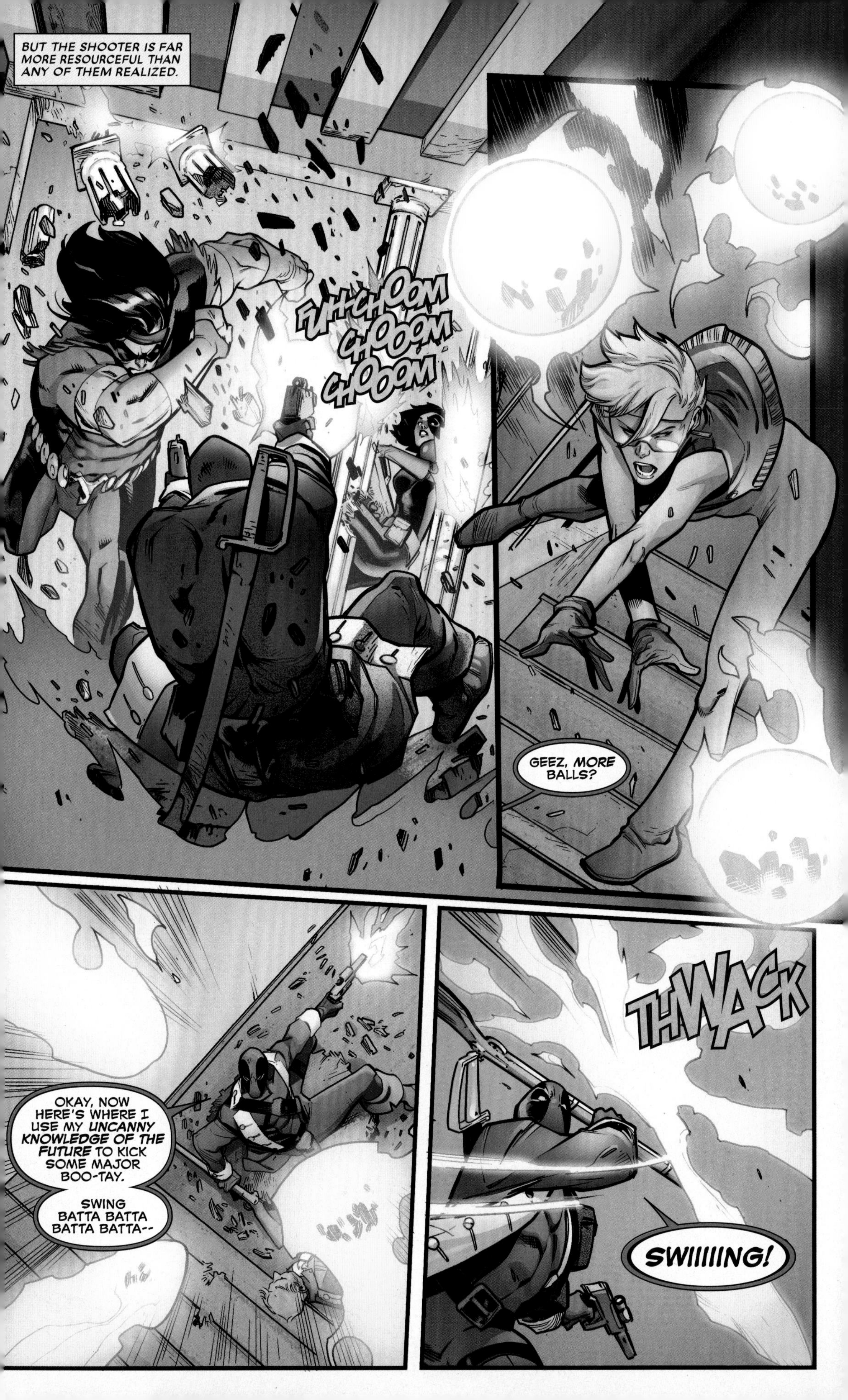
BUT THE SHOOTER IS FAR MORE RESOURCEFUL THAN ANY OF THEM REALIZED.
FUH-CHOOOM CHOOOM CHOOOM
GEEZ, MORE BALLS?
OKAY, NOW HERE'S WHERE I USE MY UNCANNY KNOWLEDGE OF THE FUTURE TO KICK SOME MAJOR BOO-TAY.
SWING BATTA BATTA BATTA BATTA--
THWACK
SWIIIIING!

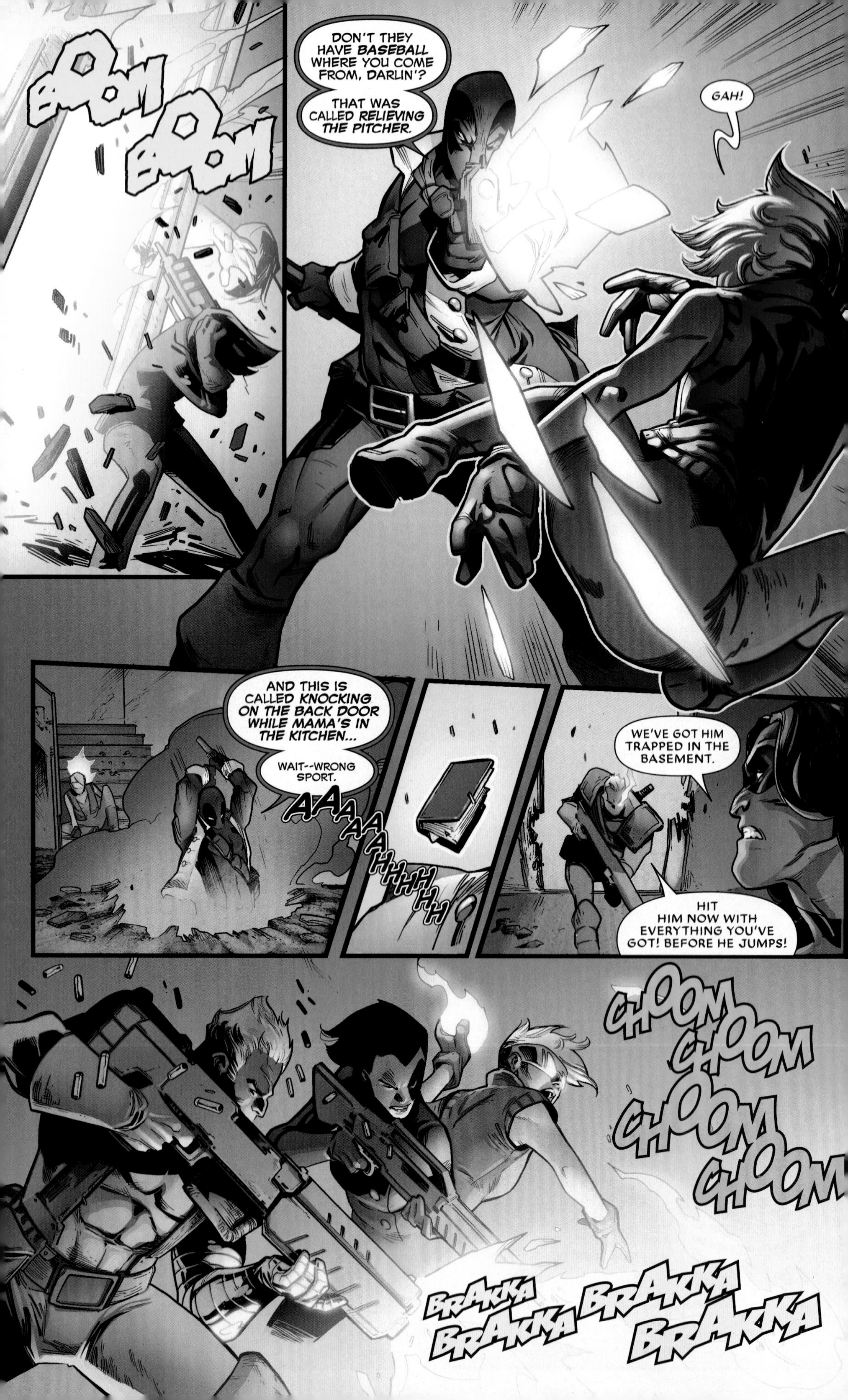
BOOM BOOM
DON'T THEY HAVE BASEBALL WHERE YOU COME FROM, DARLIN'?
THAT WAS CALLED RELIEVING THE PITCHER.
GAH!
AND THIS IS CALLED KNOCKING ON THE BACK DOOR WHILE MAMA'S IN THE KITCHEN...
WAIT--WRONG SPORT.
AAAAAAHHHHHHH
WE'VE GOT HIM TRAPPED IN THE BASEMENT.
HIT HIM NOW WITH EVERYTHING YOU'VE GOT! BEFORE HE JUMPS!
CHOOM CHOOM CHOOM CHOOM
BRAKKA BRAKKA BRAKKA BRAKKA

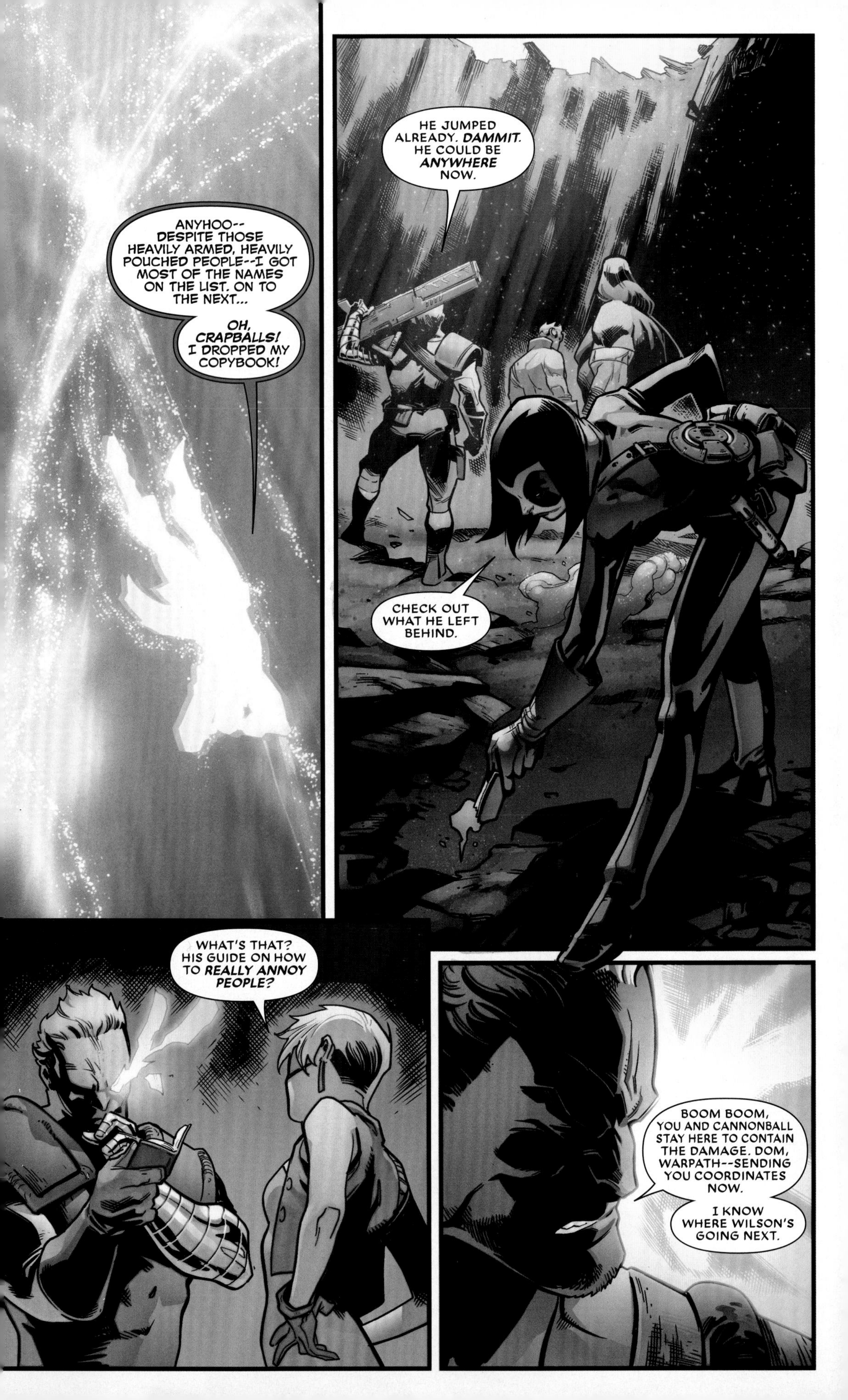
ANYHOO-- DESPITE THOSE HEAVILY ARMED, HEAVILY POUCHED PEOPLE--I GOT MOST OF THE NAMES ON THE LIST. ON TO THE NEXT...
OH, CRAPBALLS! I DROPPED MY COPYBOOK!
HE JUMPED ALREADY. DAMMIT. HE COULD BE ANYWHERE NOW.
CHECK OUT WHAT HE LEFT BEHIND.
WHAT'S THAT? HIS GUIDE ON HOW TO REALLY ANNOY PEOPLE?
BOOM BOOM, YOU AND CANNONBALL STAY HERE TO CONTAIN THE DAMAGE. DOM, WARPATH--SENDING YOU COORDINATES NOW.
I KNOW WHERE WILSON'S GOING NEXT.

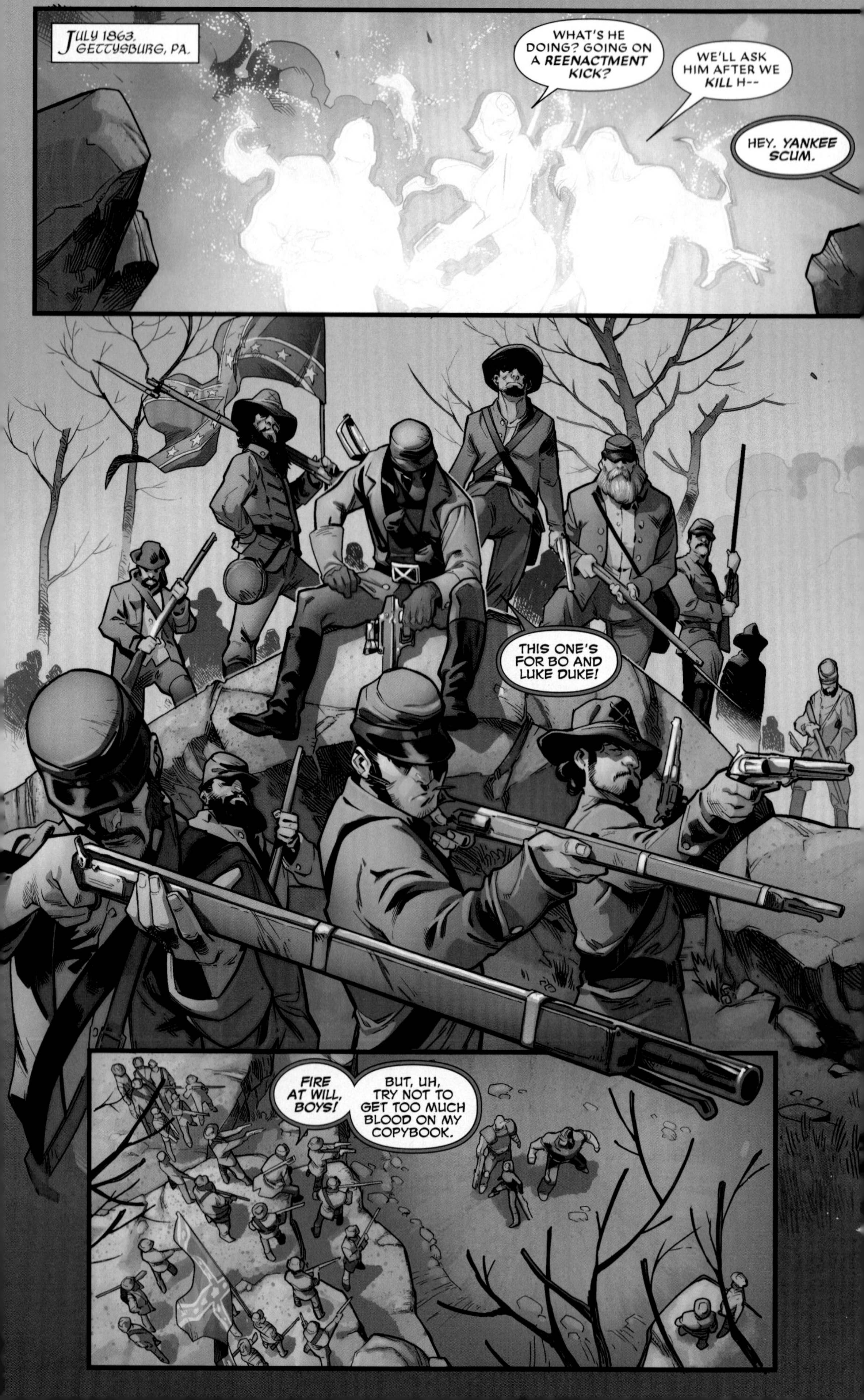
JULY 1863. GETTYSBURG, PA.
WHAT'S HE DOING? GOING ON A REENACTMENT KICK?
WE'LL ASK HIM AFTER WE KILL H--
HEY. YANKEE SCUM.
THIS ONE'S FOR BO AND LUKE DUKE!
FIRE AT WILL, BOYS!
BUT, UH, TRY NOT TO GET TOO MUCH BLOOD ON MY COPYBOOK.

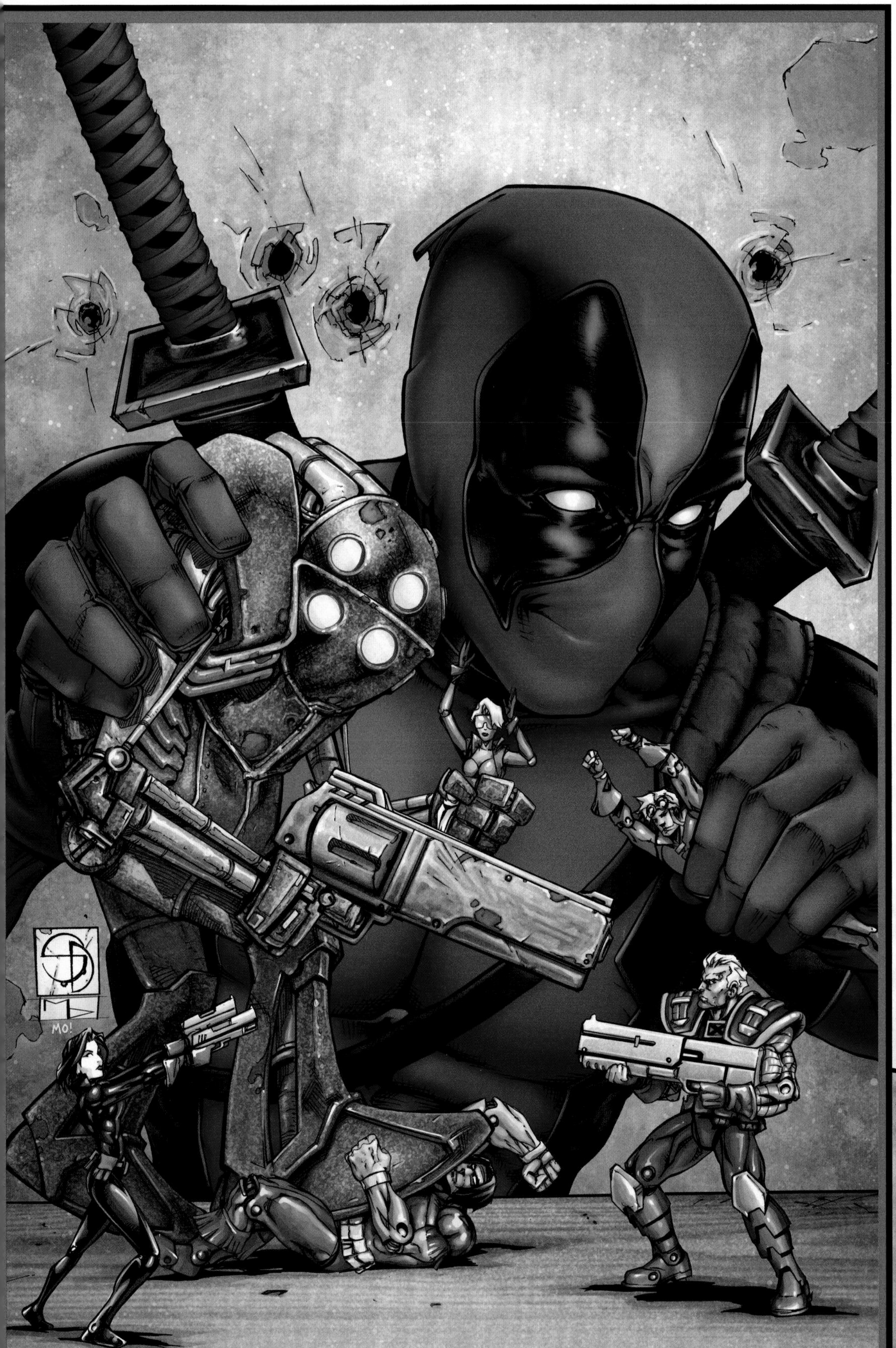
MO!

#2

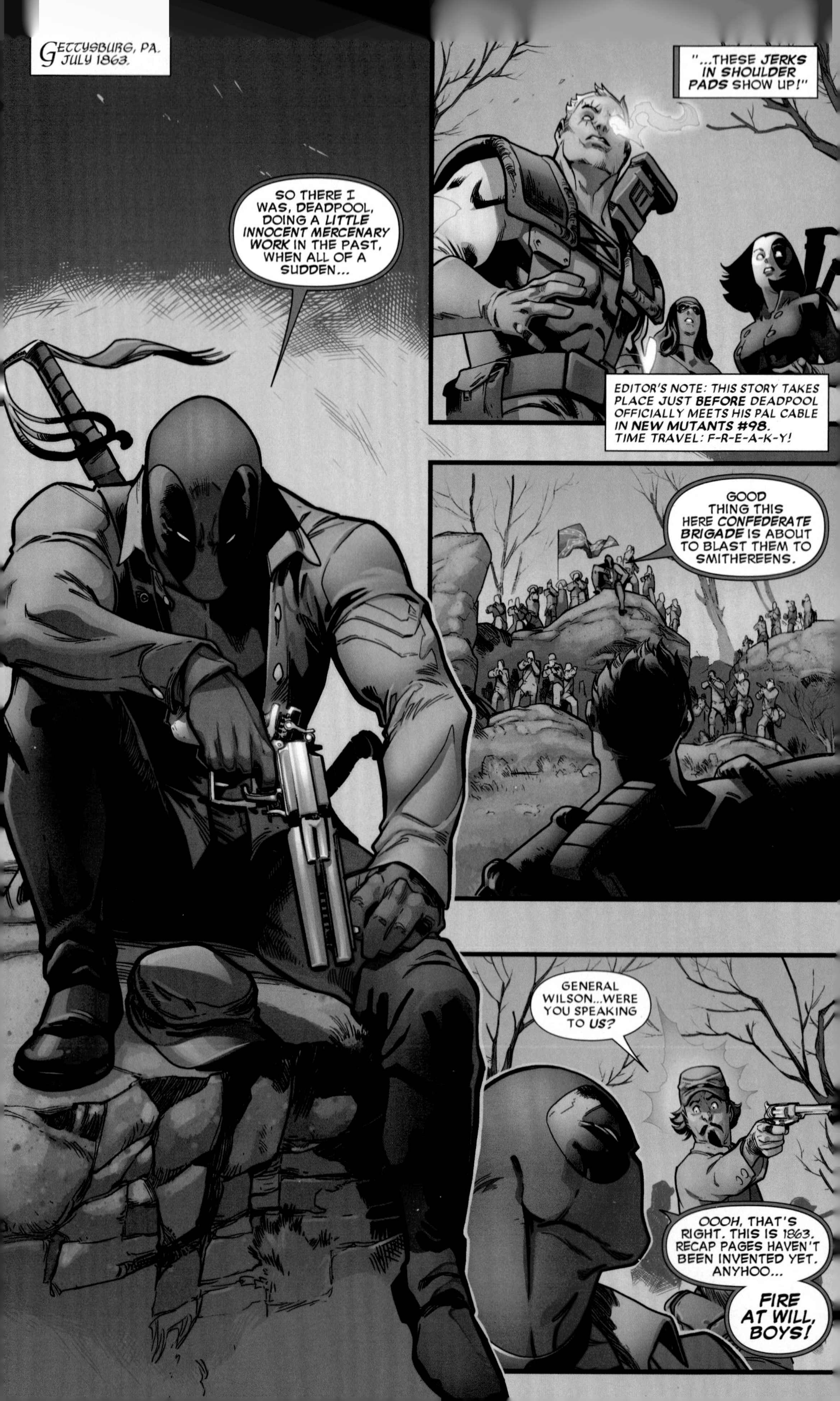

GETTYSBURG, PA. JULY 1863.
SO THERE I WAS, DEADPOOL, DOING A LITTLE INNOCENT MERCENARY WORK IN THE PAST, WHEN ALL OF A SUDDEN...
"...THESE JERKS IN SHOULDER PADS SHOW UP!"
EDITOR'S NOTE: THIS STORY TAKES PLACE JUST BEFORE DEADPOOL OFFICIALLY MEETS HIS PAL CABLE IN NEW MUTANTS #98. TIME TRAVEL: F-R-E-A-K-Y!
GOOD THING THIS HERE CONFEDERATE BRIGADE IS ABOUT TO BLAST THEM TO SMITHEREENS.
GENERAL WILSON...WERE YOU SPEAKING TO US?
OOOH, THAT'S RIGHT. THIS IS 1863. RECAP PAGES HAVEN'T BEEN INVENTED YET. ANYHOO...
FIRE AT WILL, BOYS!

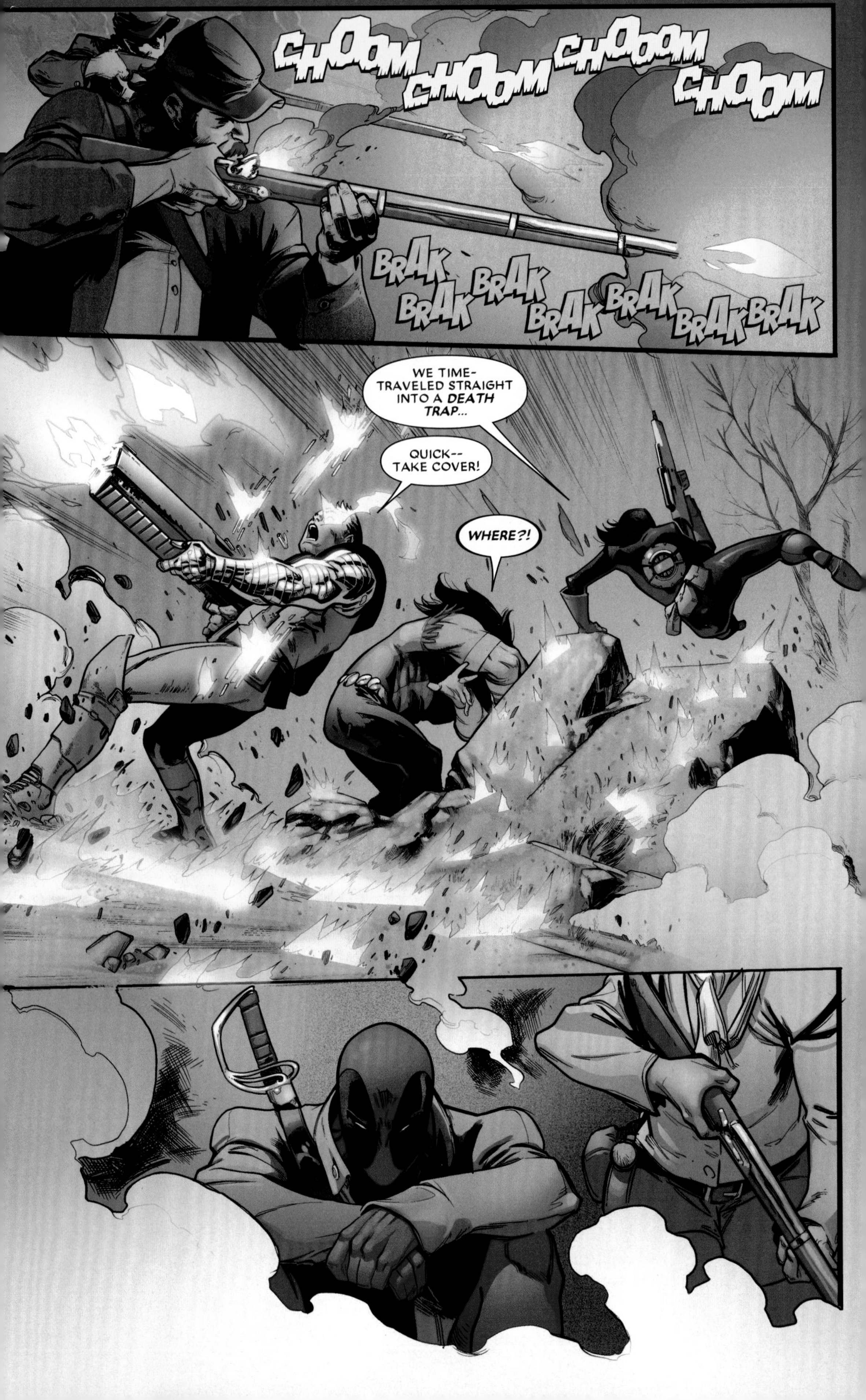
CHOOOM CHOOOM CHOOOOM CHOOOM
BRAK BRAK BRAK BRAK BRAK BRAK BRAK
WE TIME-TRAVELED STRAIGHT INTO A *DEATH TRAP*...
QUICK--TAKE COVER!
WHERE?!

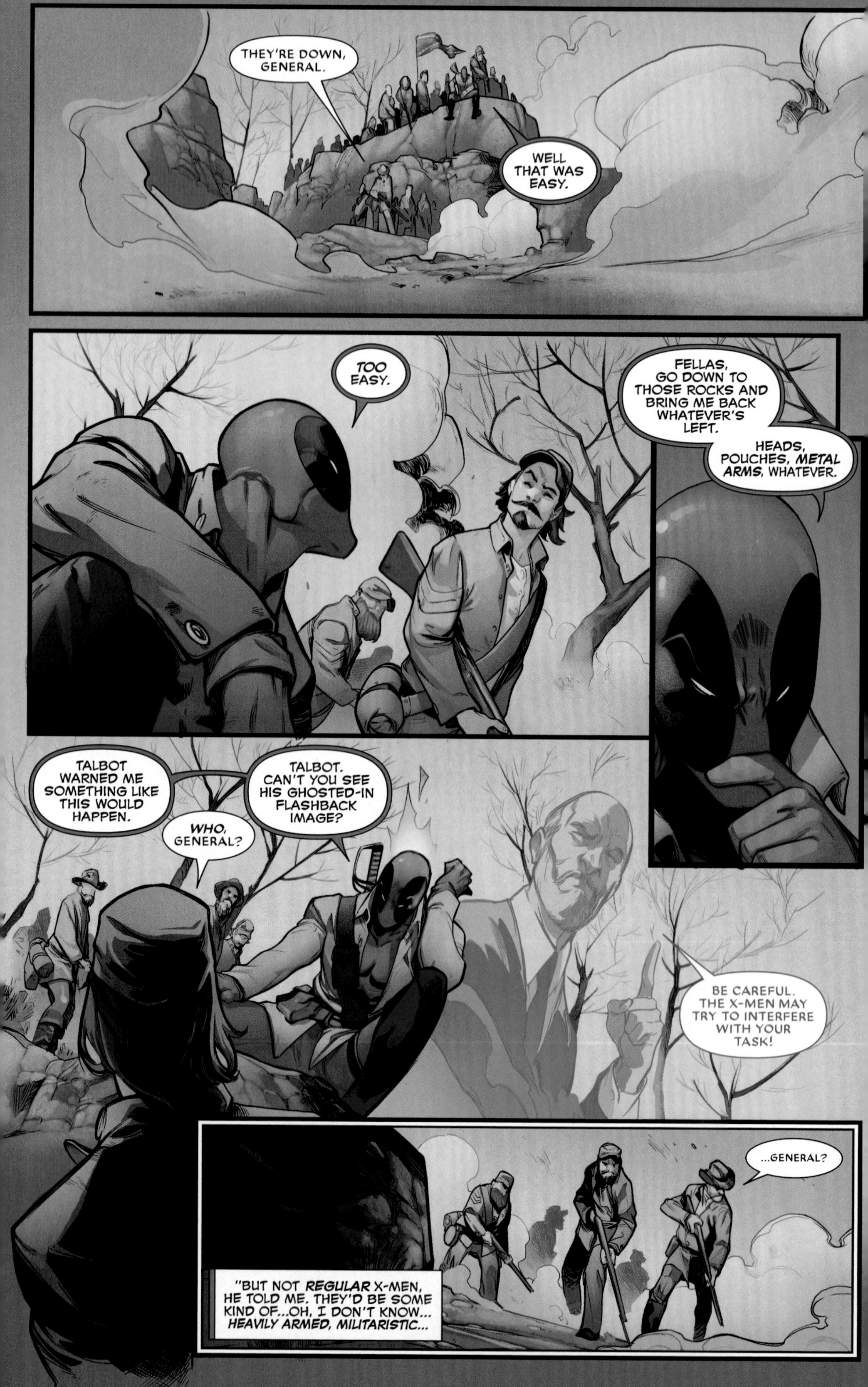
THEY'RE DOWN, GENERAL.
WELL THAT WAS EASY.
TOO EASY.
FELLAS, GO DOWN TO THOSE ROCKS AND BRING ME BACK WHATEVER'S LEFT.
HEADS, POUCHES, METAL ARMS, WHATEVER.
TALBOT WARNED ME SOMETHING LIKE THIS WOULD HAPPEN.
WHO, GENERAL?
TALBOT. CAN'T YOU SEE HIS GHOSTED-IN FLASHBACK IMAGE?
BE CAREFUL. THE X-MEN MAY TRY TO INTERFERE WITH YOUR TASK!
...GENERAL?
"BUT NOT REGULAR X-MEN, HE TOLD ME. THEY'D BE SOME KIND OF...OH, I DON'T KNOW... HEAVILY ARMED, MILITARISTIC...

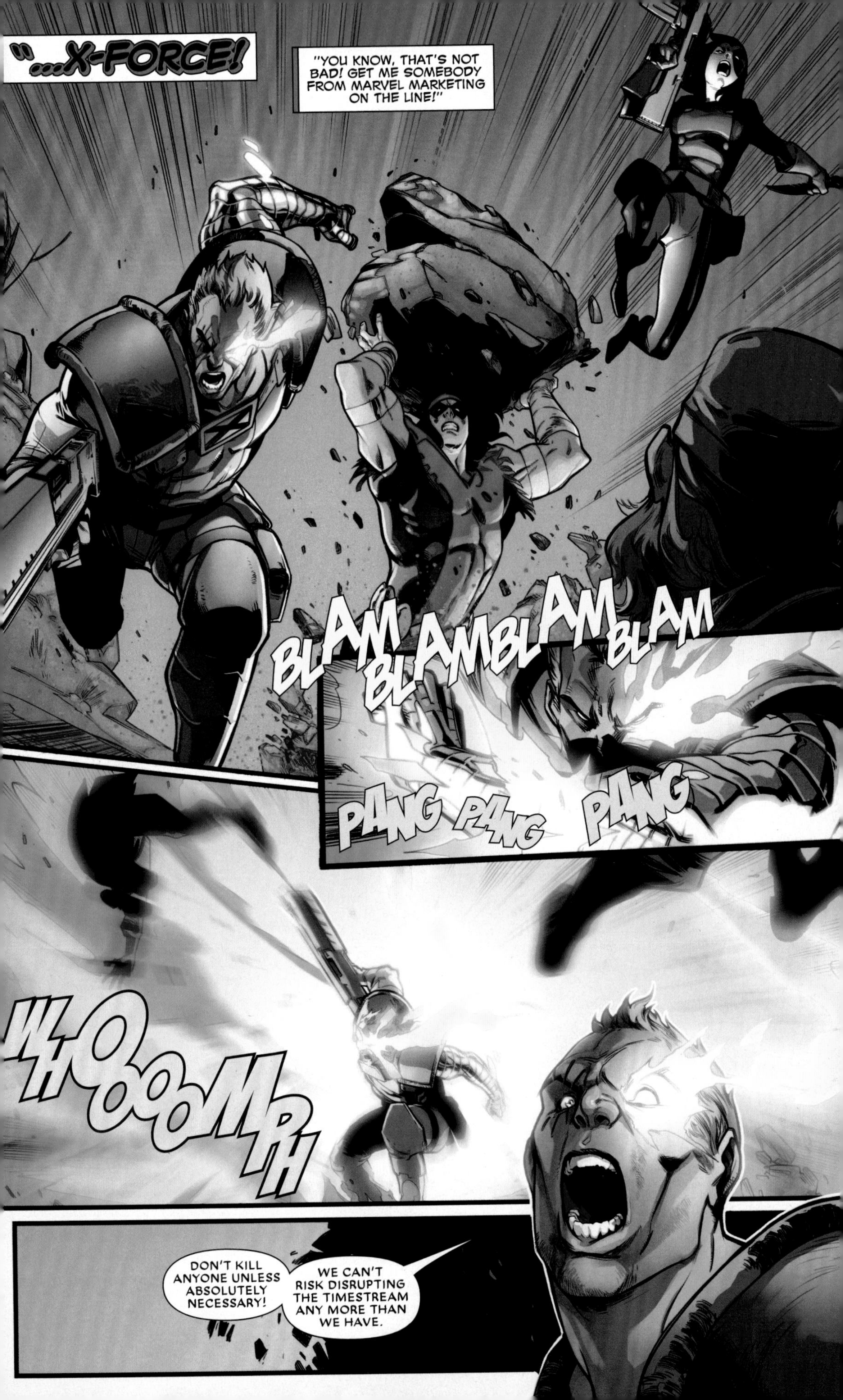

"...X-FORCE!
"YOU KNOW, THAT'S NOT BAD! GET ME SOMEBODY FROM MARVEL MARKETING ON THE LINE!"
BLAM BLAMBLAM BLAM BLAM
PANG PANG PANG
WHOOOOMPH
DON'T KILL ANYONE UNLESS ABSOLUTELY NECESSARY!
WE CAN'T RISK DISRUPTING THE TIMESTREAM ANY MORE THAN WE HAVE.

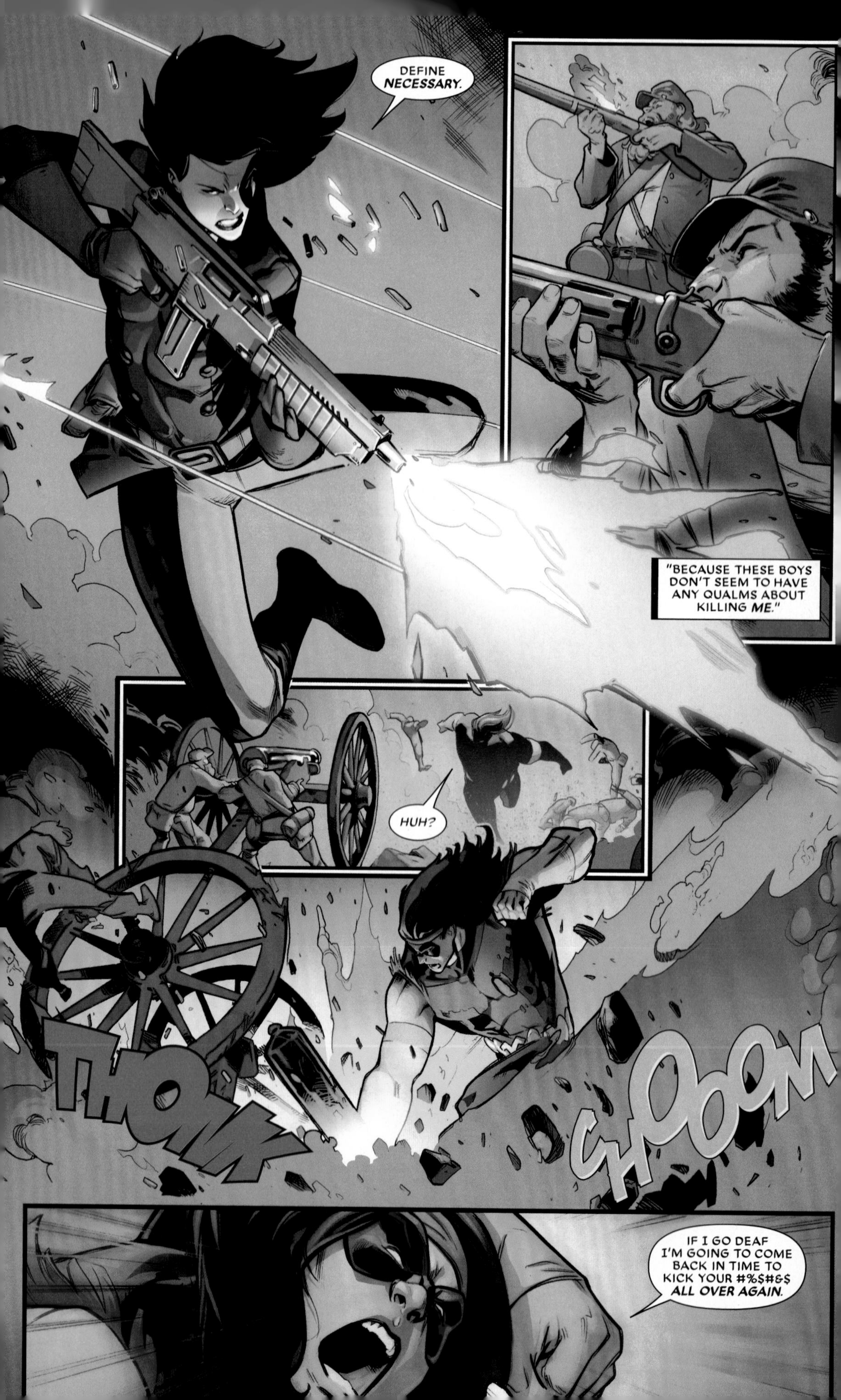
DEFINE NECESSARY.
"BECAUSE THESE BOYS DON'T SEEM TO HAVE ANY QUALMS ABOUT KILLING ME."
HUH?
THOOM
CHOOOOM
IF I GO DEAF I'M GOING TO COME BACK IN TIME TO KICK YOUR #%$#&$ ALL OVER AGAIN.

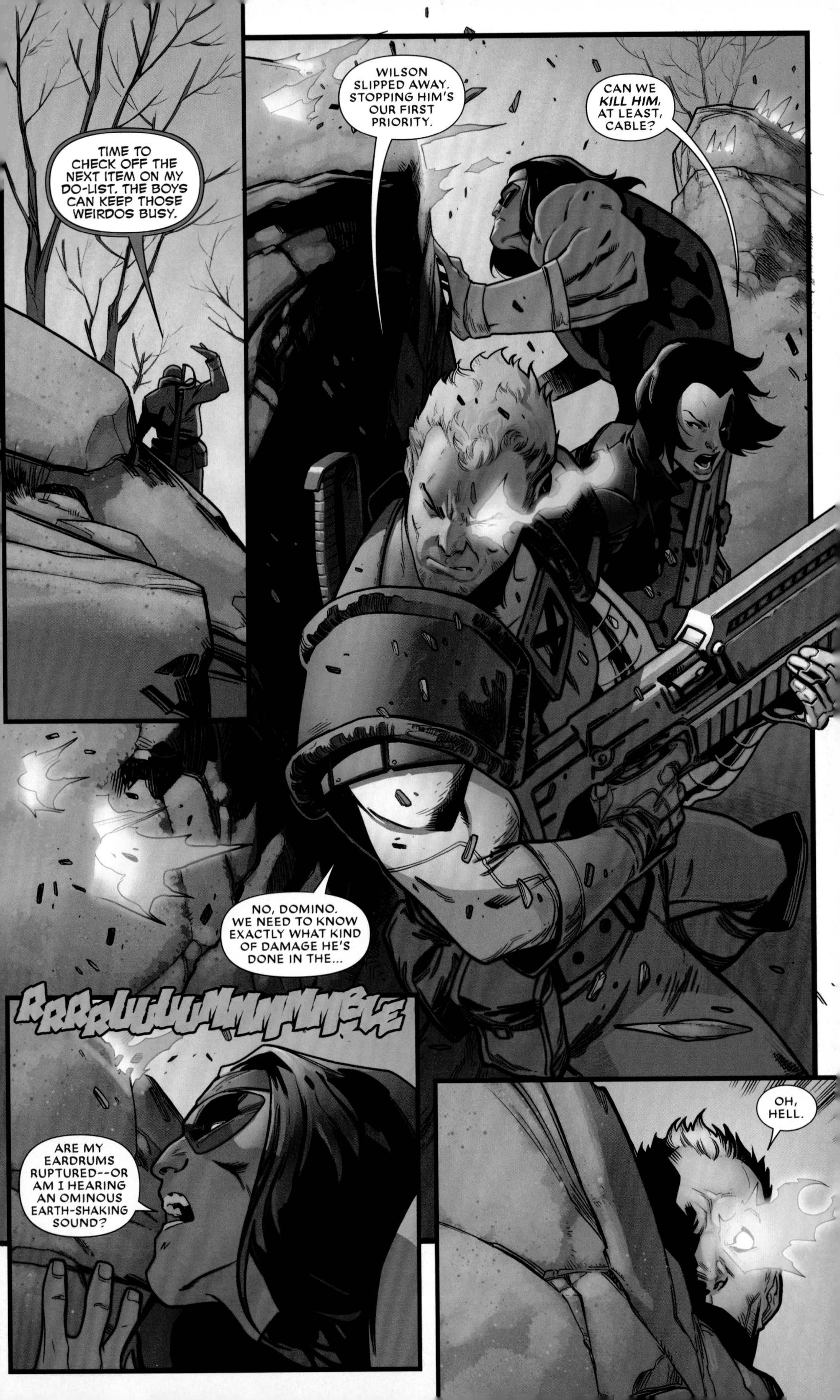
TIME TO CHECK OFF THE NEXT ITEM ON MY DO-LIST. THE BOYS CAN KEEP THOSE WEIRDOS BUSY.
WILSON SLIPPED AWAY. STOPPING HIM'S OUR FIRST PRIORITY.
CAN WE KILL HIM, AT LEAST, CABLE?
NO, DOMINO. WE NEED TO KNOW EXACTLY WHAT KIND OF DAMAGE HE'S DONE IN THE...
RRRRUUUUMMMMMMBLE
ARE MY EARDRUMS RUPTURED--OR AM I HEARING AN OMINOUS EARTH-SHAKING SOUND?
OH, HELL.

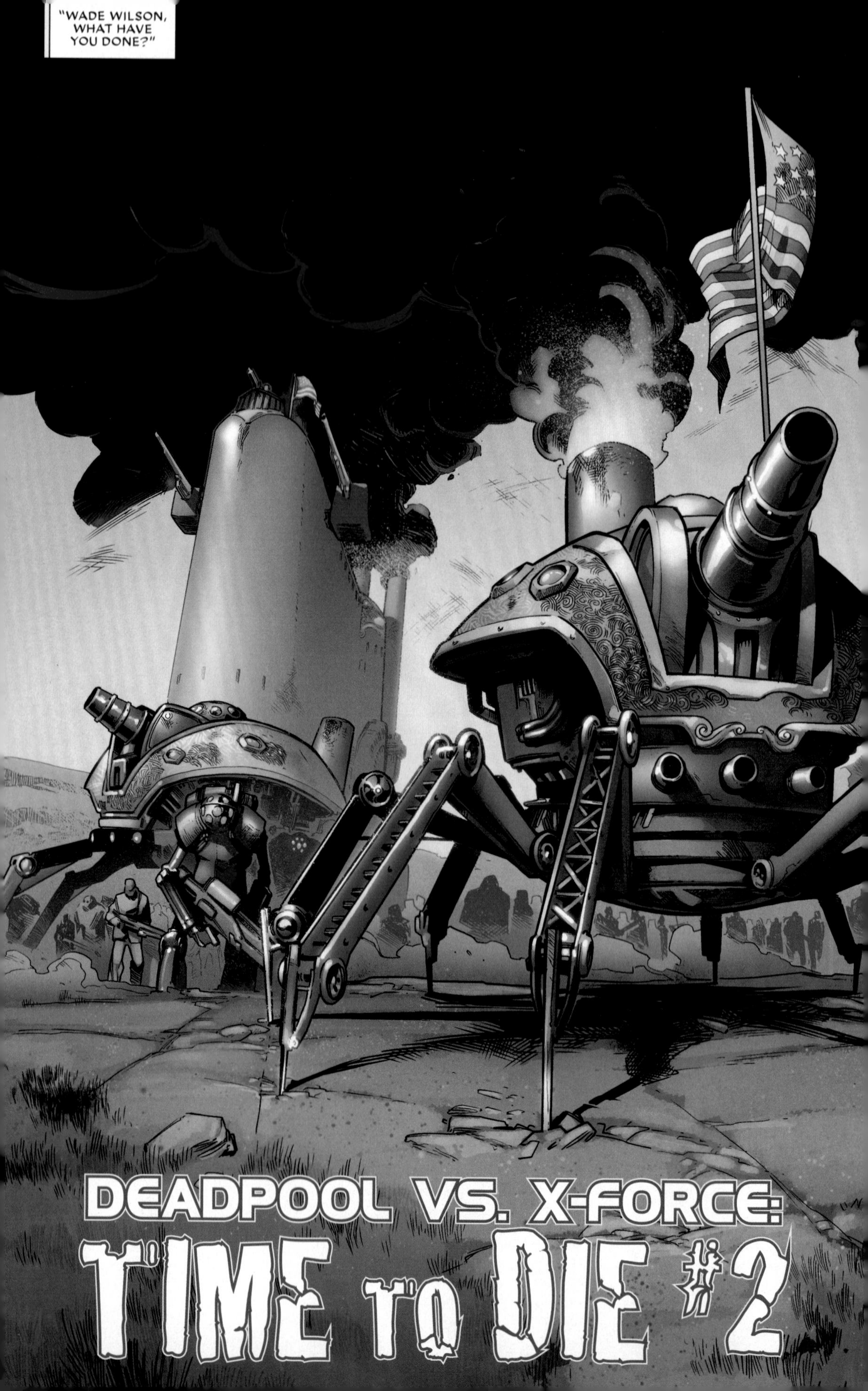
"WADE WILSON, WHAT HAVE YOU DONE?"
DEADPOOL VS. X-FORCE:
TIME TO DIE #2

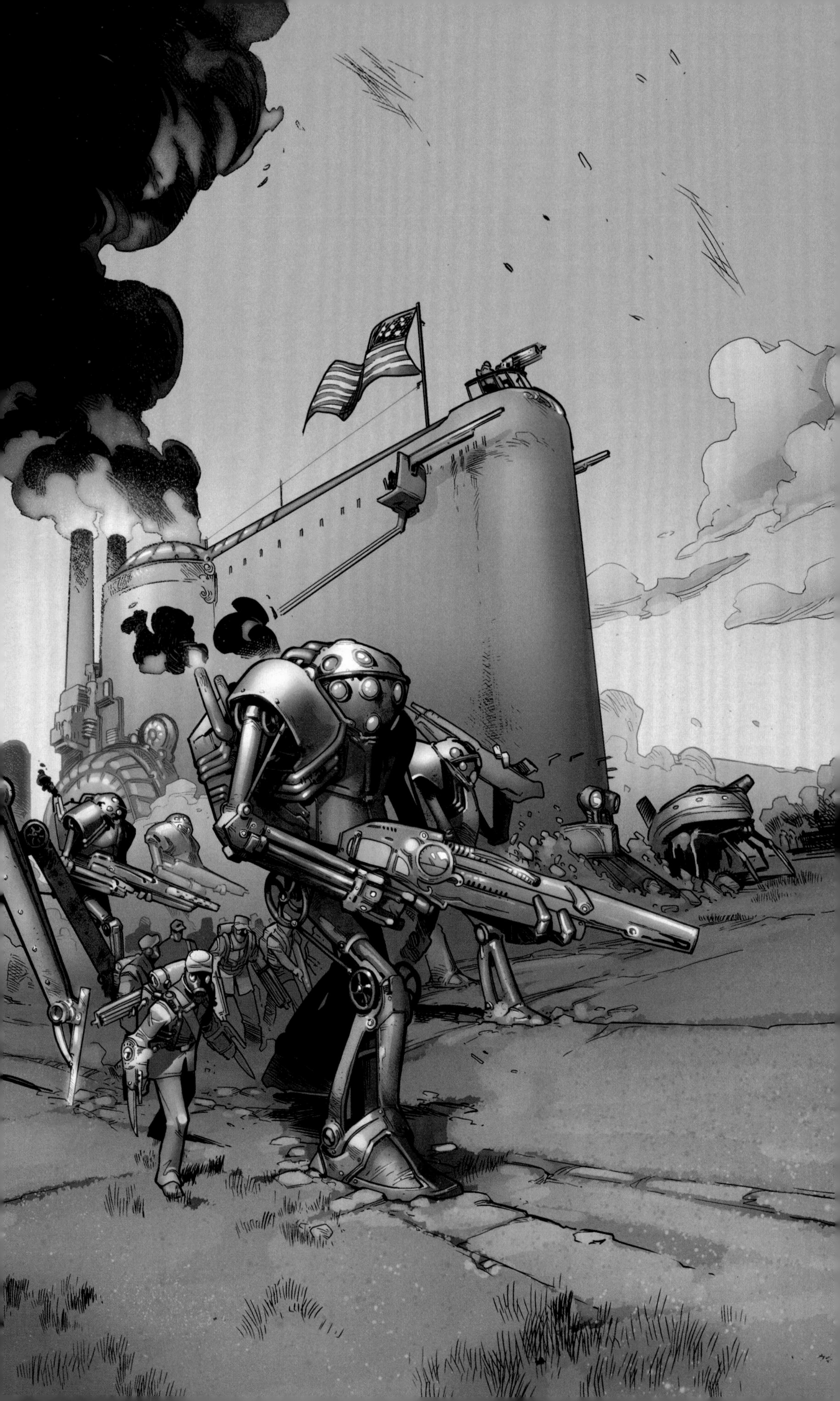

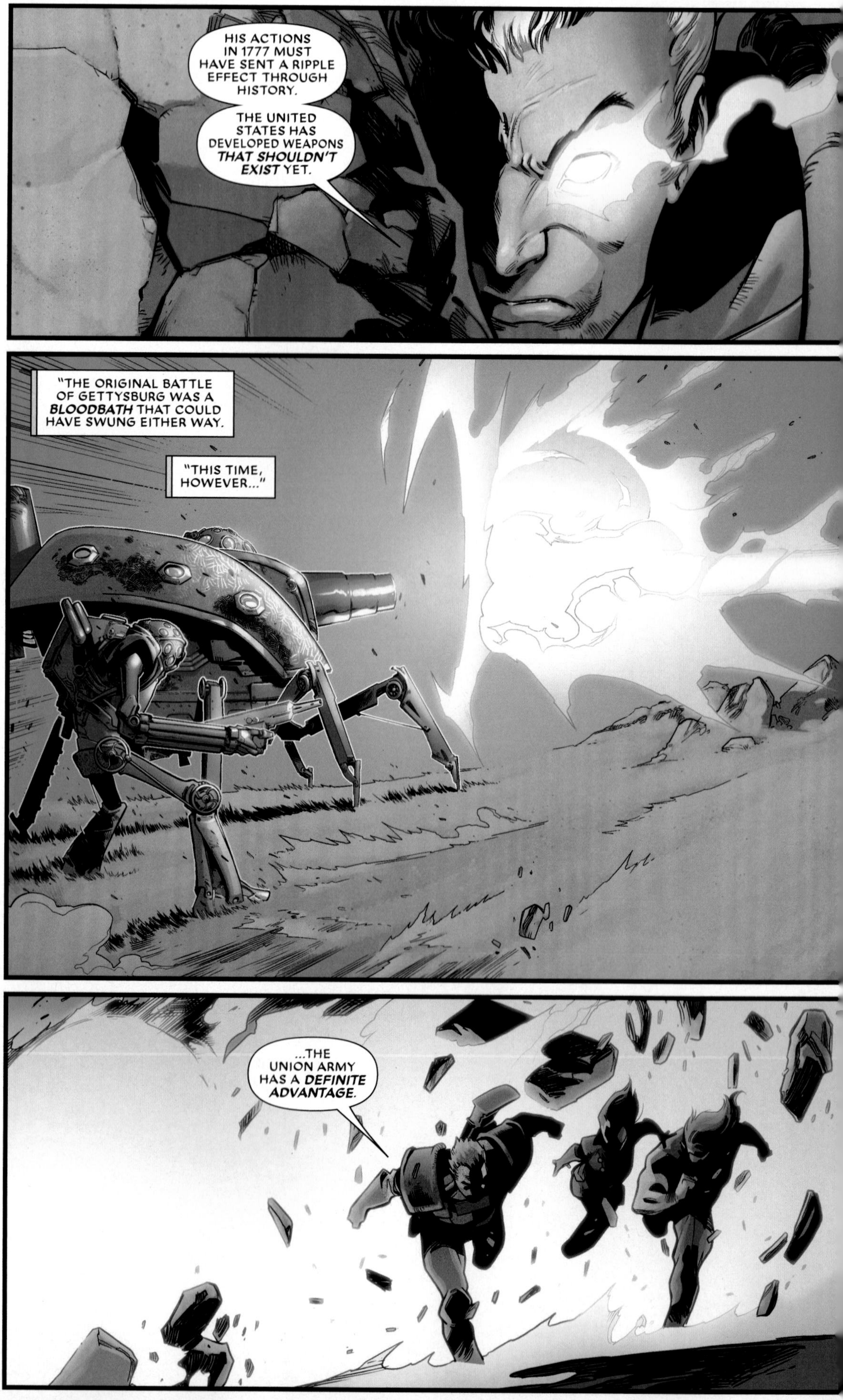
HIS ACTIONS IN 1777 MUST HAVE SENT A RIPPLE EFFECT THROUGH HISTORY.
THE UNITED STATES HAS DEVELOPED WEAPONS ***THAT SHOULDN'T EXIST*** YET.
"THE ORIGINAL BATTLE OF GETTYSBURG WAS A ***BLOODBATH*** THAT COULD HAVE SWUNG EITHER WAY.
"THIS TIME, HOWEVER..."
...THE UNION ARMY HAS A ***DEFINITE ADVANTAGE***.

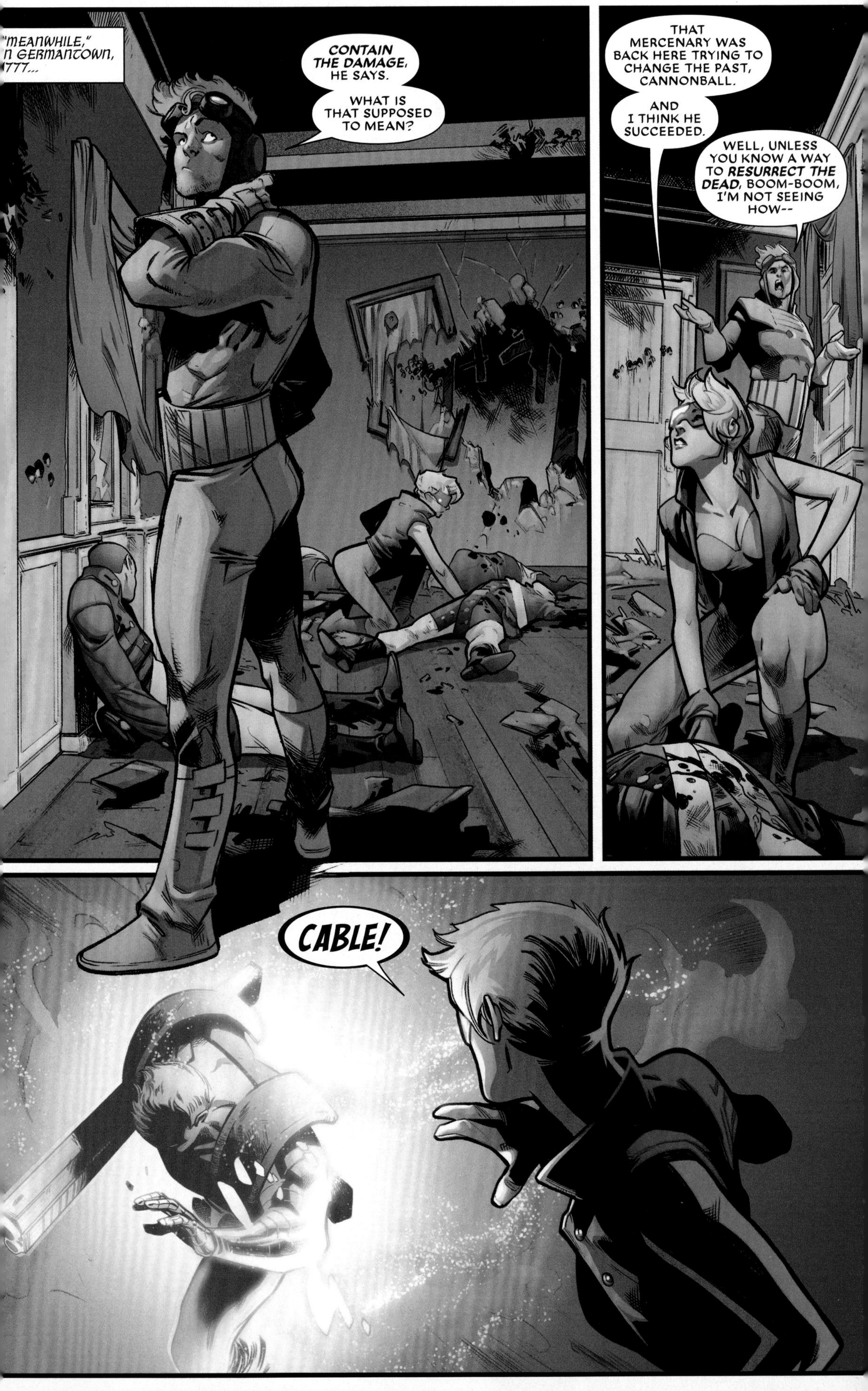
"MEANWHILE,"
n GERMANTOWN,
777...
CONTAIN THE DAMAGE, HE SAYS.
WHAT IS THAT SUPPOSED TO MEAN?
THAT MERCENARY WAS BACK HERE TRYING TO CHANGE THE PAST, CANNONBALL.
AND I THINK HE SUCCEEDED.
WELL, UNLESS YOU KNOW A WAY TO RESURRECT THE DEAD, BOOM-BOOM, I'M NOT SEEING HOW--
CABLE!

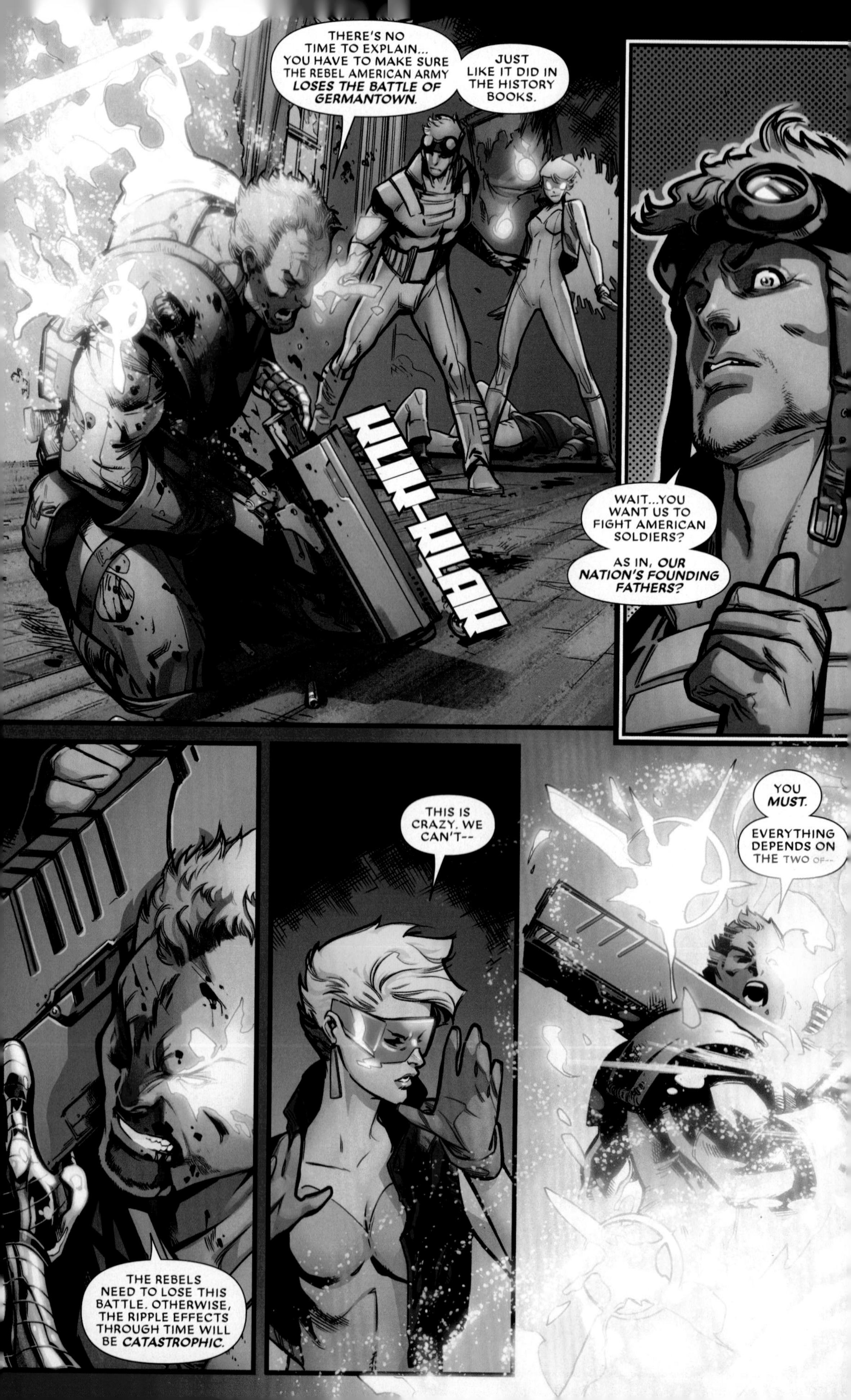
THERE'S NO TIME TO EXPLAIN... YOU HAVE TO MAKE SURE THE REBEL AMERICAN ARMY **LOSES THE BATTLE OF GERMANTOWN.**
JUST LIKE IT DID IN THE HISTORY BOOKS.
KLIK-KLAK
WAIT...YOU WANT US TO FIGHT AMERICAN SOLDIERS?
AS IN, **OUR NATION'S FOUNDING FATHERS?**
THE REBELS NEED TO LOSE THIS BATTLE. OTHERWISE, THE RIPPLE EFFECTS THROUGH TIME WILL BE **CATASTROPHIC.**
THIS IS CRAZY. WE CAN'T--
YOU **MUST.**
EVERYTHING DEPENDS ON THE TWO OF--

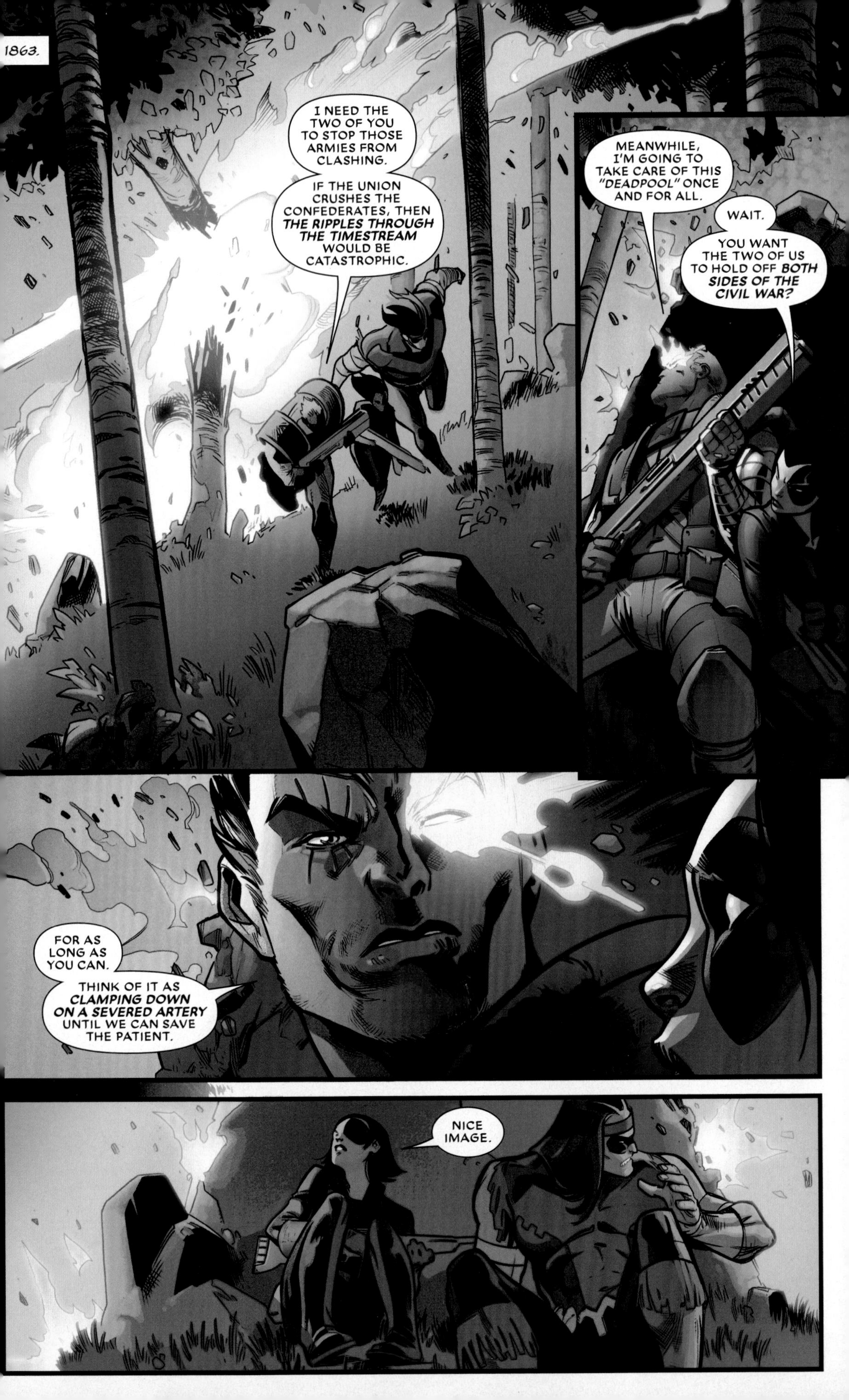

1863.
I NEED THE TWO OF YOU TO STOP THOSE ARMIES FROM CLASHING.
IF THE UNION CRUSHES THE CONFEDERATES, THEN *THE RIPPLES THROUGH THE TIMESTREAM* WOULD BE CATASTROPHIC.
MEANWHILE, I'M GOING TO TAKE CARE OF THIS *"DEADPOOL"* ONCE AND FOR ALL.
WAIT.
YOU WANT THE TWO OF US TO HOLD OFF *BOTH SIDES OF THE CIVIL WAR?*
FOR AS LONG AS YOU CAN.
THINK OF IT AS *CLAMPING DOWN ON A SEVERED ARTERY* UNTIL WE CAN SAVE THE PATIENT.
NICE IMAGE.

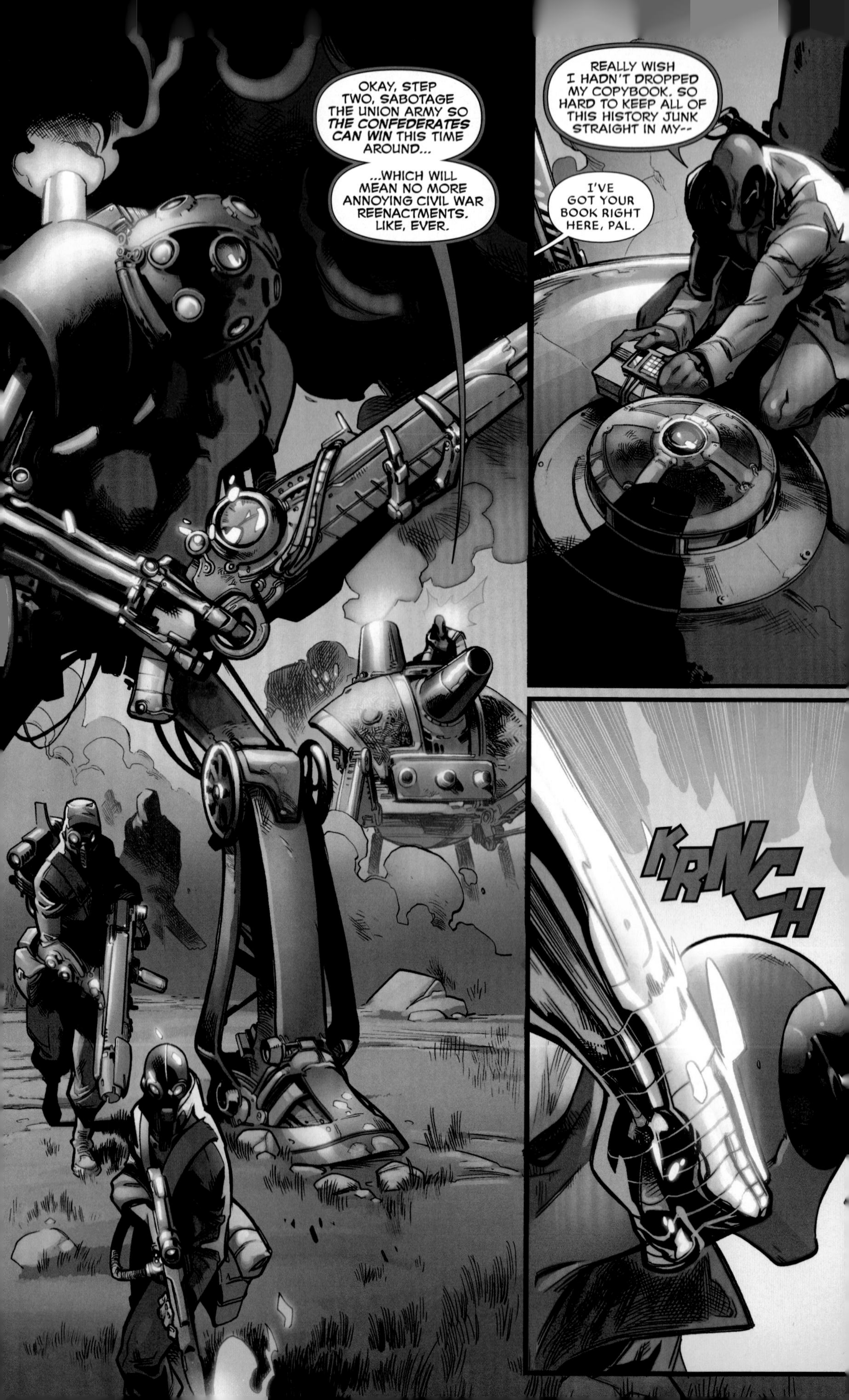
OKAY, STEP TWO, SABOTAGE THE UNION ARMY SO THE CONFEDERATES CAN WIN THIS TIME AROUND...
...WHICH WILL MEAN NO MORE ANNOYING CIVIL WAR REENACTMENTS. LIKE, EVER.
REALLY WISH I HADN'T DROPPED MY COPYBOOK. SO HARD TO KEEP ALL OF THIS HISTORY JUNK STRAIGHT IN MY--
I'VE GOT YOUR BOOK RIGHT HERE, PAL.
KRNCH

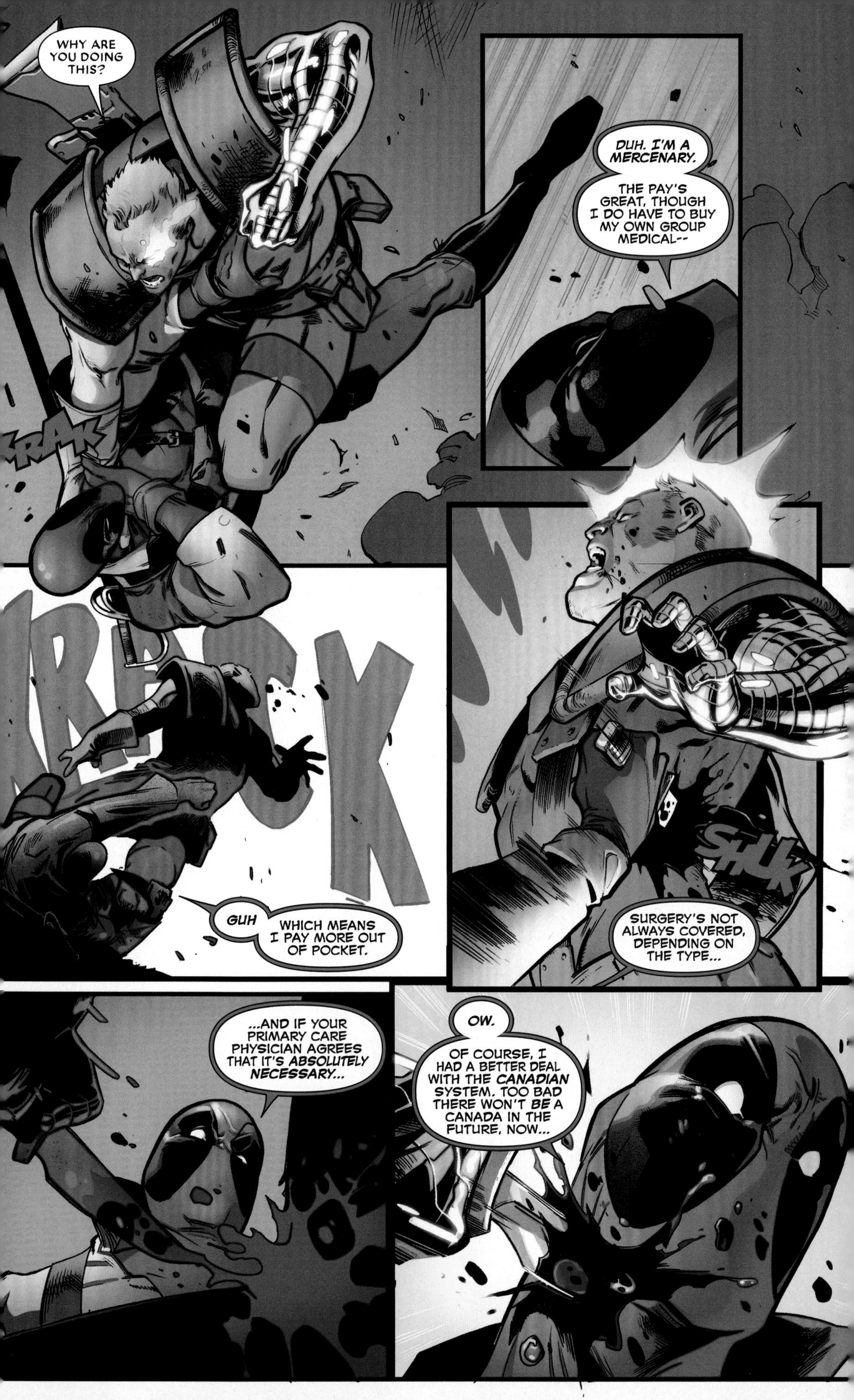
WHY ARE YOU DOING THIS?
DUH. I'M A MERCENARY.
THE PAY'S GREAT, THOUGH I DO HAVE TO BUY MY OWN GROUP MEDICAL--
GUH
WHICH MEANS I PAY MORE OUT OF POCKET.
SHUK
SURGERY'S NOT ALWAYS COVERED, DEPENDING ON THE TYPE...
...AND IF YOUR PRIMARY CARE PHYSICIAN AGREES THAT IT'S *ABSOLUTELY NECESSARY*...
OW.
OF COURSE, I HAD A BETTER DEAL WITH THE *CANADIAN* SYSTEM. TOO BAD THERE WON'T *BE* A CANADA IN THE FUTURE, NOW...

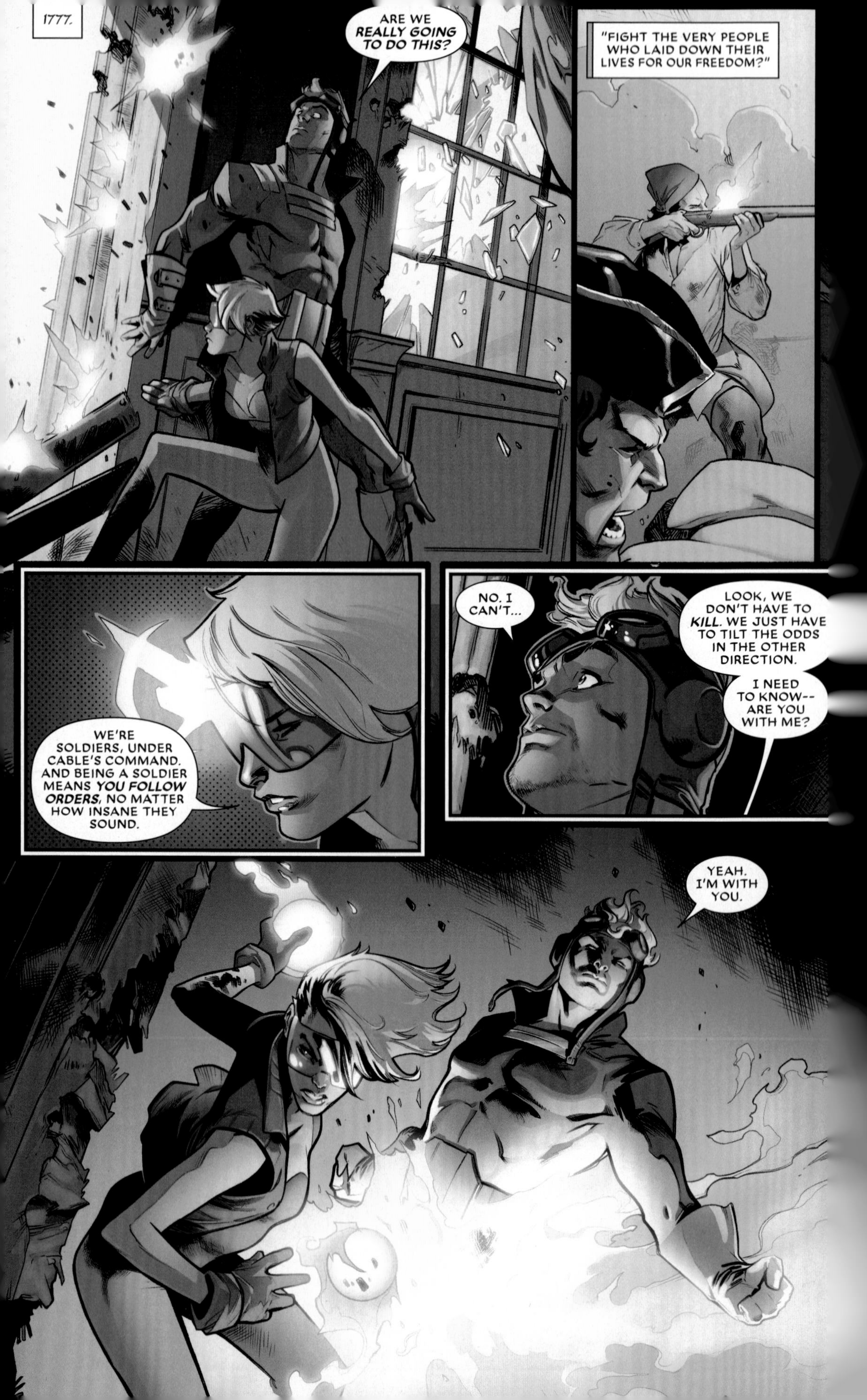
1777.
ARE WE REALLY GOING TO DO THIS?
"FIGHT THE VERY PEOPLE WHO LAID DOWN THEIR LIVES FOR OUR FREEDOM?"
WE'RE SOLDIERS, UNDER CABLE'S COMMAND. AND BEING A SOLDIER MEANS YOU FOLLOW ORDERS, NO MATTER HOW INSANE THEY SOUND.
NO. I CAN'T...
LOOK, WE DON'T HAVE TO KILL. WE JUST HAVE TO TILT THE ODDS IN THE OTHER DIRECTION.
I NEED TO KNOW--ARE YOU WITH ME?
YEAH. I'M WITH YOU.

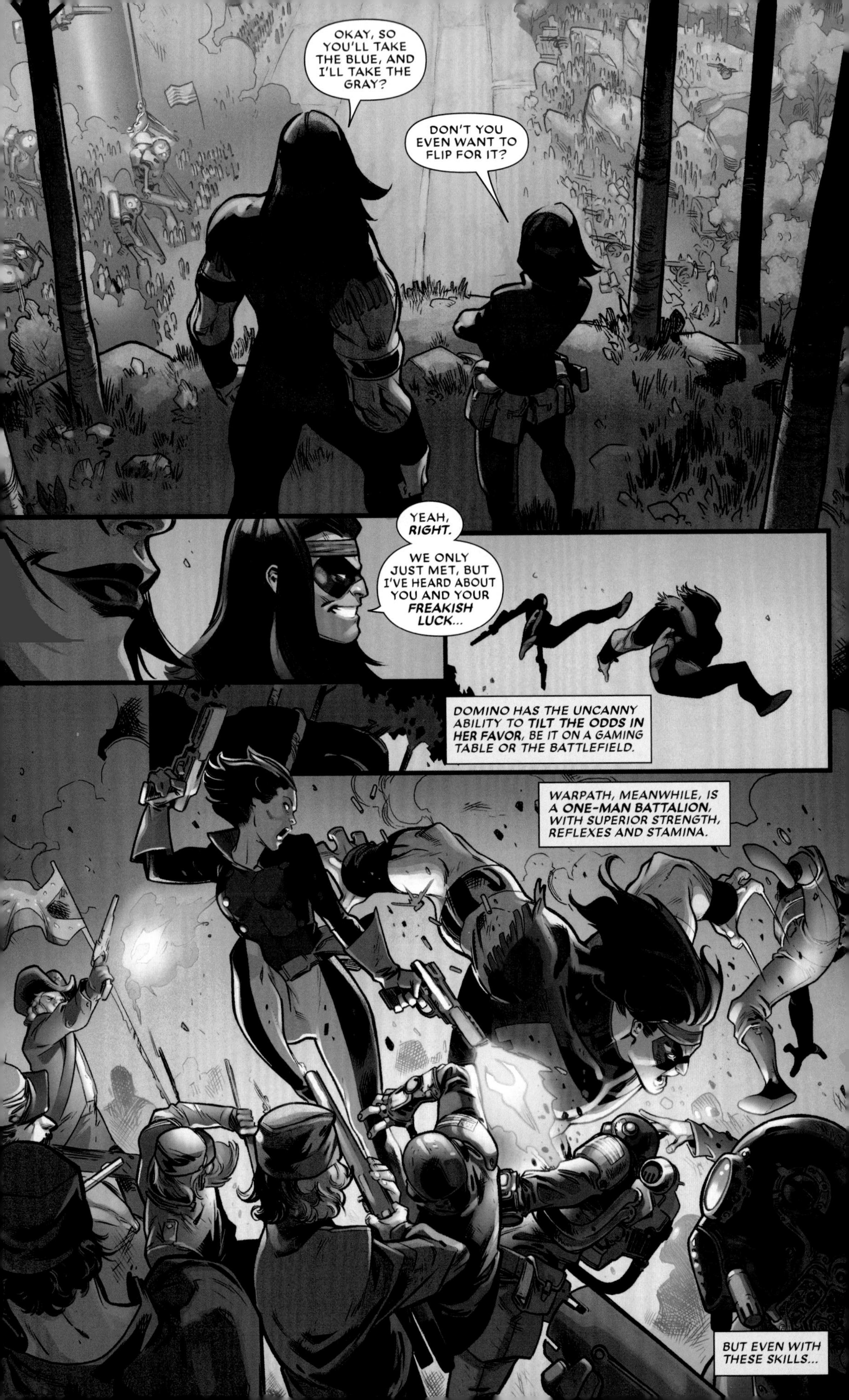
OKAY, SO YOU'LL TAKE THE BLUE, AND I'LL TAKE THE GRAY?
DON'T YOU EVEN WANT TO FLIP FOR IT?
YEAH, *RIGHT.*
WE ONLY JUST MET, BUT I'VE HEARD ABOUT YOU AND YOUR *FREAKISH LUCK...*
DOMINO HAS THE UNCANNY ABILITY TO TILT THE ODDS IN HER FAVOR, BE IT ON A GAMING TABLE OR THE BATTLEFIELD.
WARPATH, MEANWHILE, IS A ONE-MAN BATTALION, WITH SUPERIOR STRENGTH, REFLEXES AND STAMINA.
BUT EVEN WITH THESE SKILLS...

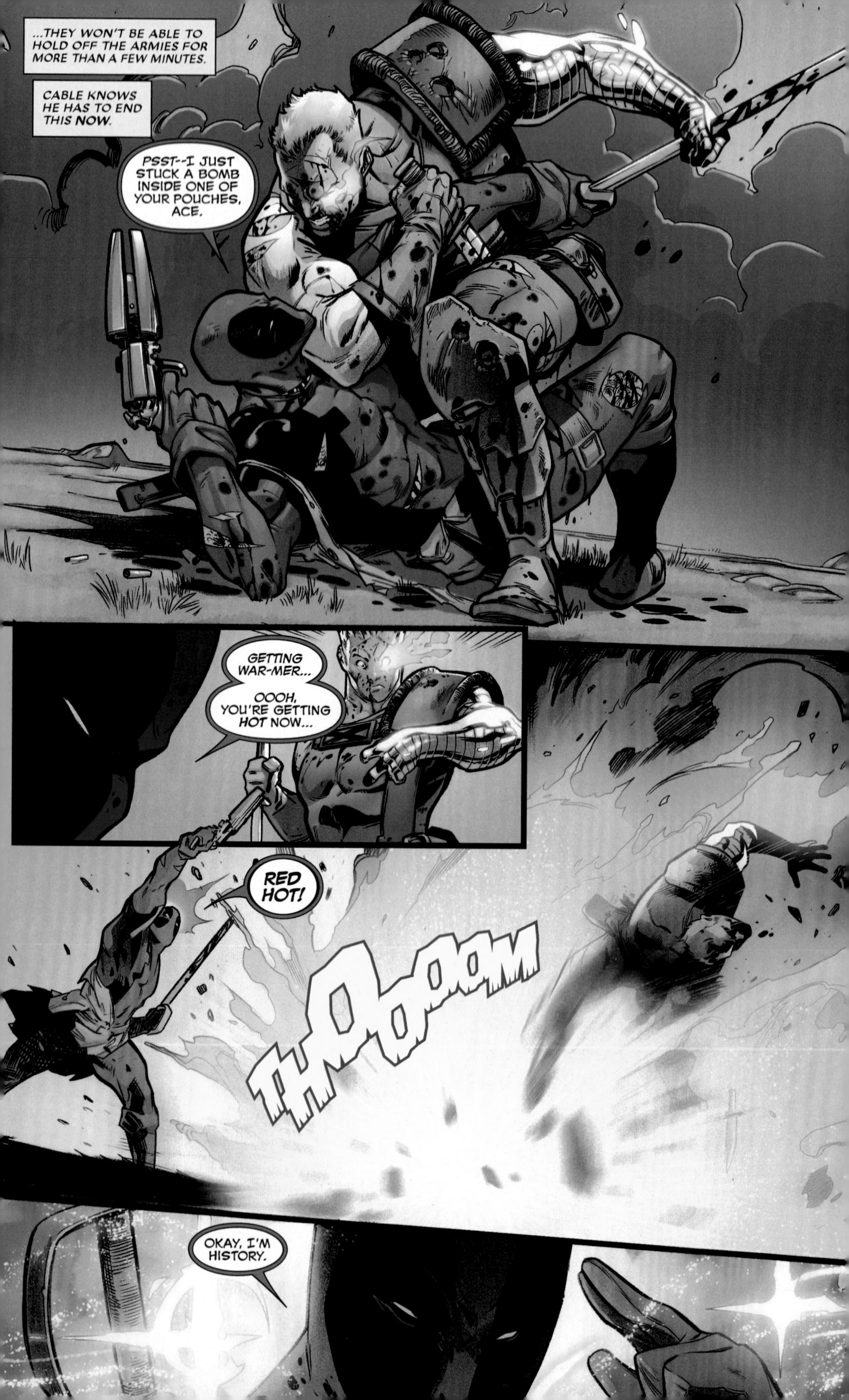
...THEY WON'T BE ABLE TO HOLD OFF THE ARMIES FOR MORE THAN A FEW MINUTES.
CABLE KNOWS HE HAS TO END THIS NOW.
PSST--I JUST STUCK A BOMB INSIDE ONE OF YOUR POUCHES, ACE.
GETTING WAR-MER...
OOOH, YOU'RE GETTING HOT NOW...
RED HOT!
THOOOOM
OKAY, I'M HISTORY.

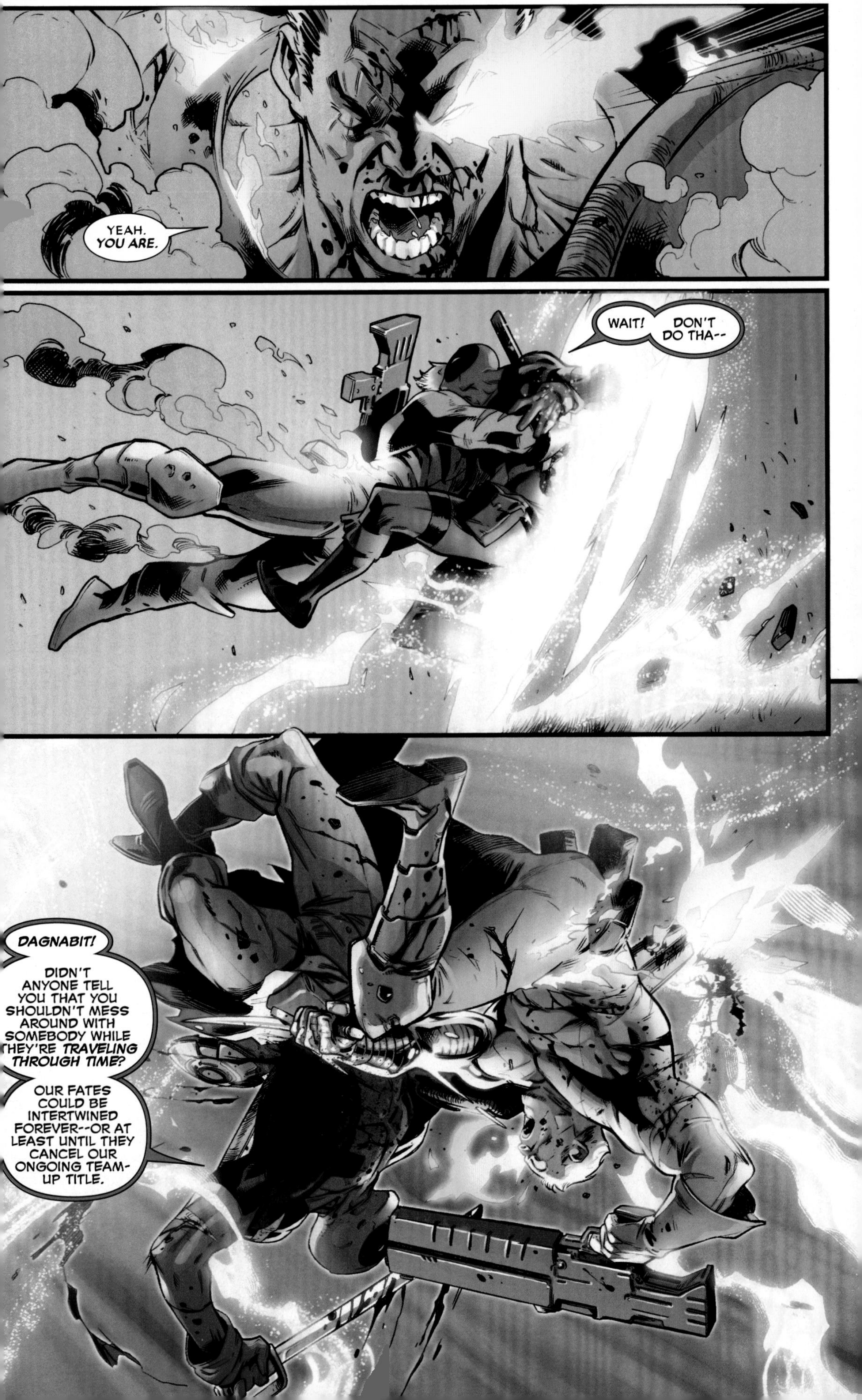
YEAH. YOU ARE.
WAIT!
DON'T DO THA--
DAGNABIT!
DIDN'T ANYONE TELL YOU THAT YOU SHOULDN'T MESS AROUND WITH SOMEBODY WHILE THEY'RE *TRAVELING THROUGH TIME?*
OUR FATES COULD BE INTERTWINED FOREVER--OR AT LEAST UNTIL THEY CANCEL OUR ONGOING TEAM-UP TITLE.

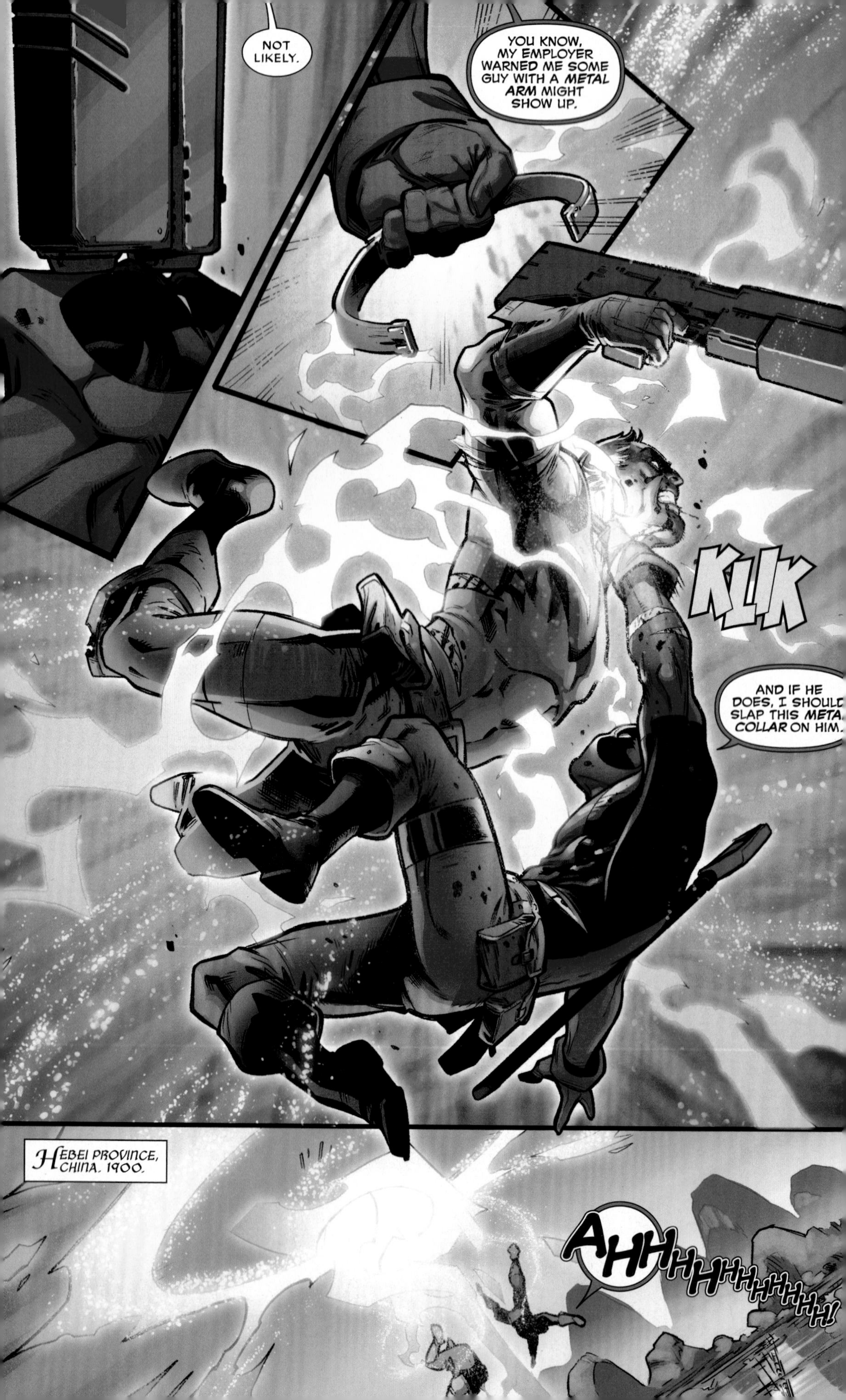
NOT LIKELY.
YOU KNOW, MY EMPLOYER WARNED ME SOME GUY WITH A METAL ARM MIGHT SHOW UP.
KLIK
AND IF HE DOES, I SHOULD SLAP THIS METAL COLLAR ON HIM.
HEBEI PROVINCE, CHINA, 1900.
AHHHHHHHHHHH!

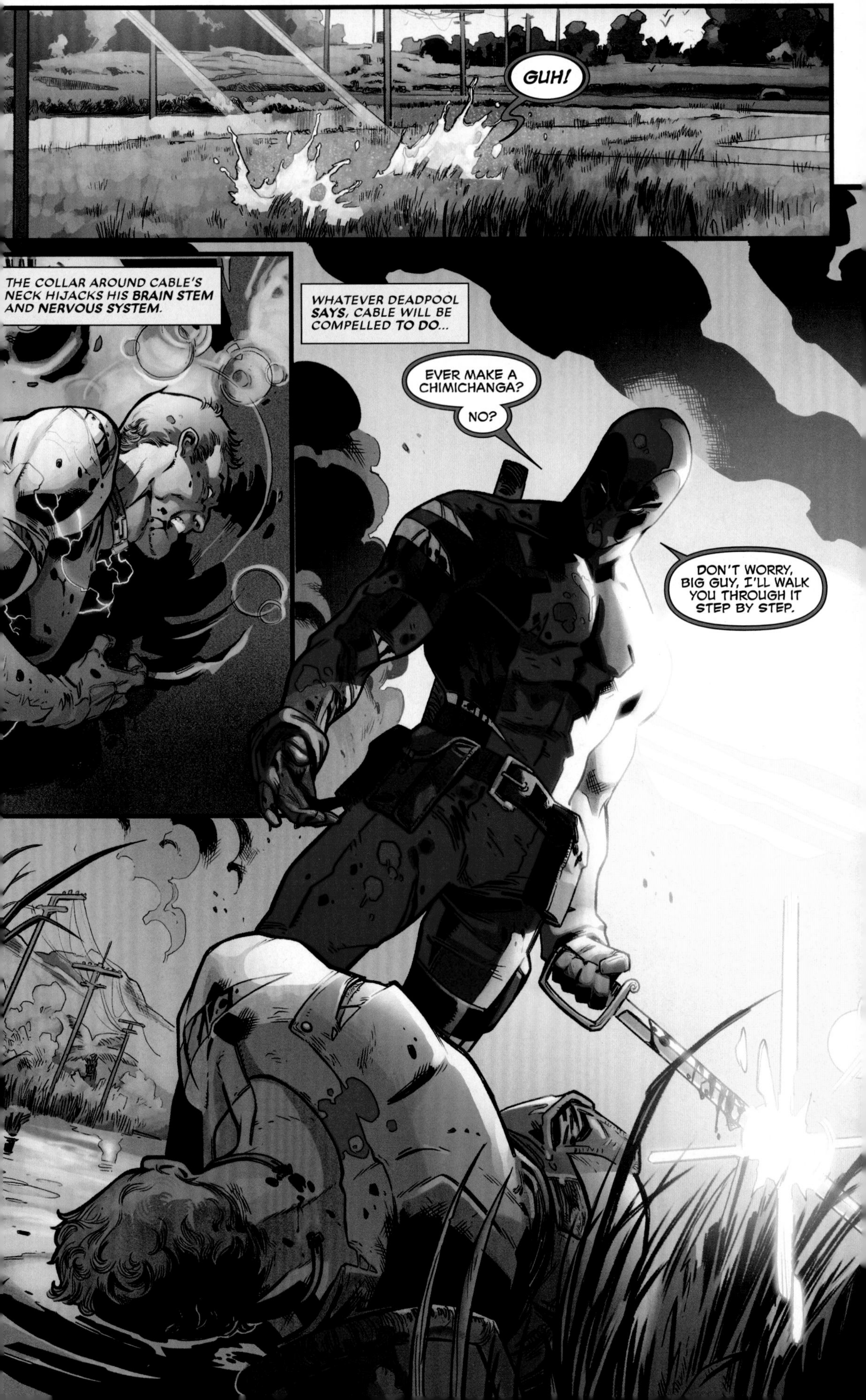
GUH!
THE COLLAR AROUND CABLE'S NECK HIJACKS HIS BRAIN STEM AND NERVOUS SYSTEM.
WHATEVER DEADPOOL SAYS, CABLE WILL BE COMPELLED TO DO...
EVER MAKE A CHIMICHANGA?
NO?
DON'T WORRY, BIG GUY, I'LL WALK YOU THROUGH IT STEP BY STEP.

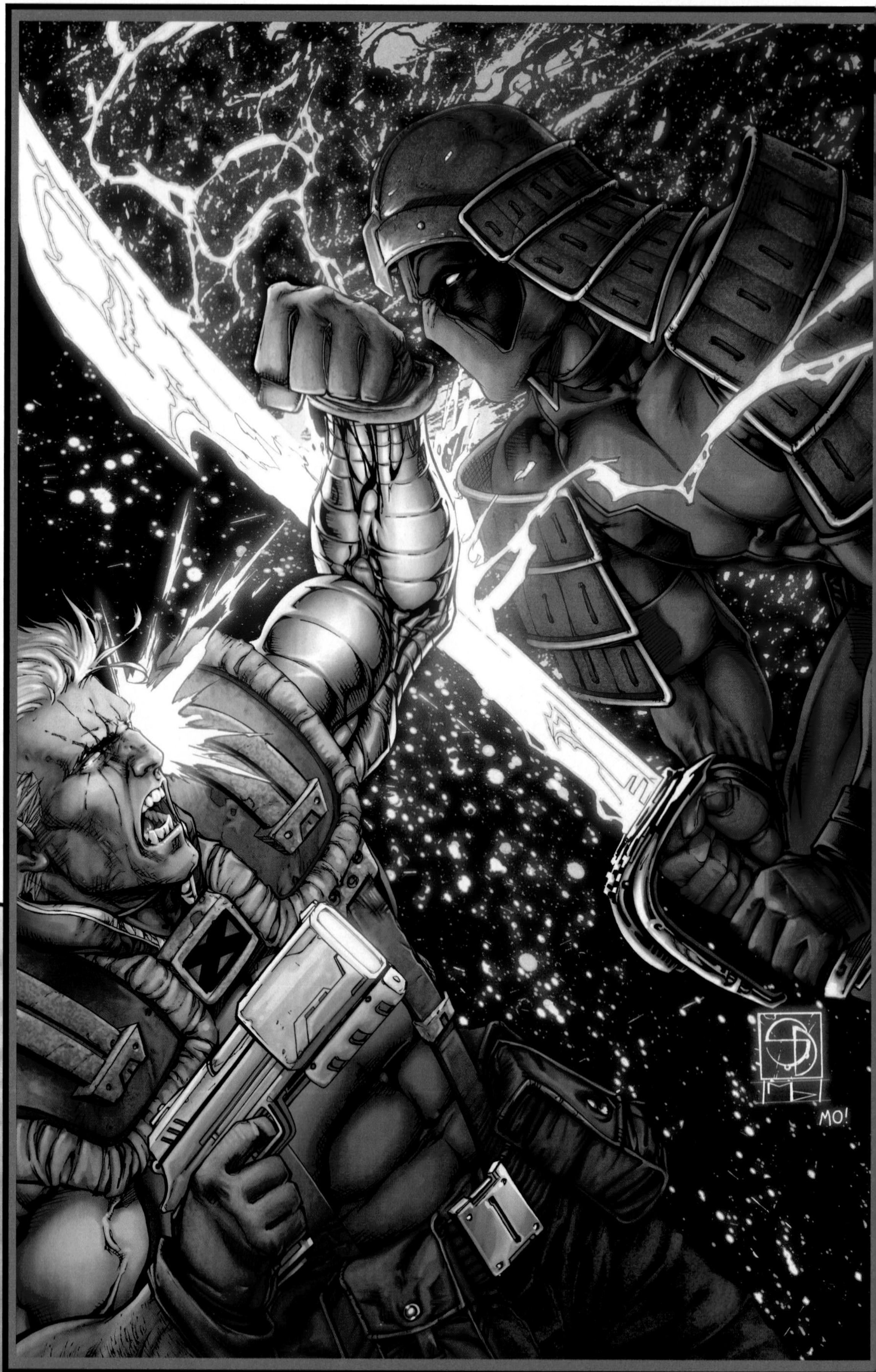

#3

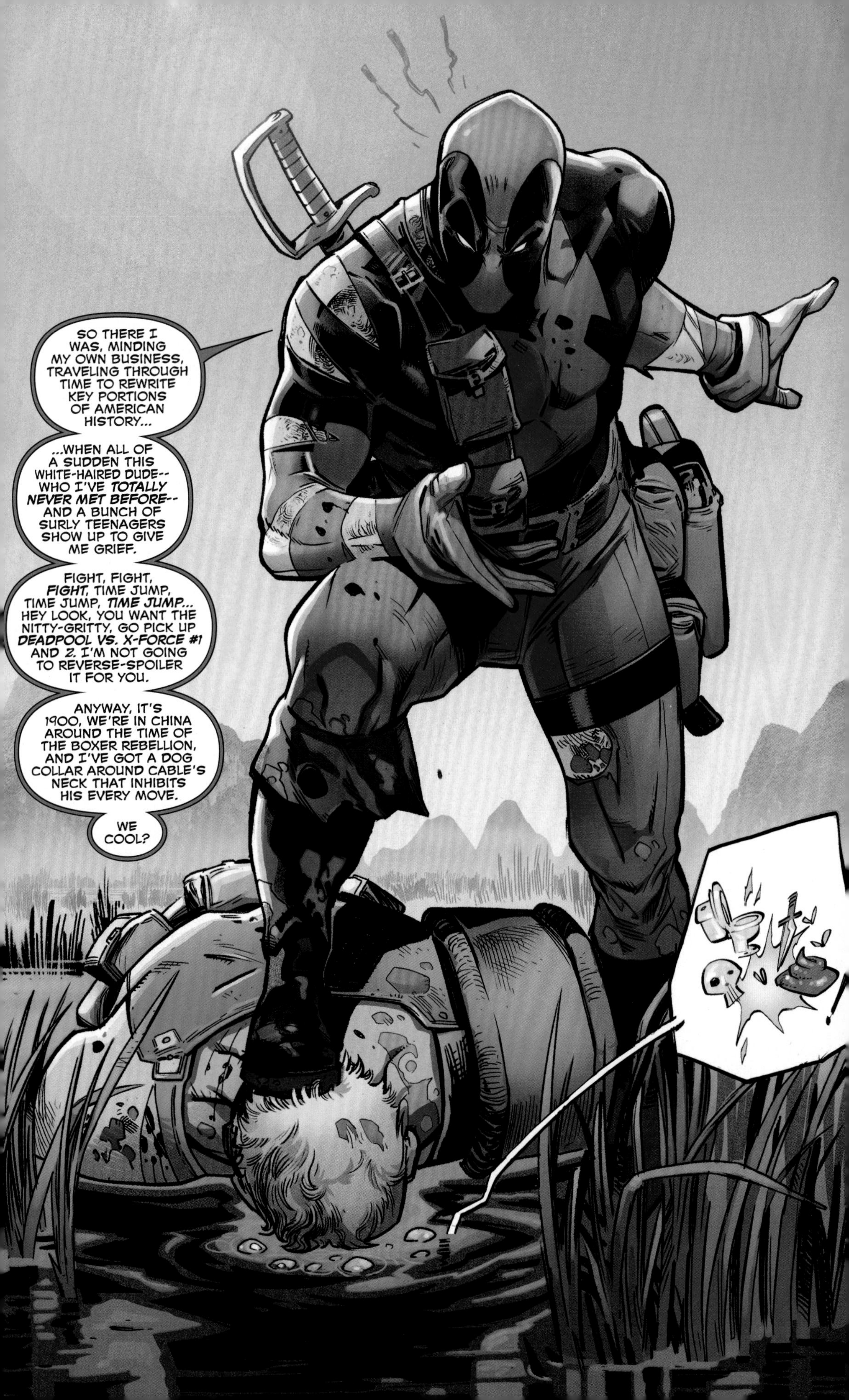
SO THERE I WAS, MINDING MY OWN BUSINESS, TRAVELING THROUGH TIME TO REWRITE KEY PORTIONS OF AMERICAN HISTORY...
...WHEN ALL OF A SUDDEN THIS WHITE-HAIRED DUDE-- WHO I'VE *TOTALLY NEVER MET BEFORE*-- AND A BUNCH OF SURLY TEENAGERS SHOW UP TO GIVE ME GRIEF.
FIGHT, FIGHT, *FIGHT*, TIME JUMP, TIME JUMP, *TIME JUMP*... HEY LOOK, YOU WANT THE NITTY-GRITTY, GO PICK UP *DEADPOOL VS. X-FORCE #1* AND 2. I'M NOT GOING TO REVERSE-SPOILER IT FOR YOU.
ANYWAY, IT'S 1900, WE'RE IN CHINA AROUND THE TIME OF THE BOXER REBELLION, AND I'VE GOT A DOG COLLAR AROUND CABLE'S NECK THAT INHIBITS HIS EVERY MOVE.
WE COOL?

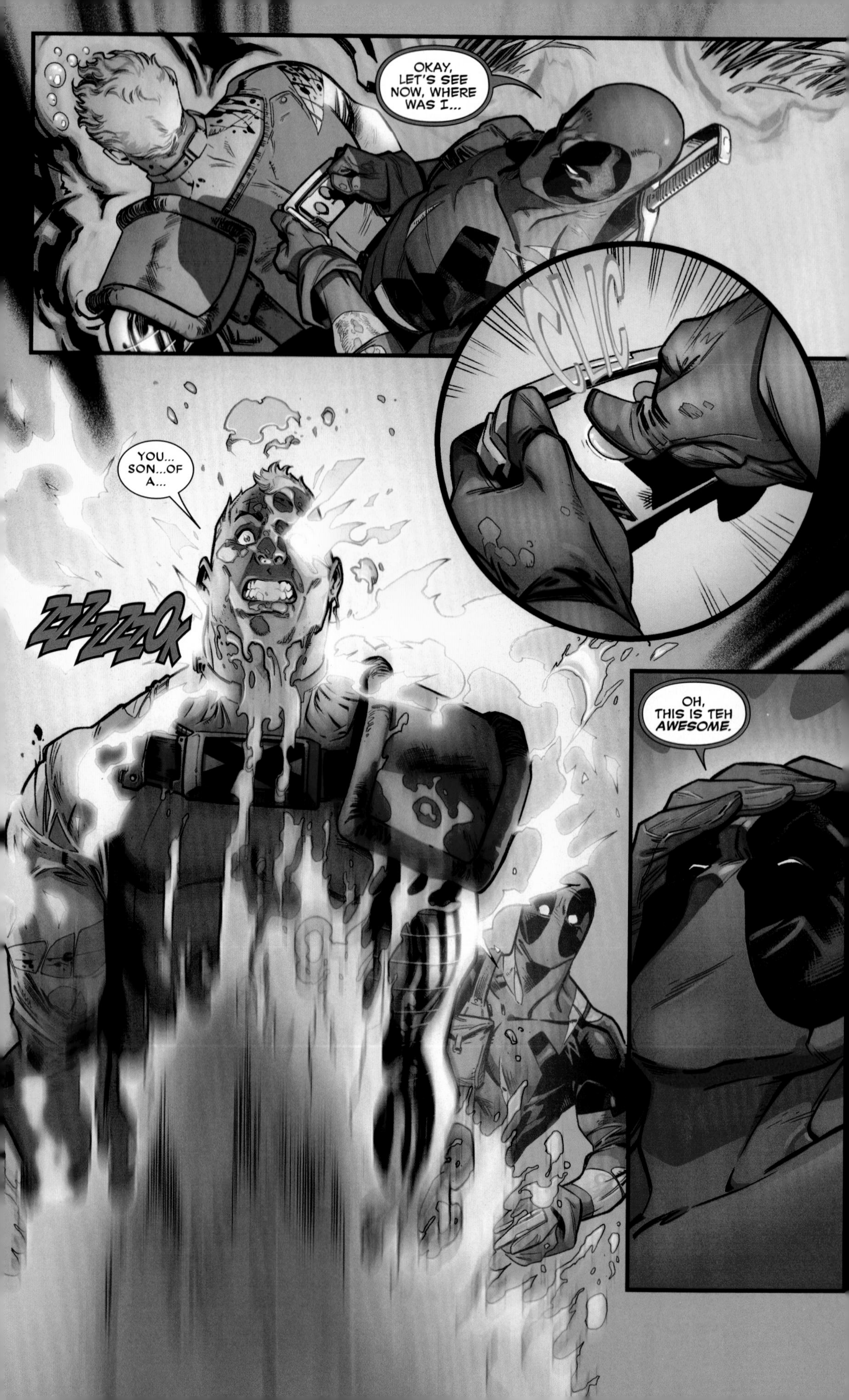
OKAY, LET'S SEE NOW, WHERE WAS I...
CLIC
YOU... SON...OF A...
ZZZZZZOK
OH, THIS IS TEH *AWESOME.*

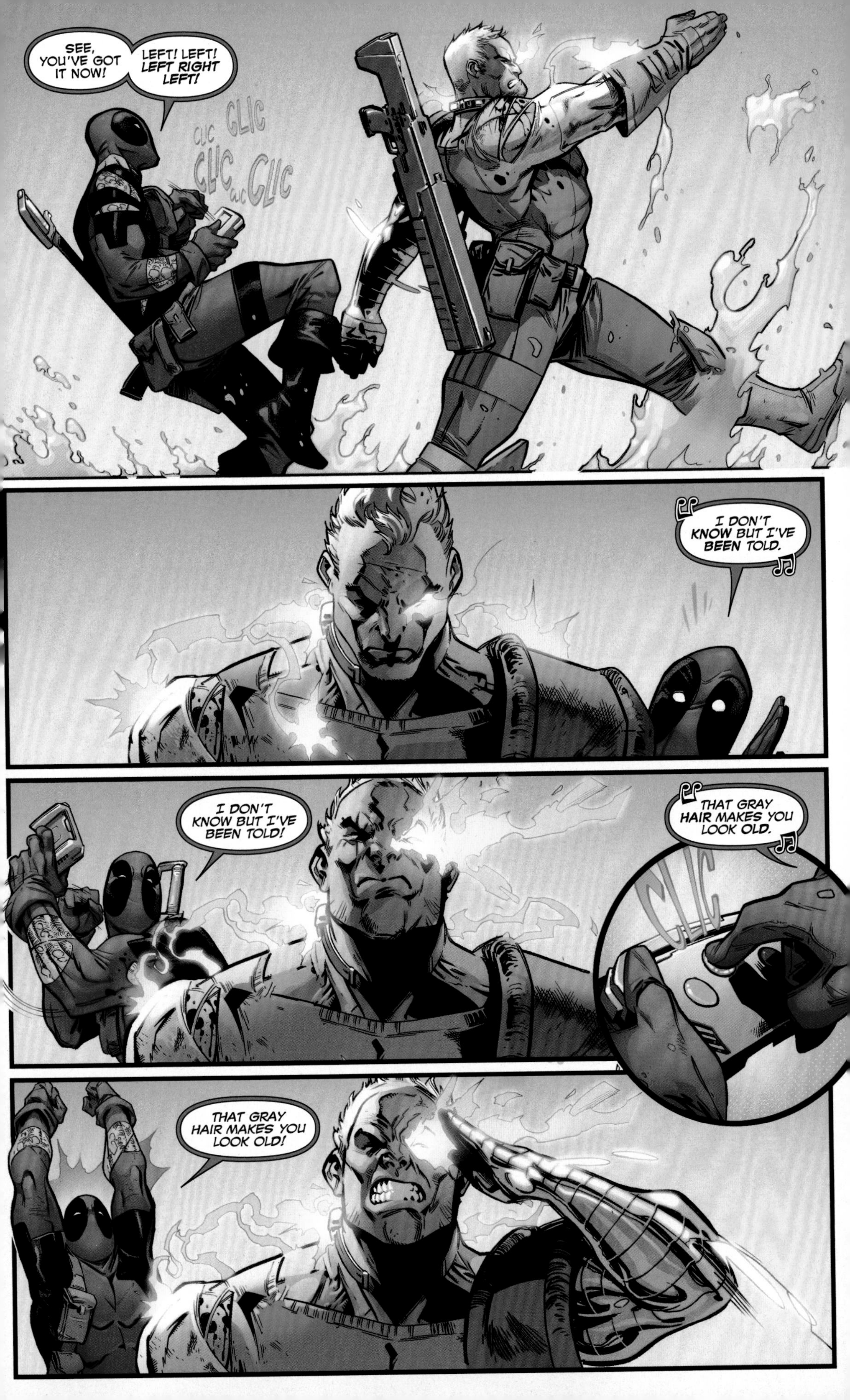
SEE, YOU'VE GOT IT NOW!
LEFT! LEFT! LEFT RIGHT LEFT!
CLIC CLIC CLIC CLIC CLIC
I DON'T KNOW BUT I'VE BEEN TOLD.
I DON'T KNOW BUT I'VE BEEN TOLD!
THAT GRAY HAIR MAKES YOU LOOK OLD.
CLIC
THAT GRAY HAIR MAKES YOU LOOK OLD!

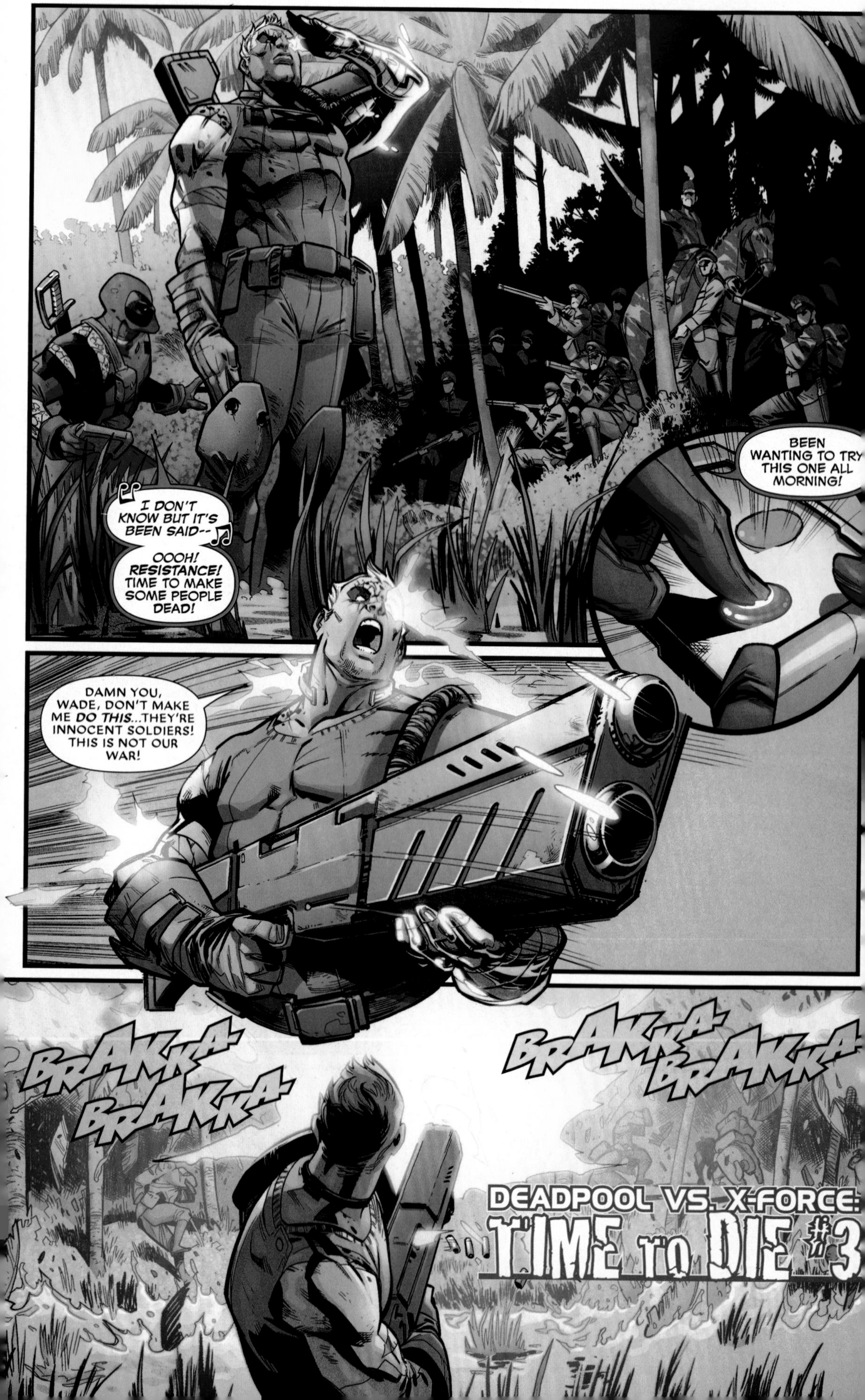

I DON'T KNOW BUT IT'S BEEN SAID--
OOOH! RESISTANCE! TIME TO MAKE SOME PEOPLE DEAD!
BEEN WANTING TO TRY THIS ONE ALL MORNING!
DAMN YOU, WADE, DON'T MAKE ME DO THIS...THEY'RE INNOCENT SOLDIERS! THIS IS NOT OUR WAR!
BRAKKA BRAKKA
BRAKKA BRAKKA
DEADPOOL VS. X-FORCE:
TIME to DIE #3

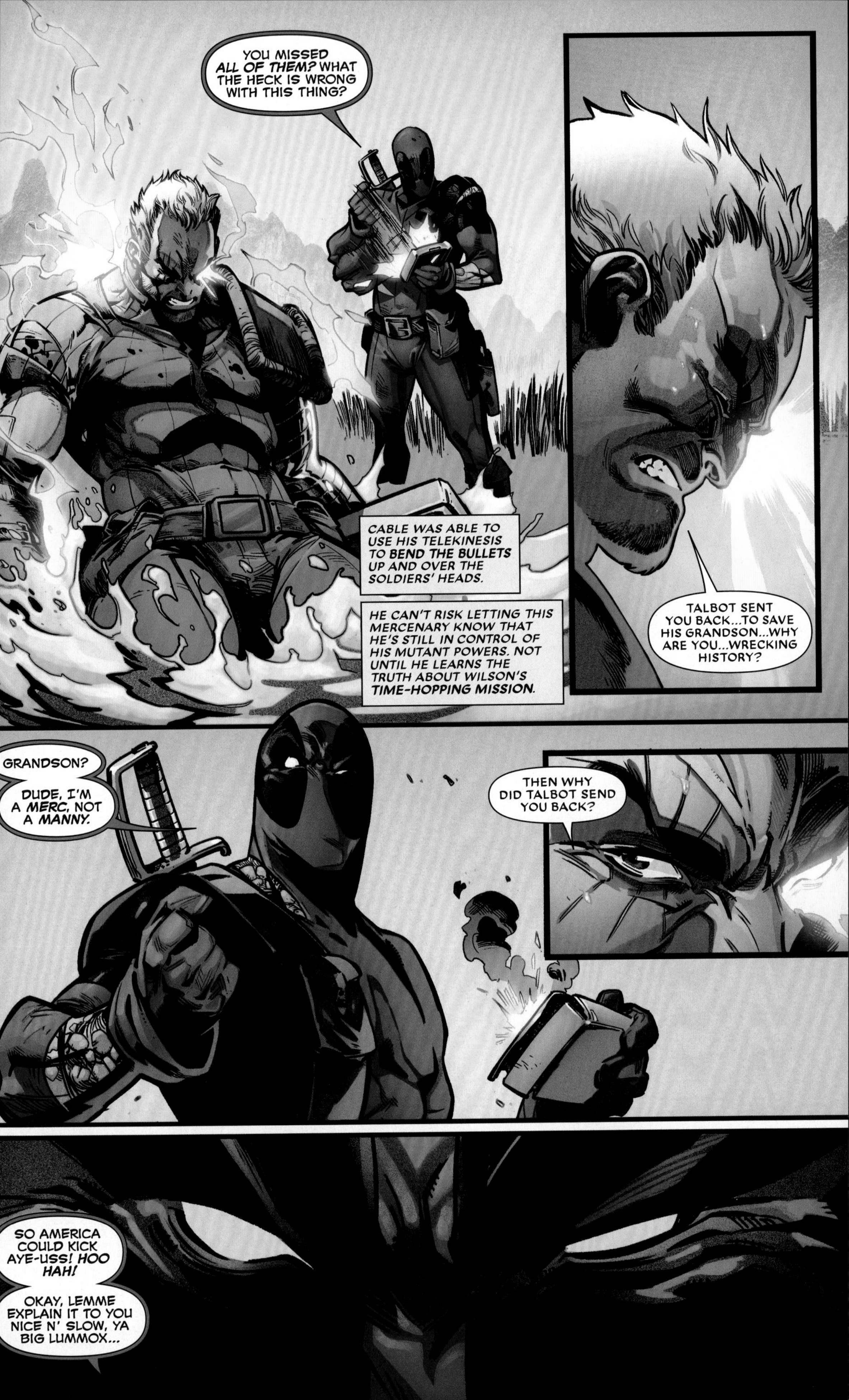
YOU MISSED ALL OF THEM? WHAT THE HECK IS WRONG WITH THIS THING?
CABLE WAS ABLE TO USE HIS TELEKINESIS TO BEND THE BULLETS UP AND OVER THE SOLDIERS' HEADS.
HE CAN'T RISK LETTING THIS MERCENARY KNOW THAT HE'S STILL IN CONTROL OF HIS MUTANT POWERS. NOT UNTIL HE LEARNS THE TRUTH ABOUT WILSON'S TIME-HOPPING MISSION.
TALBOT SENT YOU BACK...TO SAVE HIS GRANDSON...WHY ARE YOU...WRECKING HISTORY?
GRANDSON?
DUDE, I'M A MERC, NOT A MANNY.
THEN WHY DID TALBOT SEND YOU BACK?
SO AMERICA COULD KICK AYE-USS! HOO HAH!
OKAY, LEMME EXPLAIN IT TO YOU NICE N' SLOW, YA BIG LUMMOX...

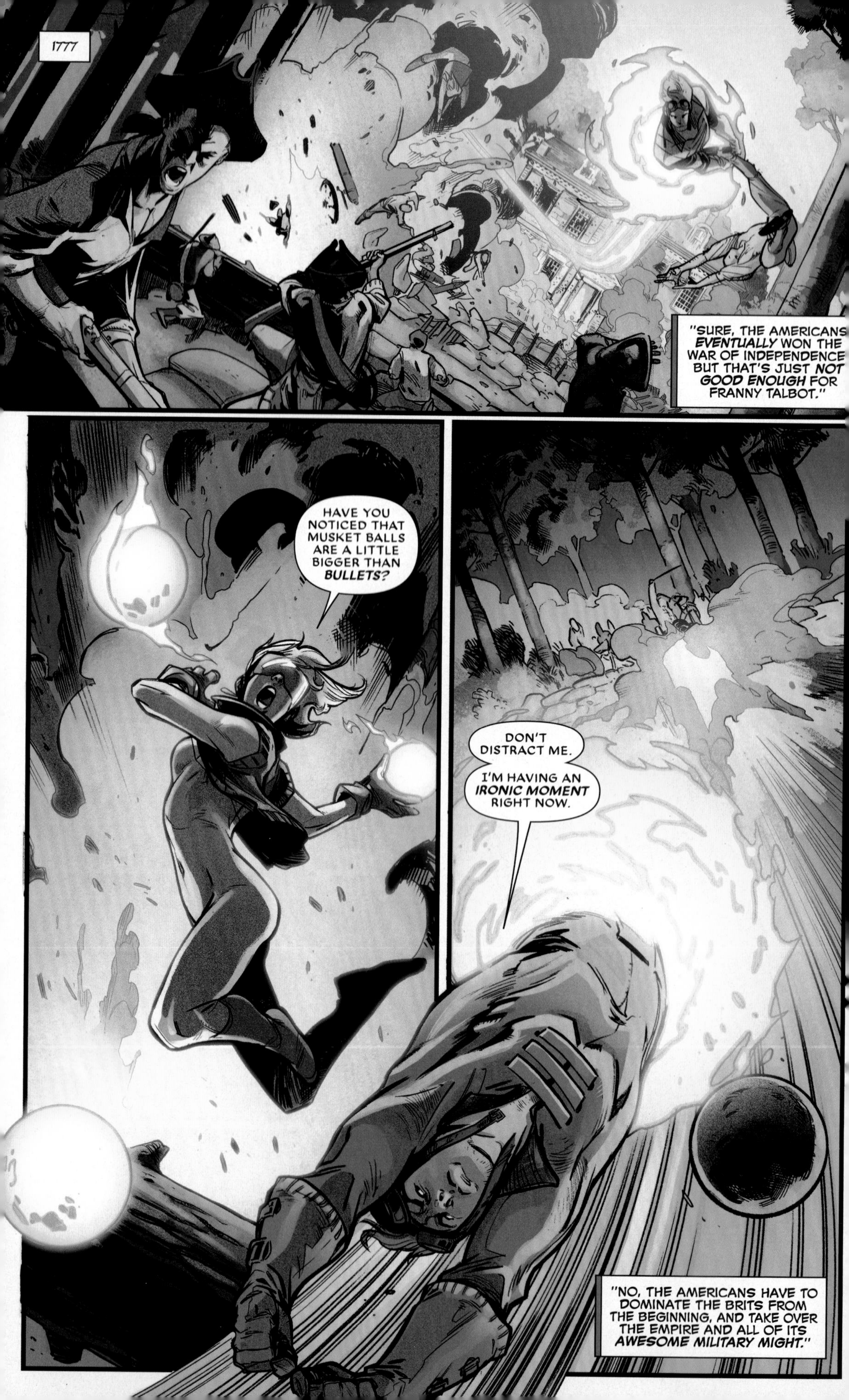
1777
"SURE, THE AMERICANS *EVENTUALLY* WON THE WAR OF INDEPENDENCE BUT THAT'S JUST *NOT GOOD ENOUGH* FOR FRANNY TALBOT."
HAVE YOU NOTICED THAT MUSKET BALLS ARE A LITTLE BIGGER THAN *BULLETS?*
DON'T DISTRACT ME.
I'M HAVING AN *IRONIC MOMENT* RIGHT NOW.
"NO, THE AMERICANS HAVE TO DOMINATE THE BRITS FROM THE BEGINNING, AND TAKE OVER THE EMPIRE AND ALL OF ITS *AWESOME MILITARY MIGHT.*"

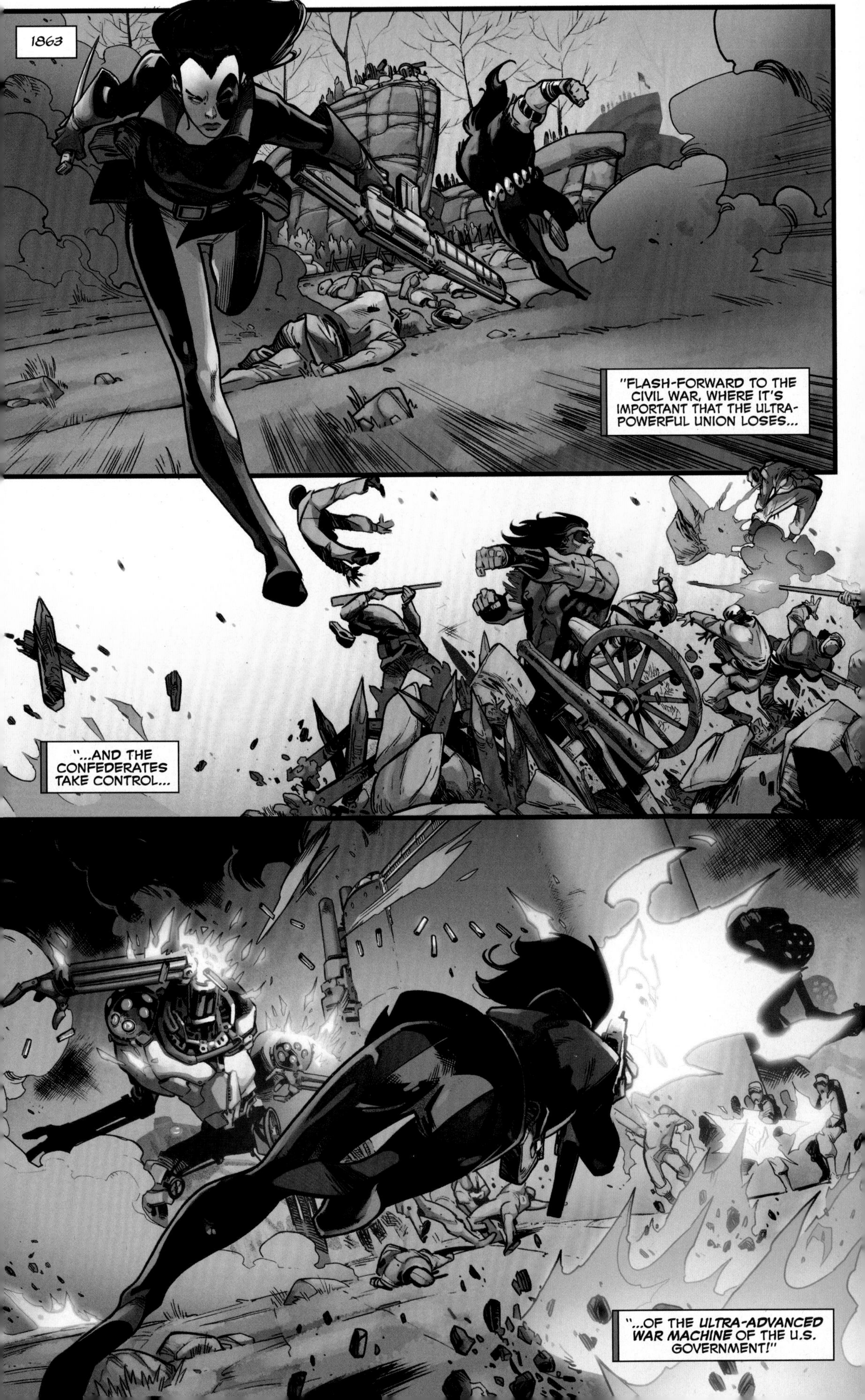
1863
"FLASH-FORWARD TO THE CIVIL WAR, WHERE IT'S IMPORTANT THAT THE ULTRA-POWERFUL UNION LOSES...
"...AND THE CONFEDERATES TAKE CONTROL...
"...OF THE *ULTRA-ADVANCED WAR MACHINE* OF THE U.S. GOVERNMENT!"

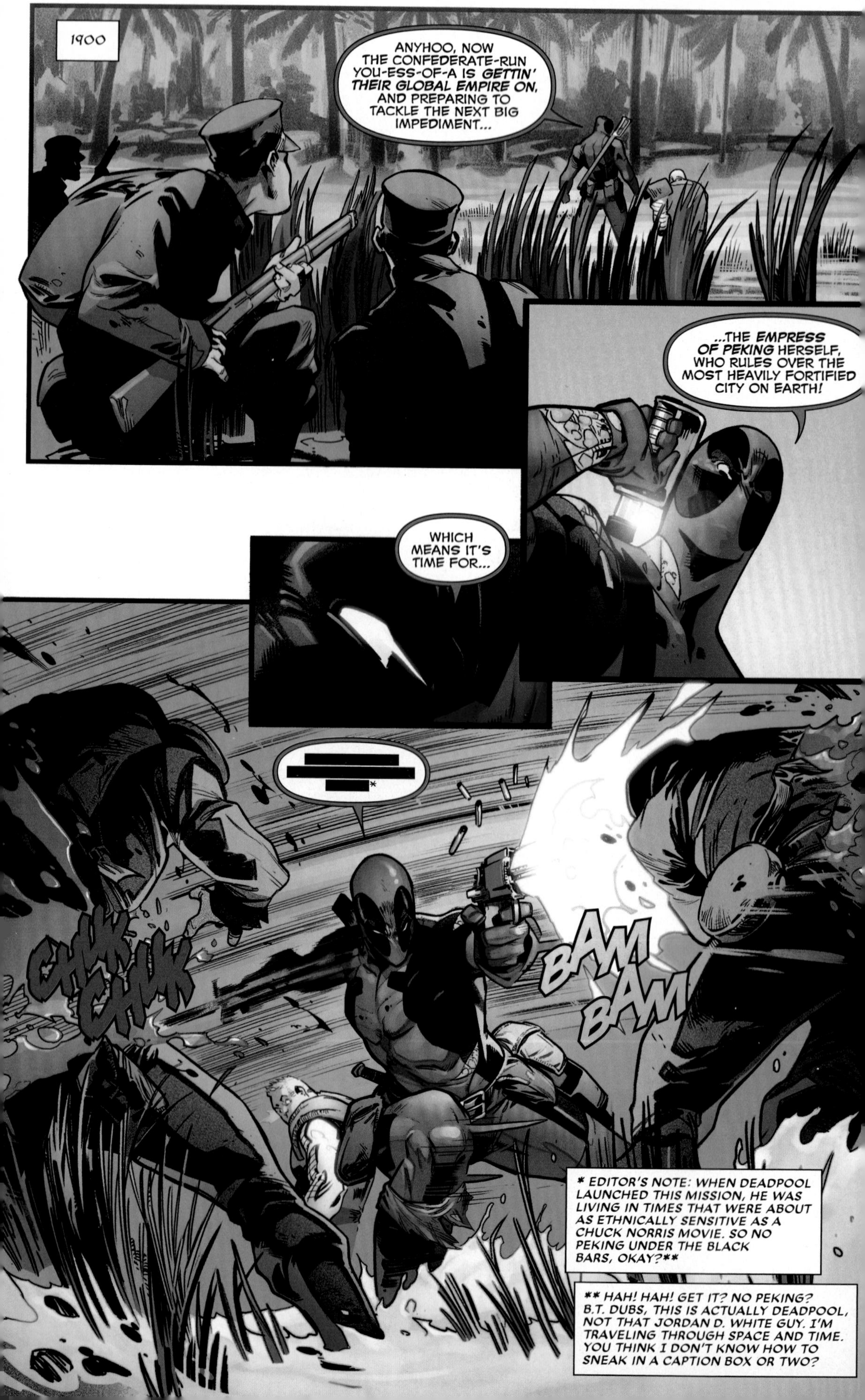
1900
ANYHOO, NOW THE CONFEDERATE-RUN YOU-ESS-OF-A IS GETTIN' THEIR GLOBAL EMPIRE ON, AND PREPARING TO TACKLE THE NEXT BIG IMPEDIMENT...
...THE EMPRESS OF PEKING HERSELF, WHO RULES OVER THE MOST HEAVILY FORTIFIED CITY ON EARTH!
WHICH MEANS IT'S TIME FOR...
[redacted]*
CHUK CHUK
BAM BAM
* EDITOR'S NOTE: WHEN DEADPOOL LAUNCHED THIS MISSION, HE WAS LIVING IN TIMES THAT WERE ABOUT AS ETHNICALLY SENSITIVE AS A CHUCK NORRIS MOVIE. SO NO PEKING UNDER THE BLACK BARS, OKAY?**
** HAH! HAH! GET IT? NO PEKING? B.T. DUBS, THIS IS ACTUALLY DEADPOOL, NOT THAT JORDAN D. WHITE GUY. I'M TRAVELING THROUGH SPACE AND TIME. YOU THINK I DON'T KNOW HOW TO SNEAK IN A CAPTION BOX OR TWO?

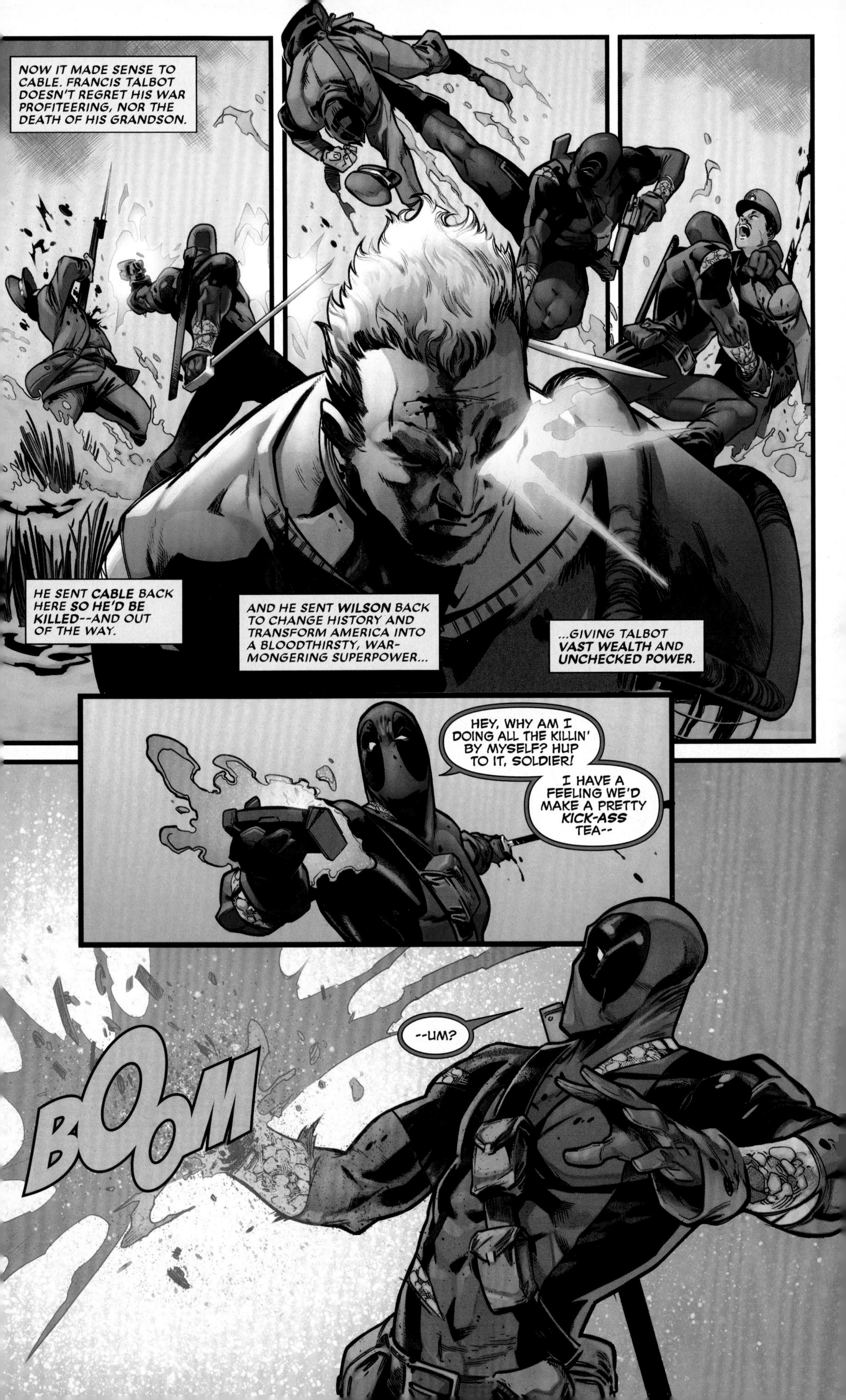
NOW IT MADE SENSE TO CABLE. FRANCIS TALBOT DOESN'T REGRET HIS WAR PROFITEERING, NOR THE DEATH OF HIS GRANDSON.
HE SENT CABLE BACK HERE SO HE'D BE KILLED--AND OUT OF THE WAY.
AND HE SENT WILSON BACK TO CHANGE HISTORY AND TRANSFORM AMERICA INTO A BLOODTHIRSTY, WAR-MONGERING SUPERPOWER...
...GIVING TALBOT VAST WEALTH AND UNCHECKED POWER.
HEY, WHY AM I DOING ALL THE KILLIN' BY MYSELF? HUP TO IT, SOLDIER!
I HAVE A FEELING WE'D MAKE A PRETTY KICK-ASS TEA--
--UM?
BOOM

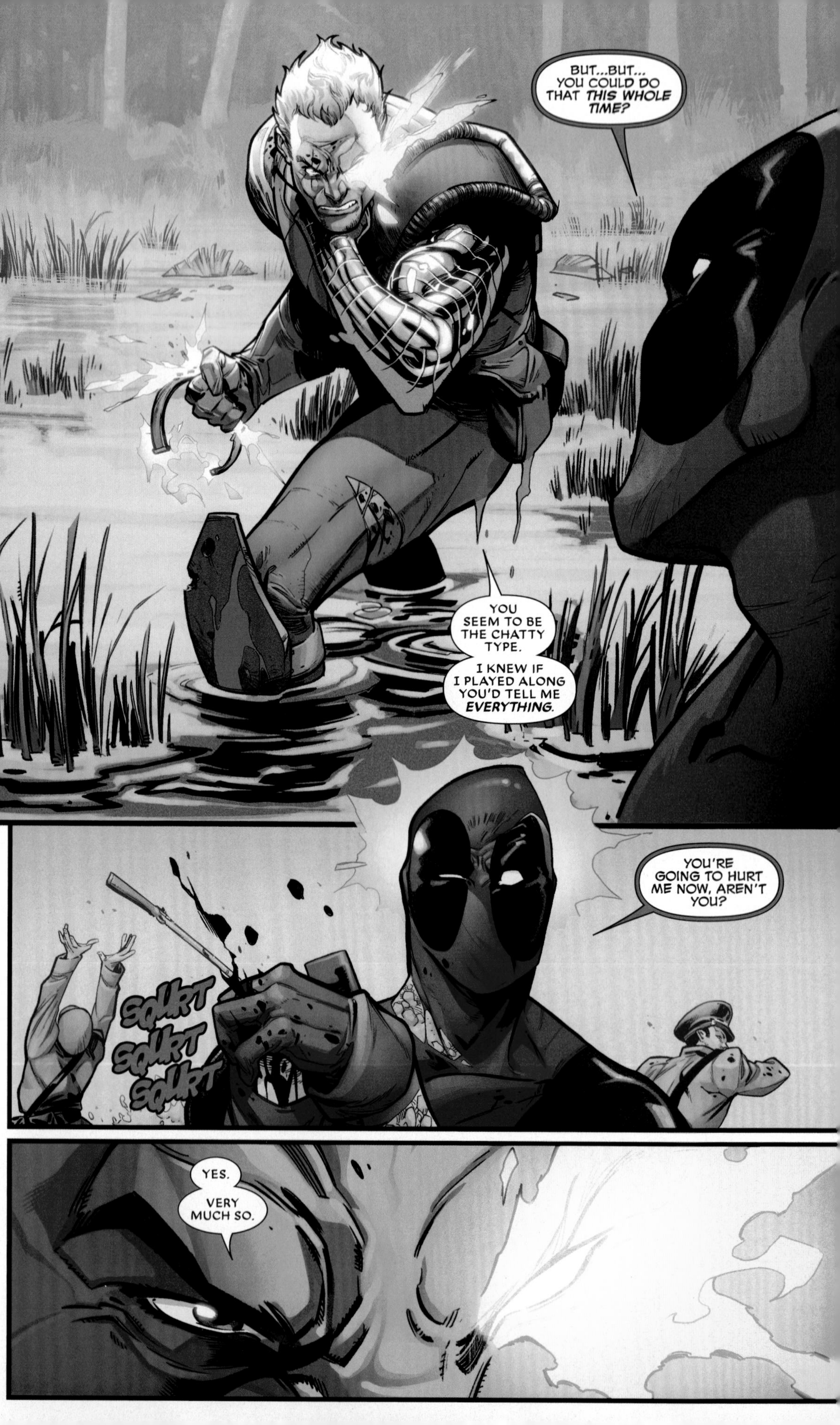
BUT...BUT... YOU COULD DO THAT THIS WHOLE TIME?
YOU SEEM TO BE THE CHATTY TYPE.
I KNEW IF I PLAYED ALONG YOU'D TELL ME EVERYTHING.
YOU'RE GOING TO HURT ME NOW, AREN'T YOU?
SQURT SQURT SQURT
YES.
VERY MUCH SO.

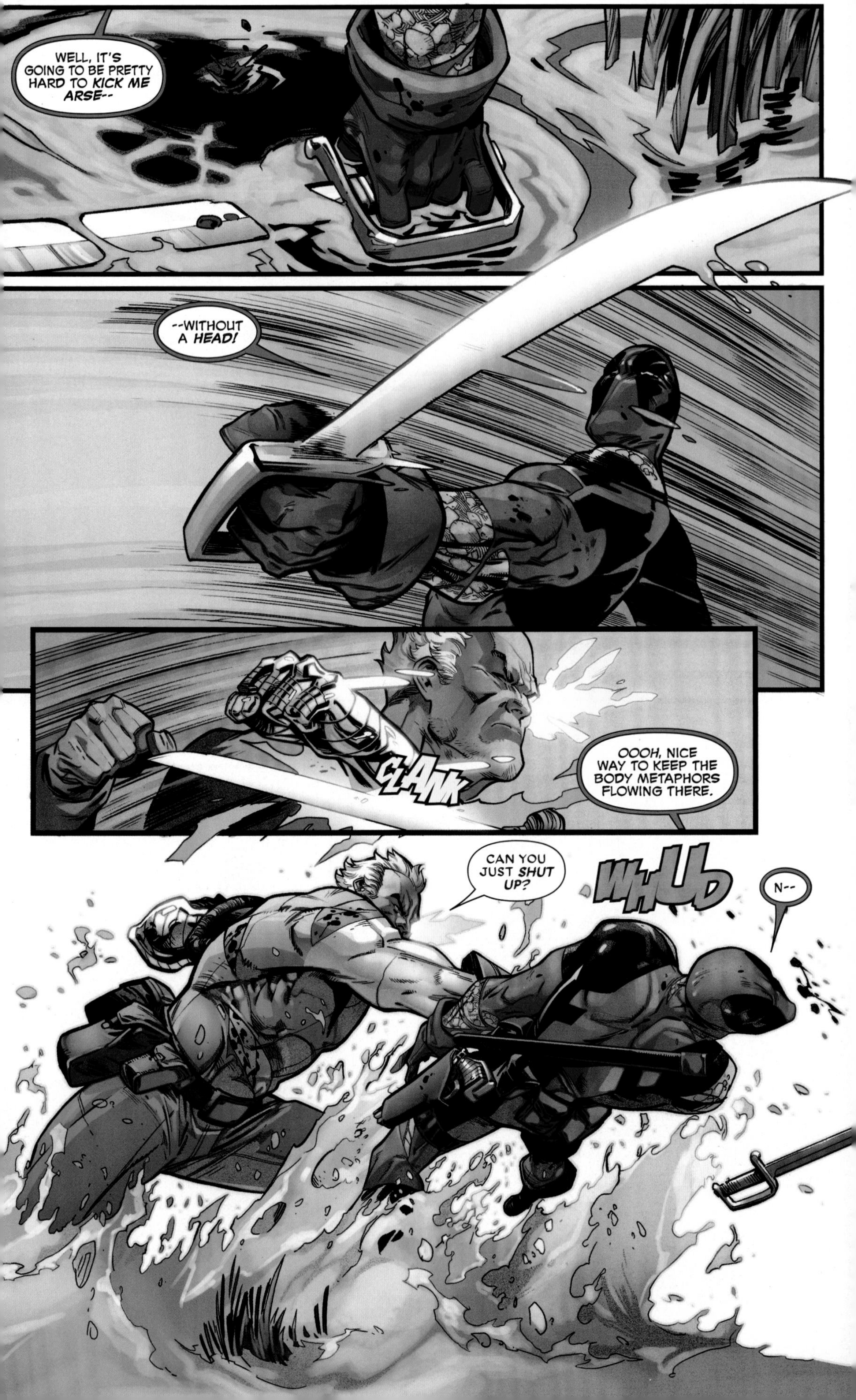
WELL, IT'S GOING TO BE PRETTY HARD TO KICK ME ARSE--
--WITHOUT A HEAD!
CLANK
OOOH, NICE WAY TO KEEP THE BODY METAPHORS FLOWING THERE.
CAN YOU JUST SHUT UP?
WHUD
N--

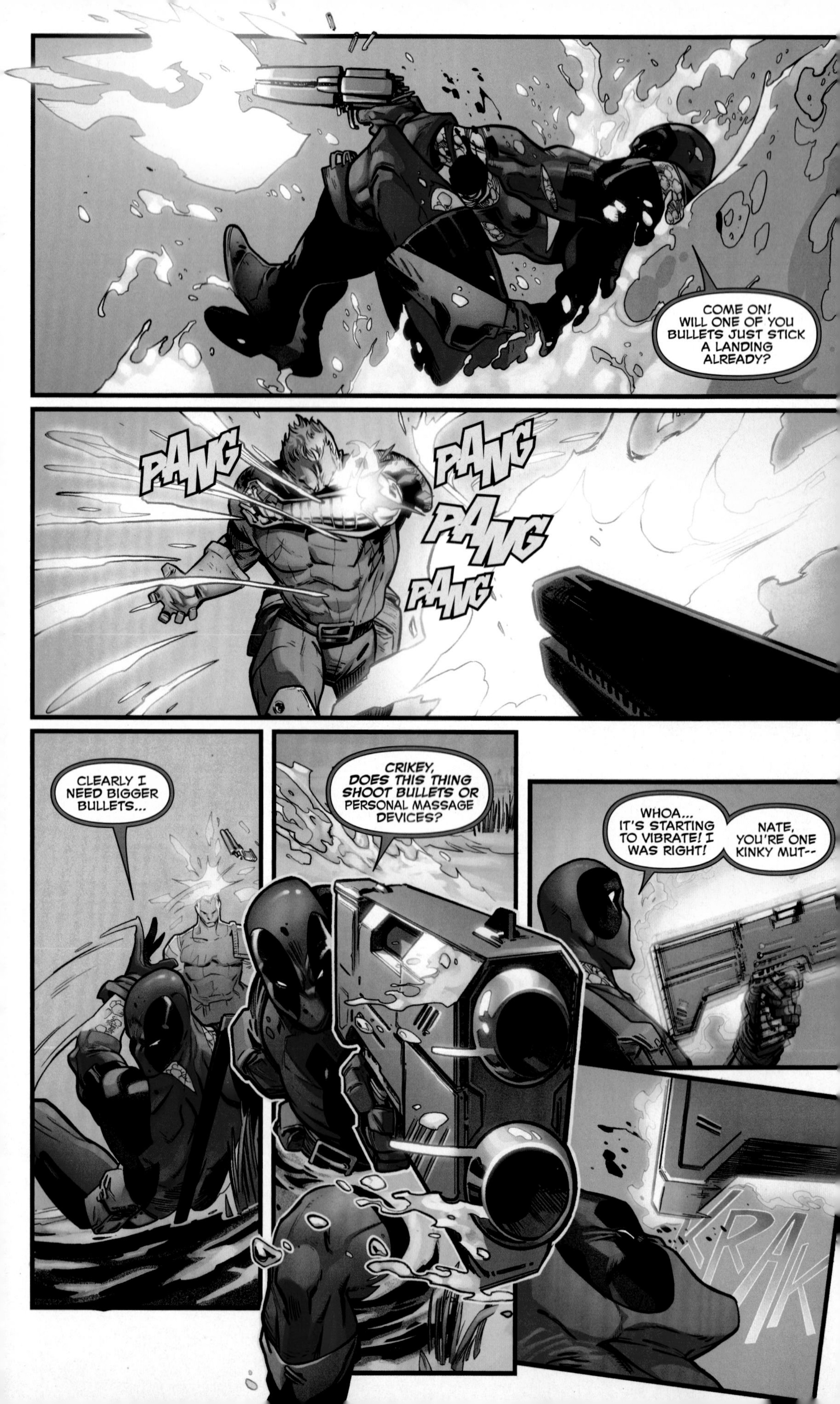
COME ON! WILL ONE OF YOU BULLETS JUST STICK A LANDING ALREADY?
PANG
PANG
PANG
PANG
CLEARLY I NEED BIGGER BULLETS...
CRIKEY, DOES THIS THING SHOOT BULLETS OR PERSONAL MASSAGE DEVICES?
WHOA... IT'S STARTING TO VIBRATE! I WAS RIGHT!
NATE, YOU'RE ONE KINKY MUT--
KRAK

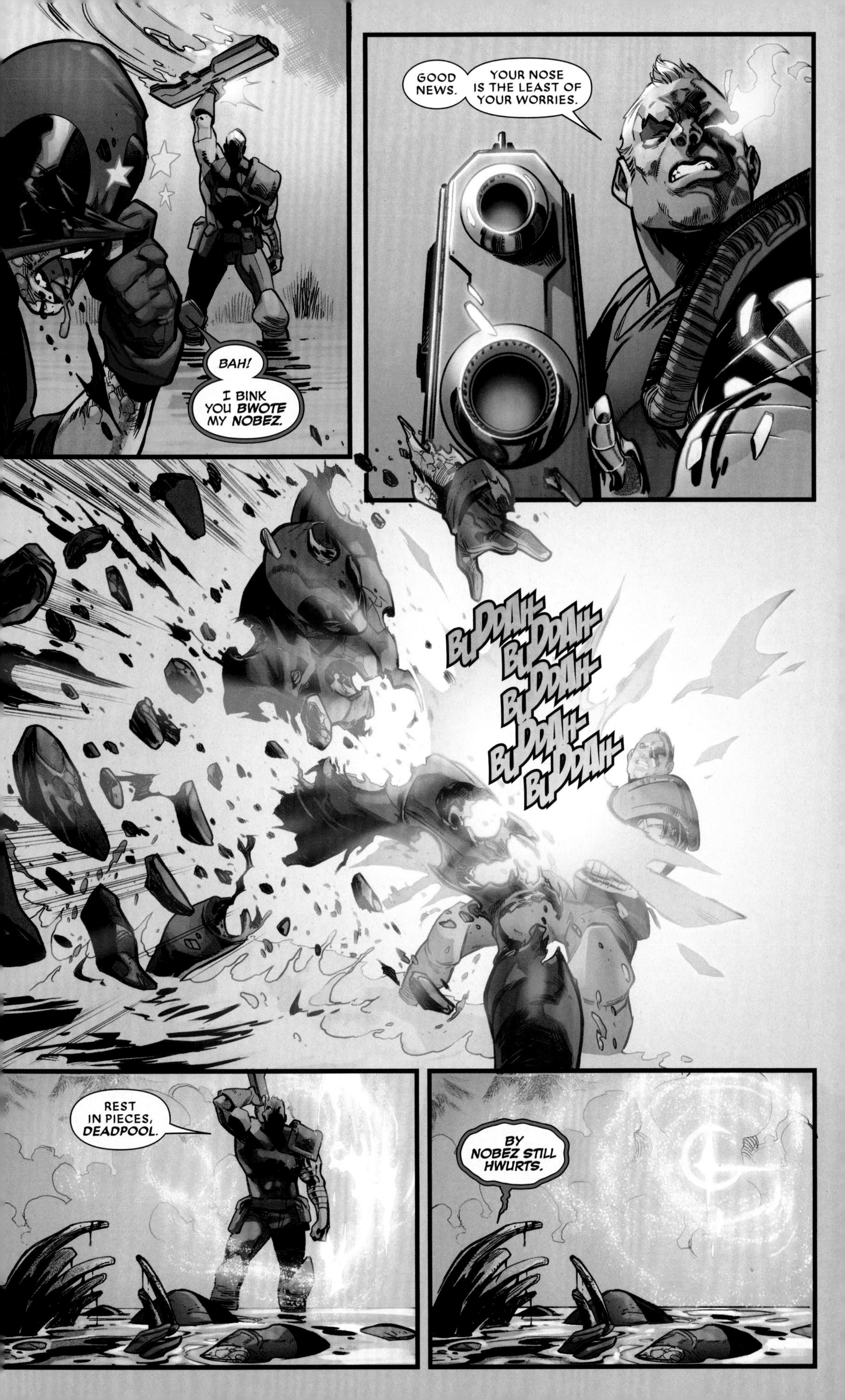
BAH!
I BINK YOU BWOTE MY NOBEZ.
GOOD NEWS.
YOUR NOSE IS THE LEAST OF YOUR WORRIES.
BUDDAH-BUDDAH-BUDDAH-BUDDAH-BUDDAH-
REST IN PIECES, DEADPOOL.
BY NOBEZ STILL HWURTS.

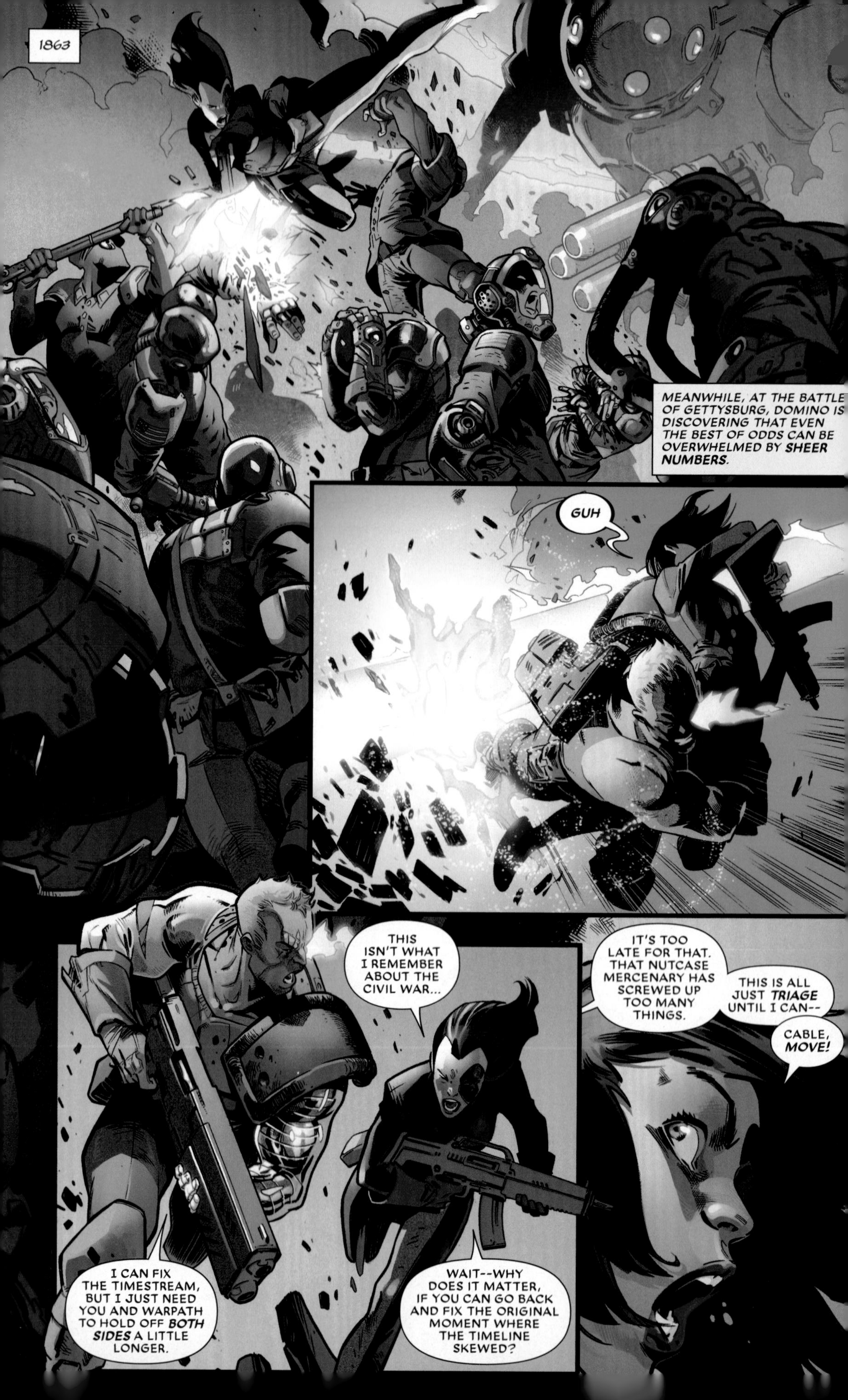
1863
MEANWHILE, AT THE BATTLE OF GETTYSBURG, DOMINO IS DISCOVERING THAT EVEN THE BEST OF ODDS CAN BE OVERWHELMED BY SHEER NUMBERS.
GUH
THIS ISN'T WHAT I REMEMBER ABOUT THE CIVIL WAR...
I CAN FIX THE TIMESTREAM, BUT I JUST NEED YOU AND WARPATH TO HOLD OFF BOTH SIDES A LITTLE LONGER.
WAIT--WHY DOES IT MATTER, IF YOU CAN GO BACK AND FIX THE ORIGINAL MOMENT WHERE THE TIMELINE SKEWED?
IT'S TOO LATE FOR THAT. THAT NUTCASE MERCENARY HAS SCREWED UP TOO MANY THINGS.
THIS IS ALL JUST TRIAGE UNTIL I CAN--
CABLE, MOVE!

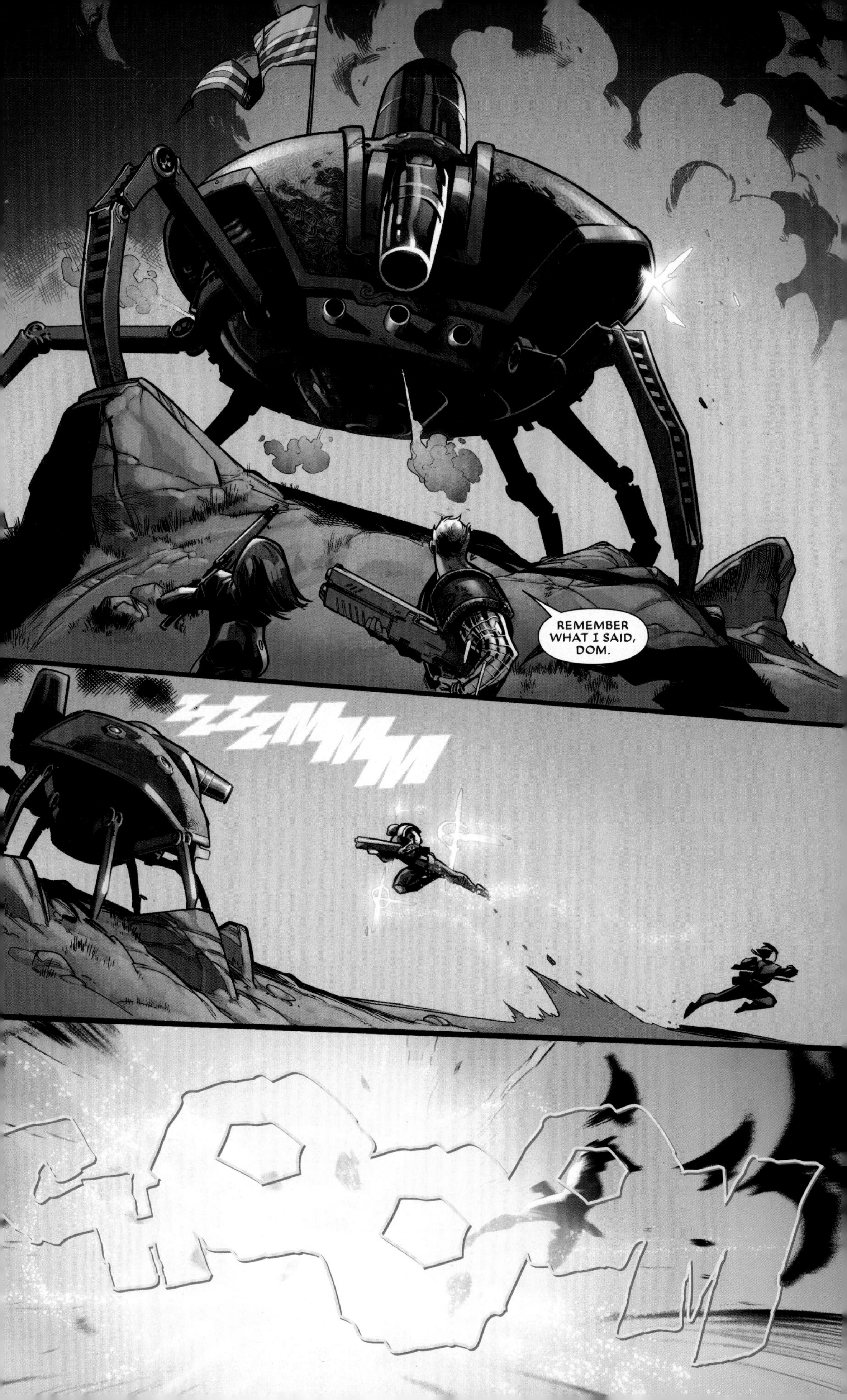
REMEMBER WHAT I SAID, DOM.
ZZZZMMMM
CHOOOM

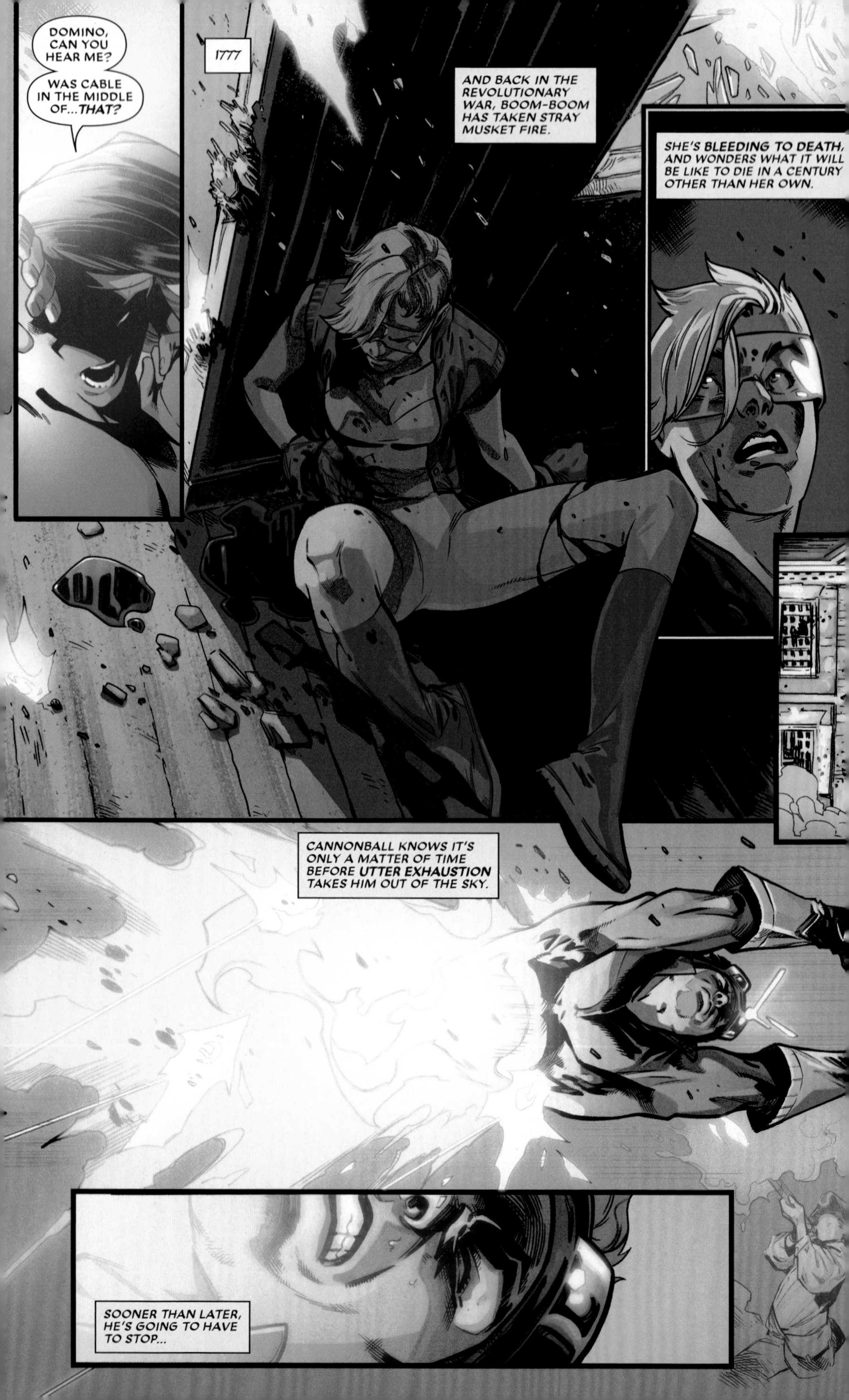
DOMINO, CAN YOU HEAR ME?
WAS CABLE IN THE MIDDLE OF...THAT?
1777
AND BACK IN THE REVOLUTIONARY WAR, BOOM-BOOM HAS TAKEN STRAY MUSKET FIRE.
SHE'S BLEEDING TO DEATH, AND WONDERS WHAT IT WILL BE LIKE TO DIE IN A CENTURY OTHER THAN HER OWN.
CANNONBALL KNOWS IT'S ONLY A MATTER OF TIME BEFORE UTTER EXHAUSTION TAKES HIM OUT OF THE SKY.
SOONER THAN LATER, HE'S GOING TO HAVE TO STOP...

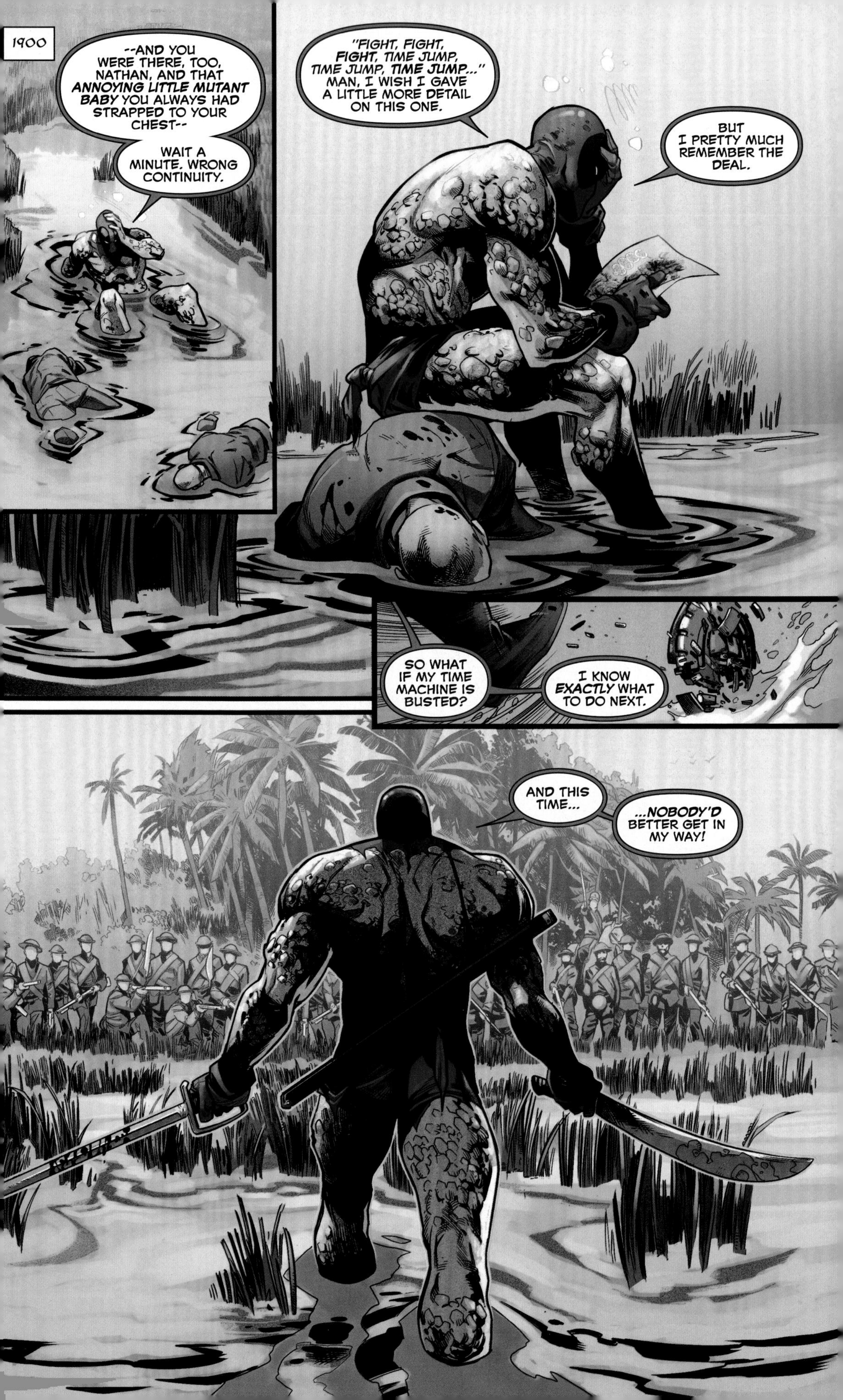
1900
--AND YOU WERE THERE, TOO, NATHAN, AND THAT ANNOYING LITTLE MUTANT BABY YOU ALWAYS HAD STRAPPED TO YOUR CHEST--
WAIT A MINUTE. WRONG CONTINUITY.
"FIGHT, FIGHT, FIGHT, TIME JUMP, TIME JUMP, TIME JUMP..." MAN, I WISH I GAVE A LITTLE MORE DETAIL ON THIS ONE.
BUT I PRETTY MUCH REMEMBER THE DEAL.
SO WHAT IF MY TIME MACHINE IS BUSTED?
I KNOW EXACTLY WHAT TO DO NEXT.
AND THIS TIME...
...NOBODY'D BETTER GET IN MY WAY!

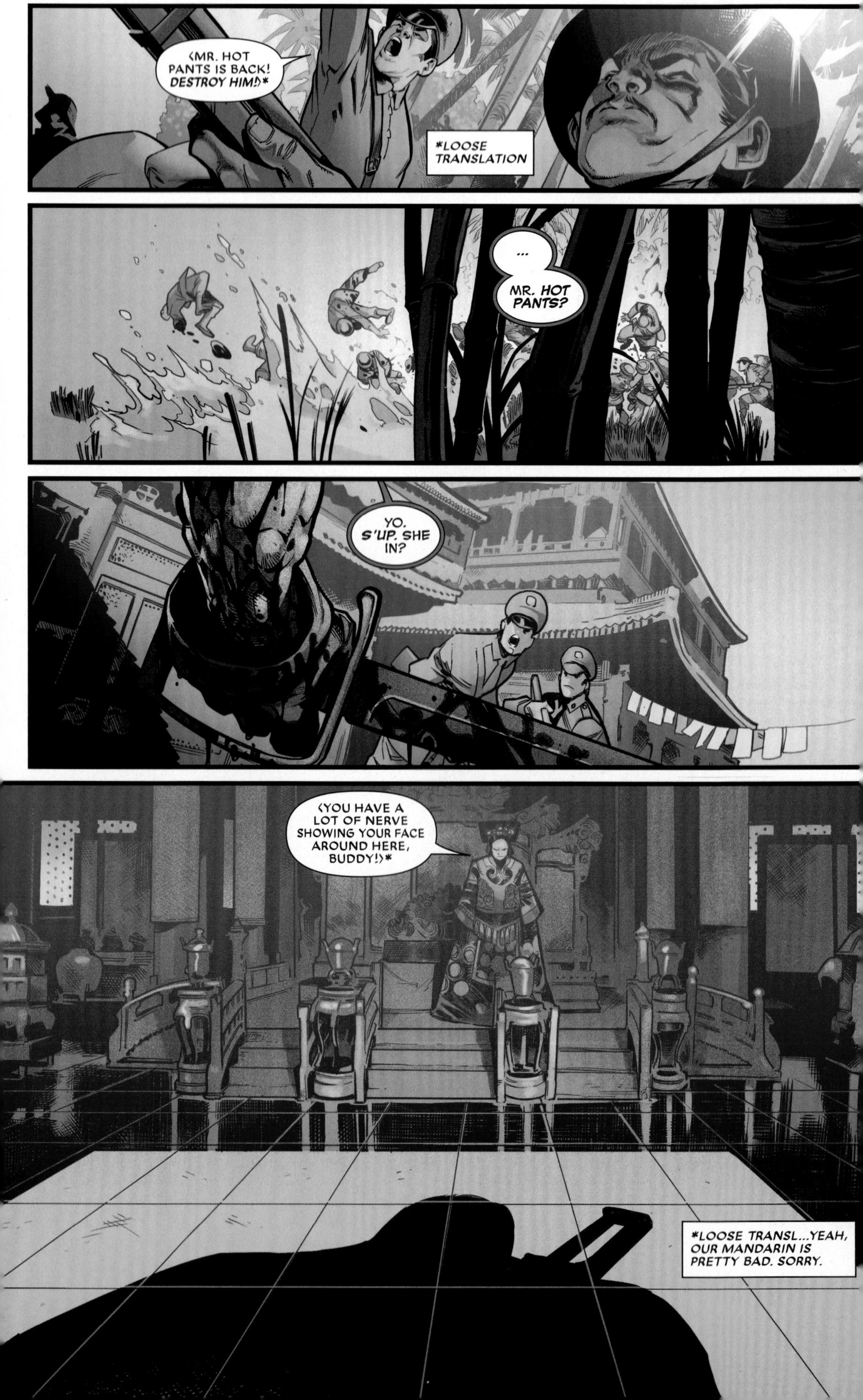
‹MR. HOT PANTS IS BACK! DESTROY HIM!›*
*LOOSE TRANSLATION
...
MR. HOT PANTS?
YO. S'UP. SHE IN?
‹YOU HAVE A LOT OF NERVE SHOWING YOUR FACE AROUND HERE, BUDDY!›*
*LOOSE TRANSL...YEAH, OUR MANDARIN IS PRETTY BAD. SORRY.

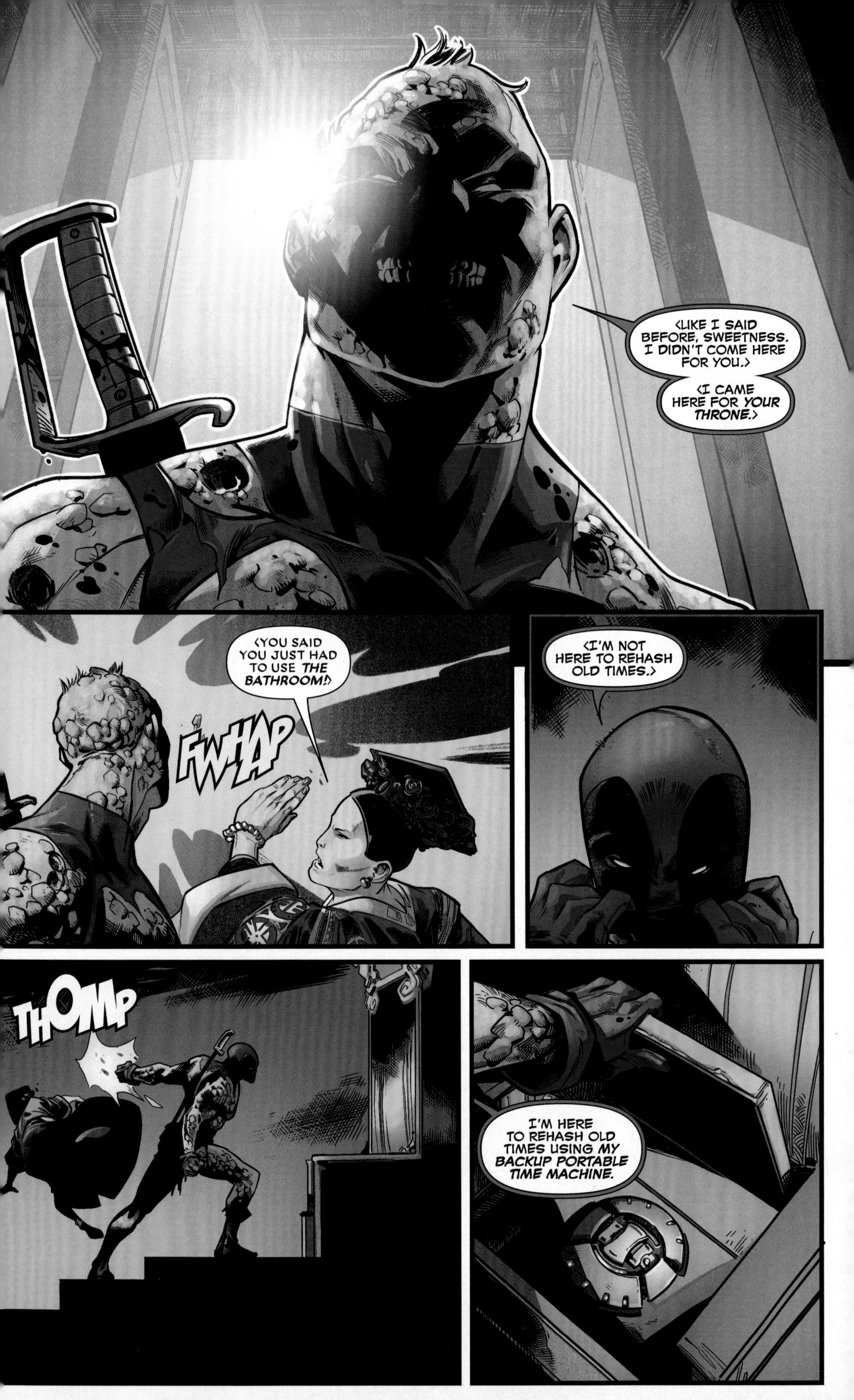
<LIKE I SAID BEFORE, SWEETNESS. I DIDN'T COME HERE FOR YOU.>
<I CAME HERE FOR *YOUR THRONE.*>
<YOU SAID YOU JUST HAD TO USE *THE BATHROOM!*>
FWHAP
<I'M NOT HERE TO REHASH OLD TIMES.>
THOMP
I'M HERE TO REHASH OLD TIMES USING MY *BACKUP PORTABLE TIME MACHINE.*

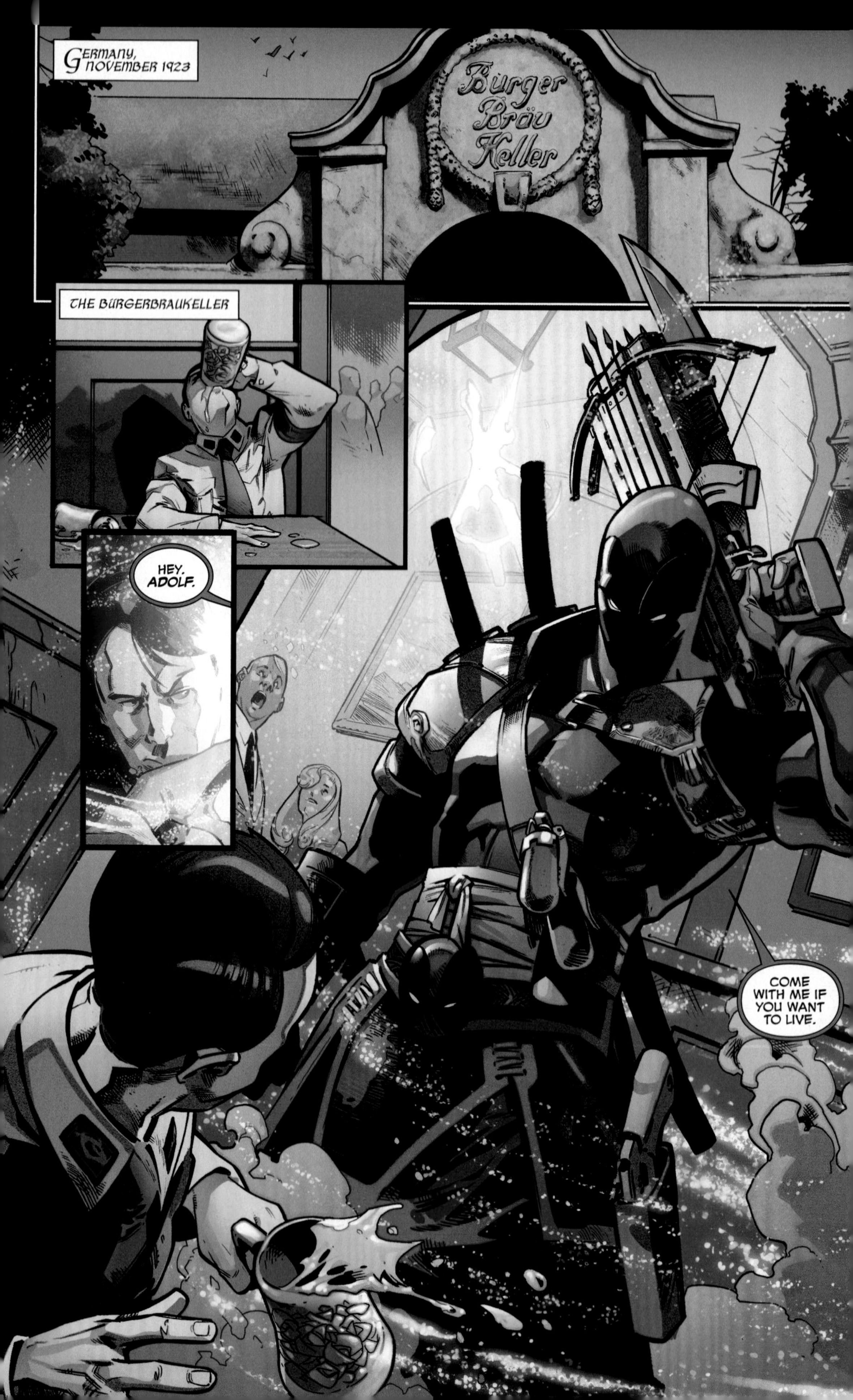
GERMANY, NOVEMBER 1923
Bürger Bräu Keller
THE BÜRGERBRAUKELLER
HEY. ADOLF.
COME WITH ME IF YOU WANT TO LIVE.

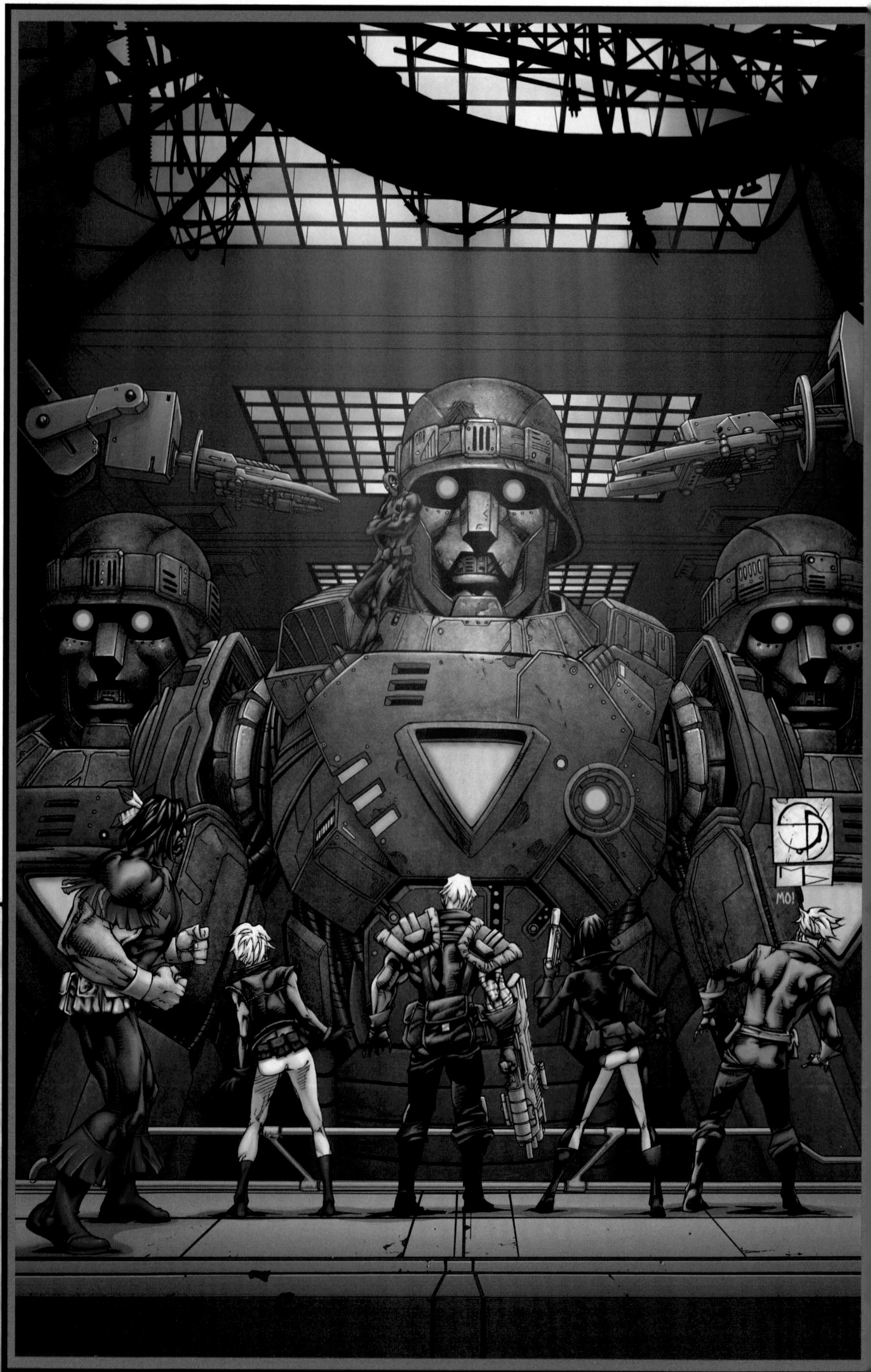
MO!

#4

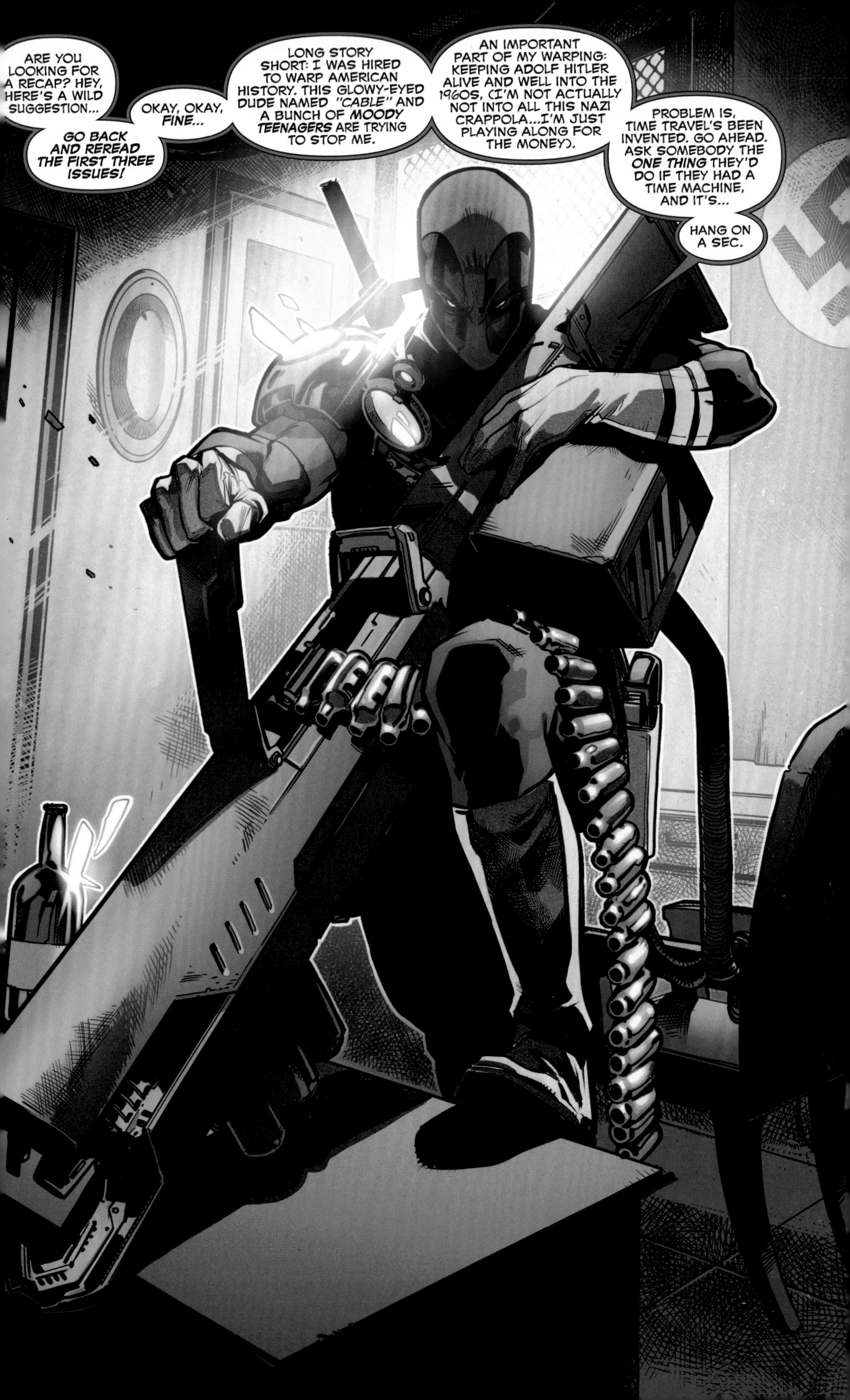
ARE YOU LOOKING FOR A RECAP? HEY, HERE'S A WILD SUGGESTION...
GO BACK AND REREAD THE FIRST THREE ISSUES!
OKAY, OKAY, FINE...
LONG STORY SHORT: I WAS HIRED TO WARP AMERICAN HISTORY. THIS GLOWY-EYED DUDE NAMED "CABLE" AND A BUNCH OF MOODY TEENAGERS ARE TRYING TO STOP ME.
AN IMPORTANT PART OF MY WARPING: KEEPING ADOLF HITLER ALIVE AND WELL INTO THE 1960S. (I'M NOT ACTUALLY NOT INTO ALL THIS NAZI CRAPPOLA...I'M JUST PLAYING ALONG FOR THE MONEY).
PROBLEM IS, TIME TRAVEL'S BEEN INVENTED. GO AHEAD. ASK SOMEBODY THE ONE THING THEY'D DO IF THEY HAD A TIME MACHINE, AND IT'S...
HANG ON A SEC.

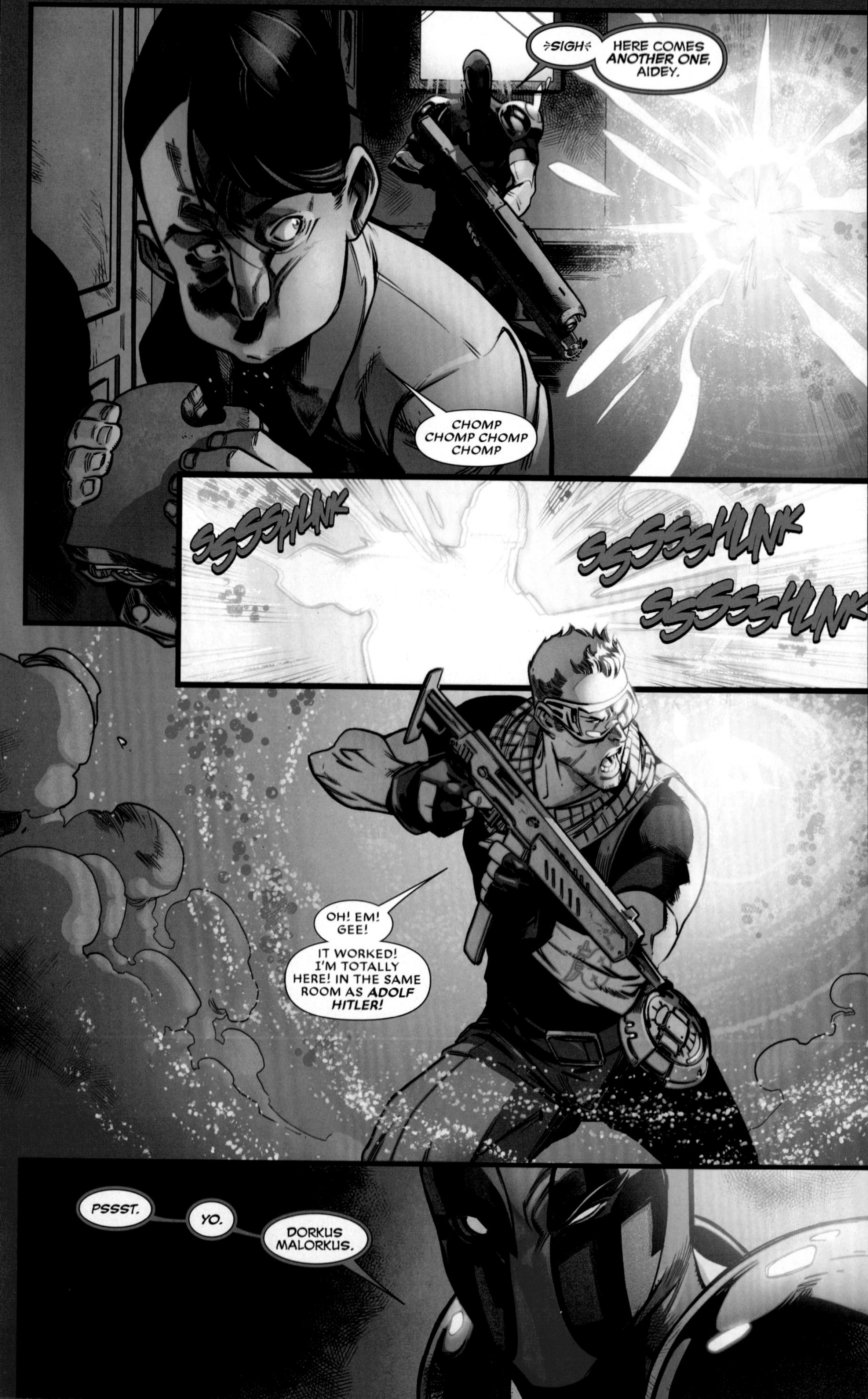

⊱SIGH⊰
HERE COMES ANOTHER ONE, AIDEY.
CHOMP CHOMP CHOMP CHOMP
SSSSHUNK
SSSSSHUNK
SSSSSHUNK
OH! EM! GEE!
IT WORKED! I'M TOTALLY HERE! IN THE SAME ROOM AS ADOLF HITLER!
PSSST.
YO.
DORKUS MALORKUS.

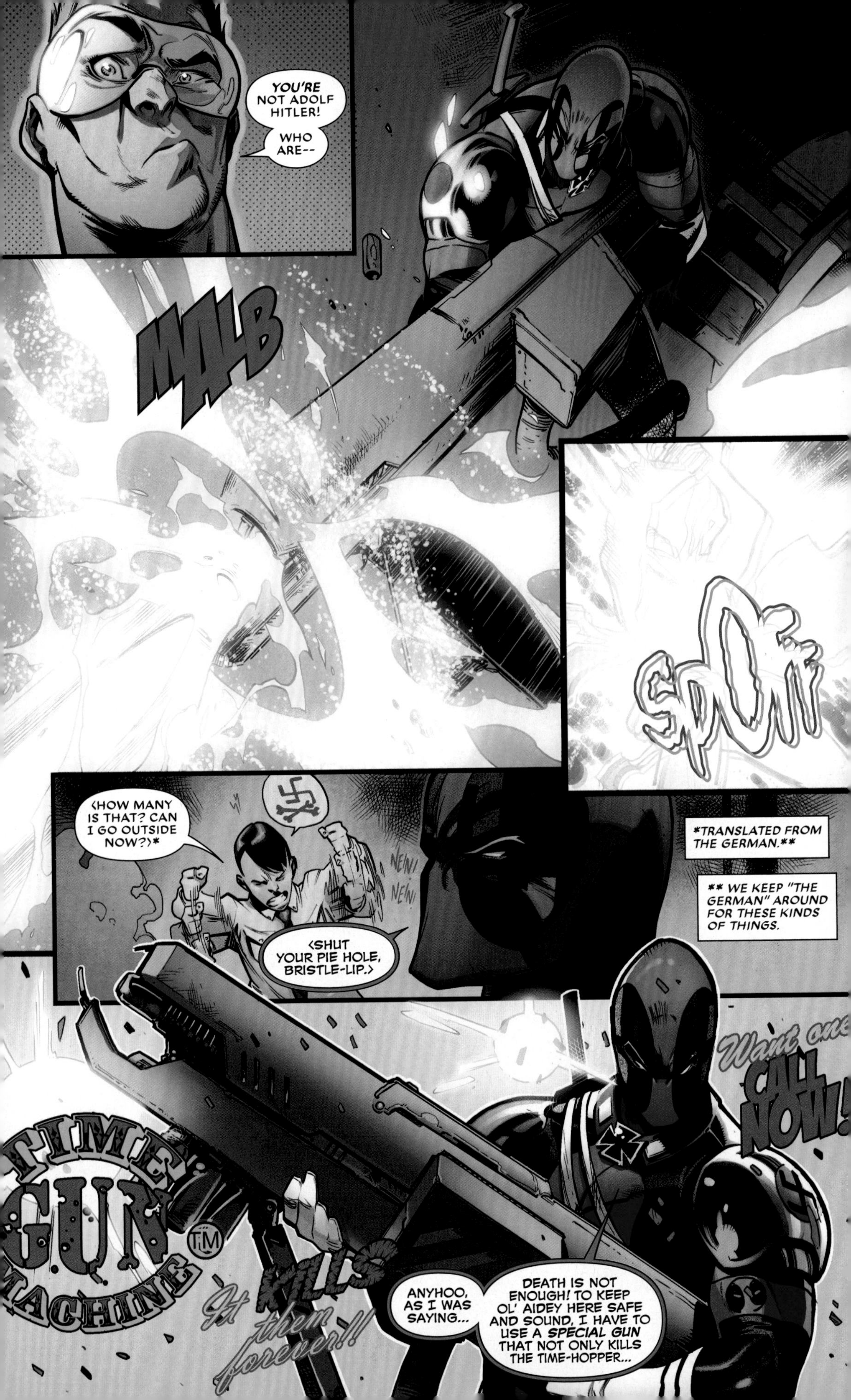

YOU'RE NOT ADOLF HITLER!
WHO ARE--
BLAM
SPLAT
‹HOW MANY IS THAT? CAN I GO OUTSIDE NOW?›*
NEIN! NEIN!
‹SHUT YOUR PIE HOLE, BRISTLE-LIP.›
*TRANSLATED FROM THE GERMAN.**
** WE KEEP "THE GERMAN" AROUND FOR THESE KINDS OF THINGS.
Want one CALL NOW!
TIME MACHINE GUN TM
It KILLS them forever!!
ANYHOO, AS I WAS SAYING...
DEATH IS NOT ENOUGH! TO KEEP OL' AIDEY HERE SAFE AND SOUND, I HAVE TO USE A SPECIAL GUN THAT NOT ONLY KILLS THE TIME-HOPPER...

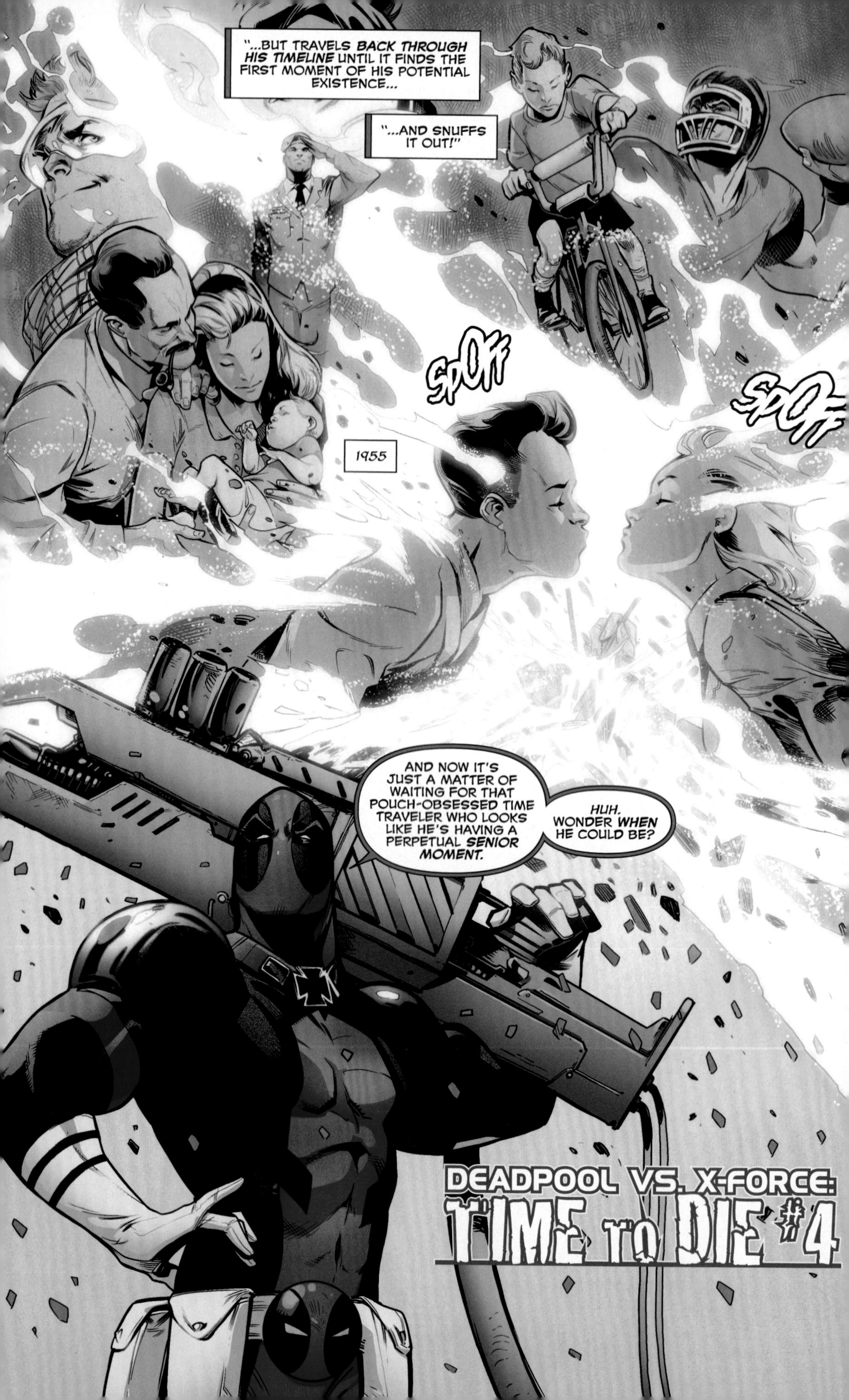
"...BUT TRAVELS BACK THROUGH HIS TIMELINE UNTIL IT FINDS THE FIRST MOMENT OF HIS POTENTIAL EXISTENCE...
"...AND SNUFFS IT OUT!"
SPOFF
SPOFF
1955
AND NOW IT'S JUST A MATTER OF WAITING FOR THAT POUCH-OBSESSED TIME TRAVELER WHO LOOKS LIKE HE'S HAVING A PERPETUAL SENIOR MOMENT.
HUH. WONDER WHEN HE COULD BE?
DEADPOOL VS. X-FORCE:
TIME TO DIE #4

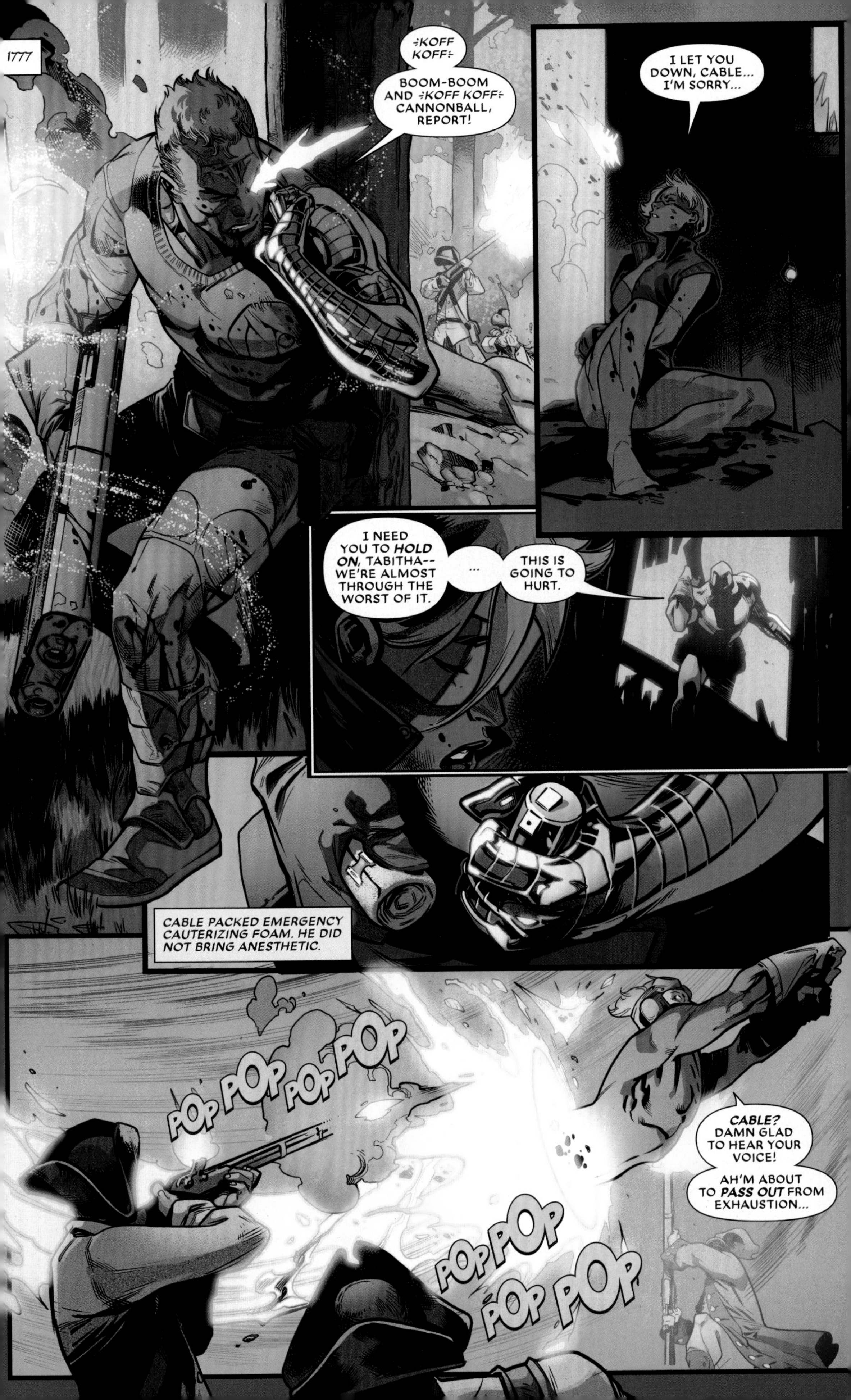
1777
=KOFF KOFF=
BOOM-BOOM AND =KOFF KOFF= CANNONBALL, REPORT!
I LET YOU DOWN, CABLE... I'M SORRY...
I NEED YOU TO **HOLD ON**, TABITHA-- WE'RE ALMOST THROUGH THE WORST OF IT.
...
THIS IS GOING TO HURT.
CABLE PACKED EMERGENCY CAUTERIZING FOAM. HE DID NOT BRING ANESTHETIC.
POP POP POP POP
CABLE? DAMN GLAD TO HEAR YOUR VOICE!
AH'M ABOUT TO ***PASS OUT*** FROM EXHAUSTION...
POP POP
POP POP

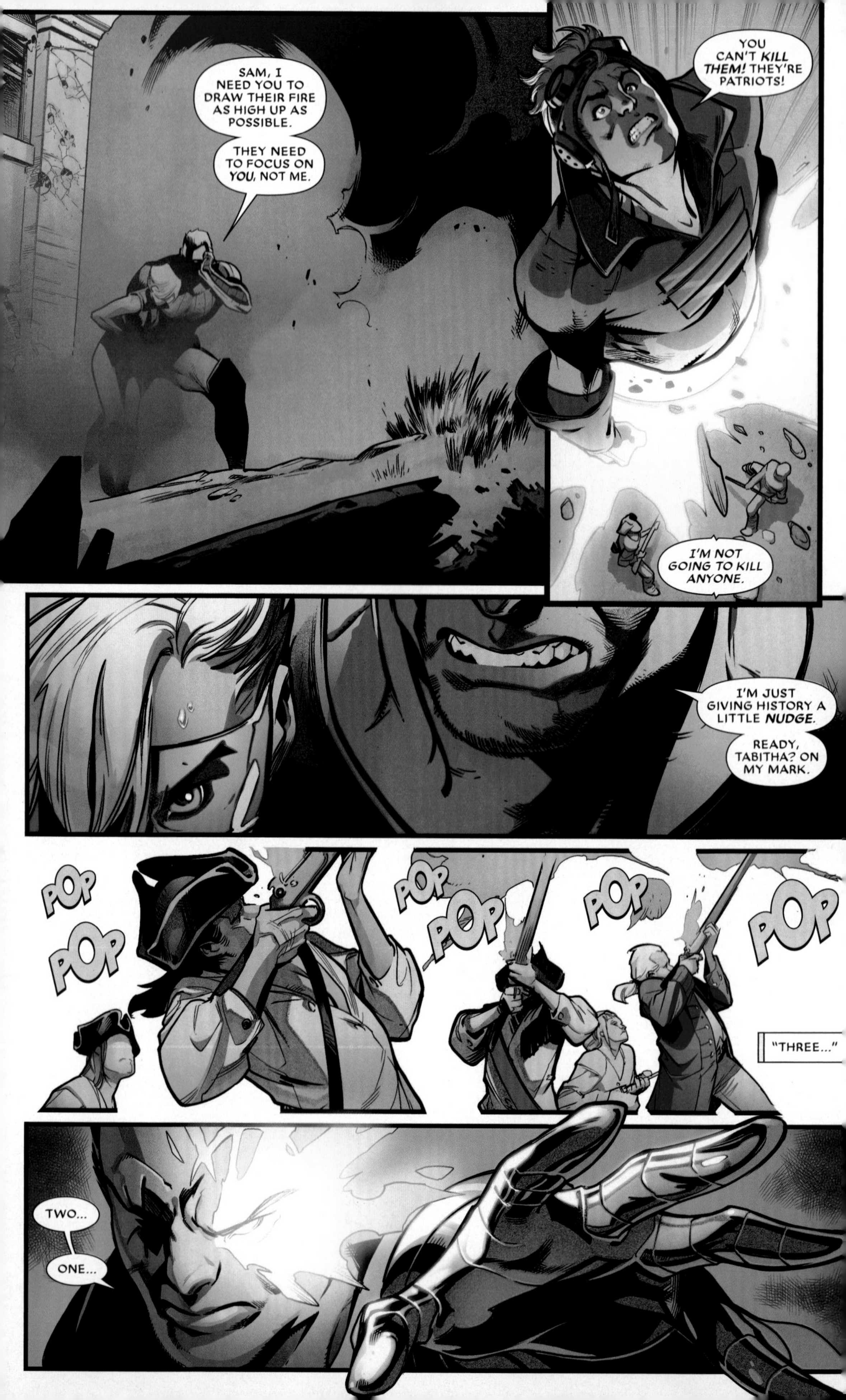
SAM, I NEED YOU TO DRAW THEIR FIRE AS HIGH UP AS POSSIBLE.
THEY NEED TO FOCUS ON YOU, NOT ME.
YOU CAN'T KILL THEM! THEY'RE PATRIOTS!
I'M NOT GOING TO KILL ANYONE.
I'M JUST GIVING HISTORY A LITTLE NUDGE.
READY, TABITHA? ON MY MARK.
POP
POP
POP
POP
POP
POP
"THREE..."
TWO...
ONE...

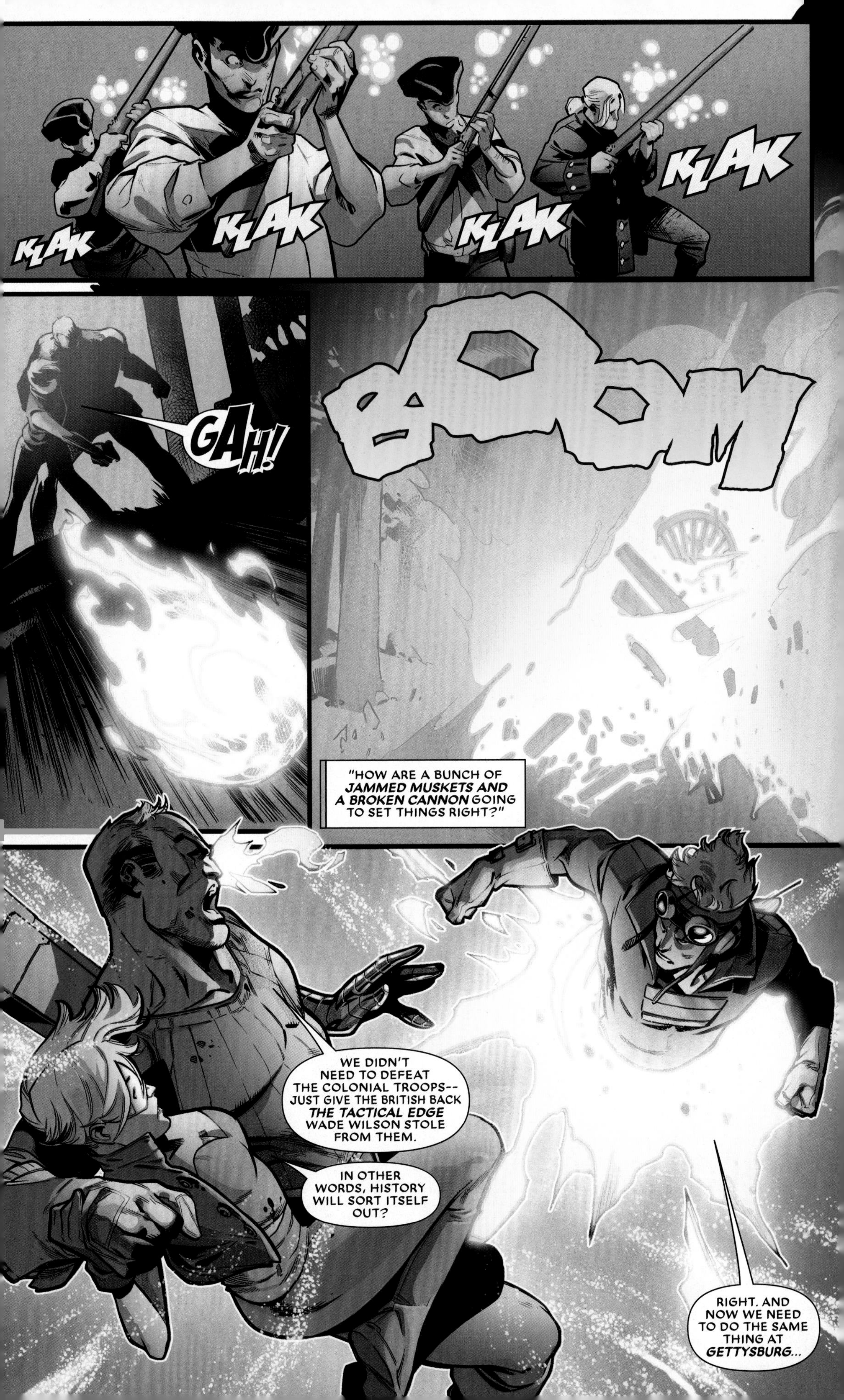
KLAK
KLAK
KLAK
KLAK
GAH!
BOOM
"HOW ARE A BUNCH OF *JAMMED MUSKETS AND A BROKEN CANNON* GOING TO SET THINGS RIGHT?"
WE DIDN'T NEED TO DEFEAT THE COLONIAL TROOPS-- JUST GIVE THE BRITISH BACK *THE TACTICAL EDGE* WADE WILSON STOLE FROM THEM.
IN OTHER WORDS, HISTORY WILL SORT ITSELF OUT?
RIGHT. AND NOW WE NEED TO DO THE SAME THING AT *GETTYSBURG*...

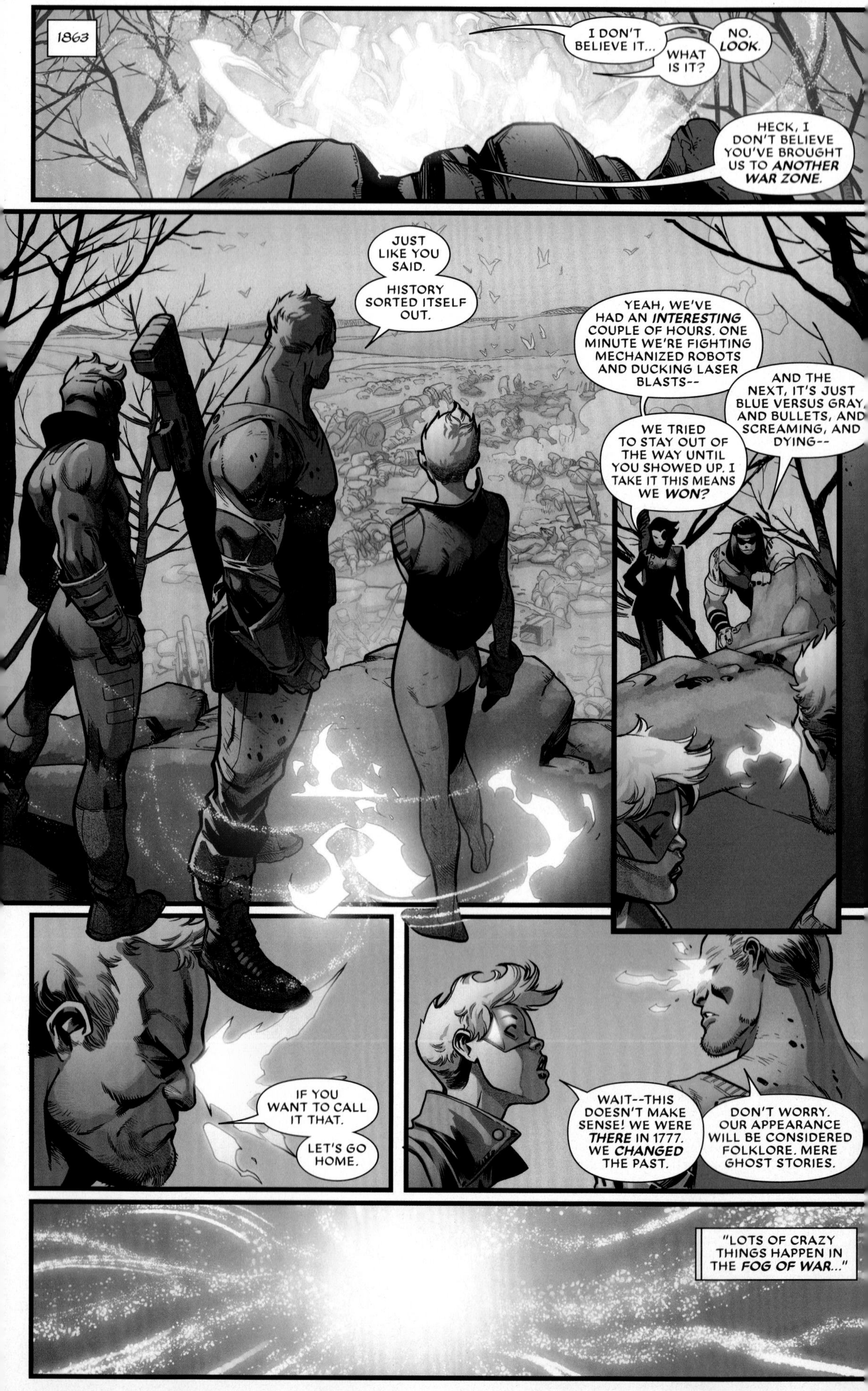
1863
I DON'T BELIEVE IT...
WHAT IS IT?
NO. LOOK.
HECK, I DON'T BELIEVE YOU'VE BROUGHT US TO ANOTHER WAR ZONE.
JUST LIKE YOU SAID.
HISTORY SORTED ITSELF OUT.
YEAH, WE'VE HAD AN INTERESTING COUPLE OF HOURS. ONE MINUTE WE'RE FIGHTING MECHANIZED ROBOTS AND DUCKING LASER BLASTS--
AND THE NEXT, IT'S JUST BLUE VERSUS GRAY, AND BULLETS, AND SCREAMING, AND DYING--
WE TRIED TO STAY OUT OF THE WAY UNTIL YOU SHOWED UP. I TAKE IT THIS MEANS WE WON?
IF YOU WANT TO CALL IT THAT.
LET'S GO HOME.
WAIT--THIS DOESN'T MAKE SENSE! WE WERE THERE IN 1777. WE CHANGED THE PAST.
DON'T WORRY. OUR APPEARANCE WILL BE CONSIDERED FOLKLORE. MERE GHOST STORIES.
"LOTS OF CRAZY THINGS HAPPEN IN THE FOG OF WAR..."

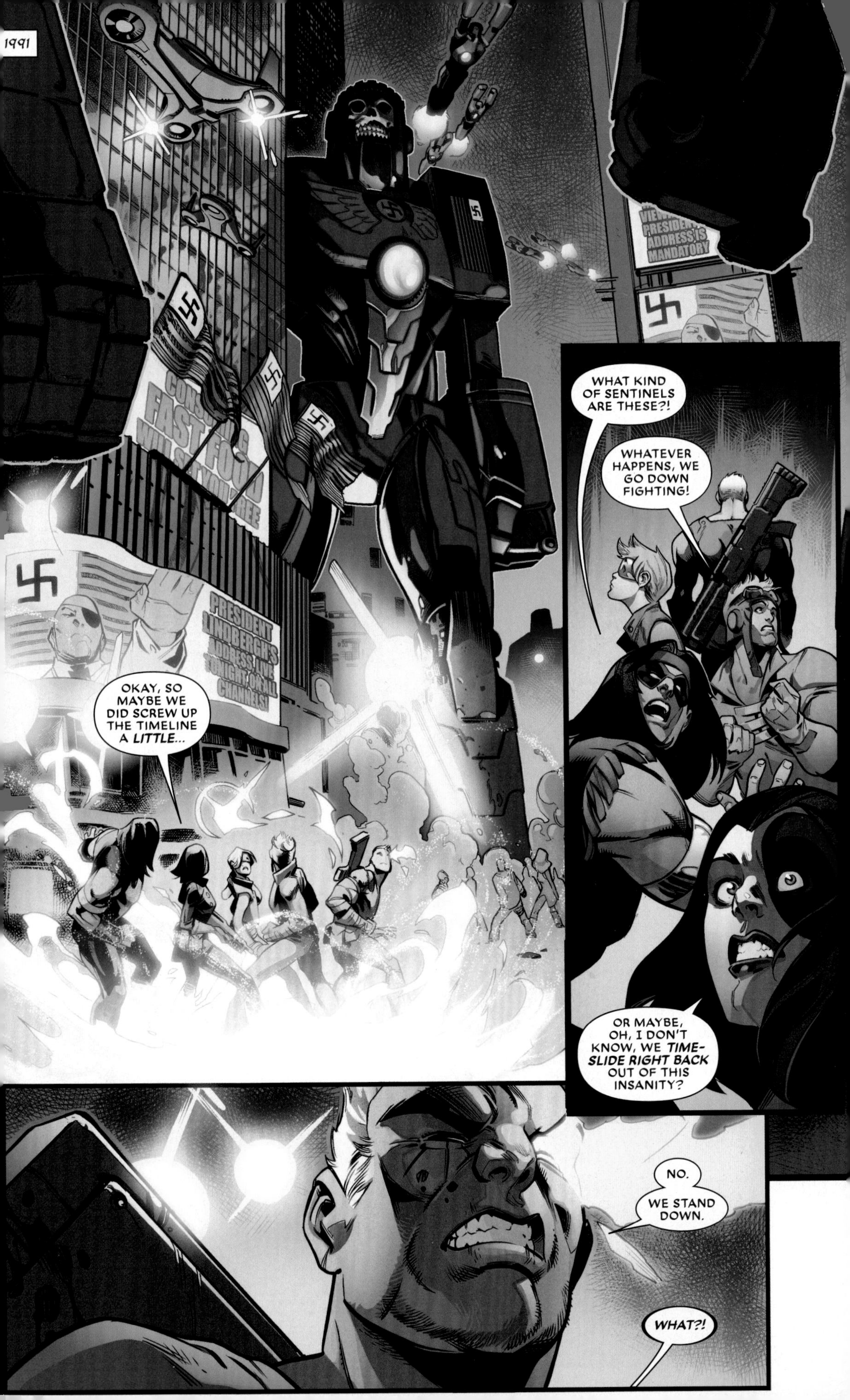
1991
PRESIDENT LINDBERGH'S ADDRESS LIVE TONIGHT ON ALL CHANNELS!
OKAY, SO MAYBE WE DID SCREW UP THE TIMELINE A *LITTLE*...
WHAT KIND OF SENTINELS ARE THESE?!
WHATEVER HAPPENS, WE GO DOWN FIGHTING!
OR MAYBE, OH, I DON'T KNOW, WE *TIME-SLIDE RIGHT BACK* OUT OF THIS INSANITY?
NO.
WE STAND DOWN.
WHAT?!

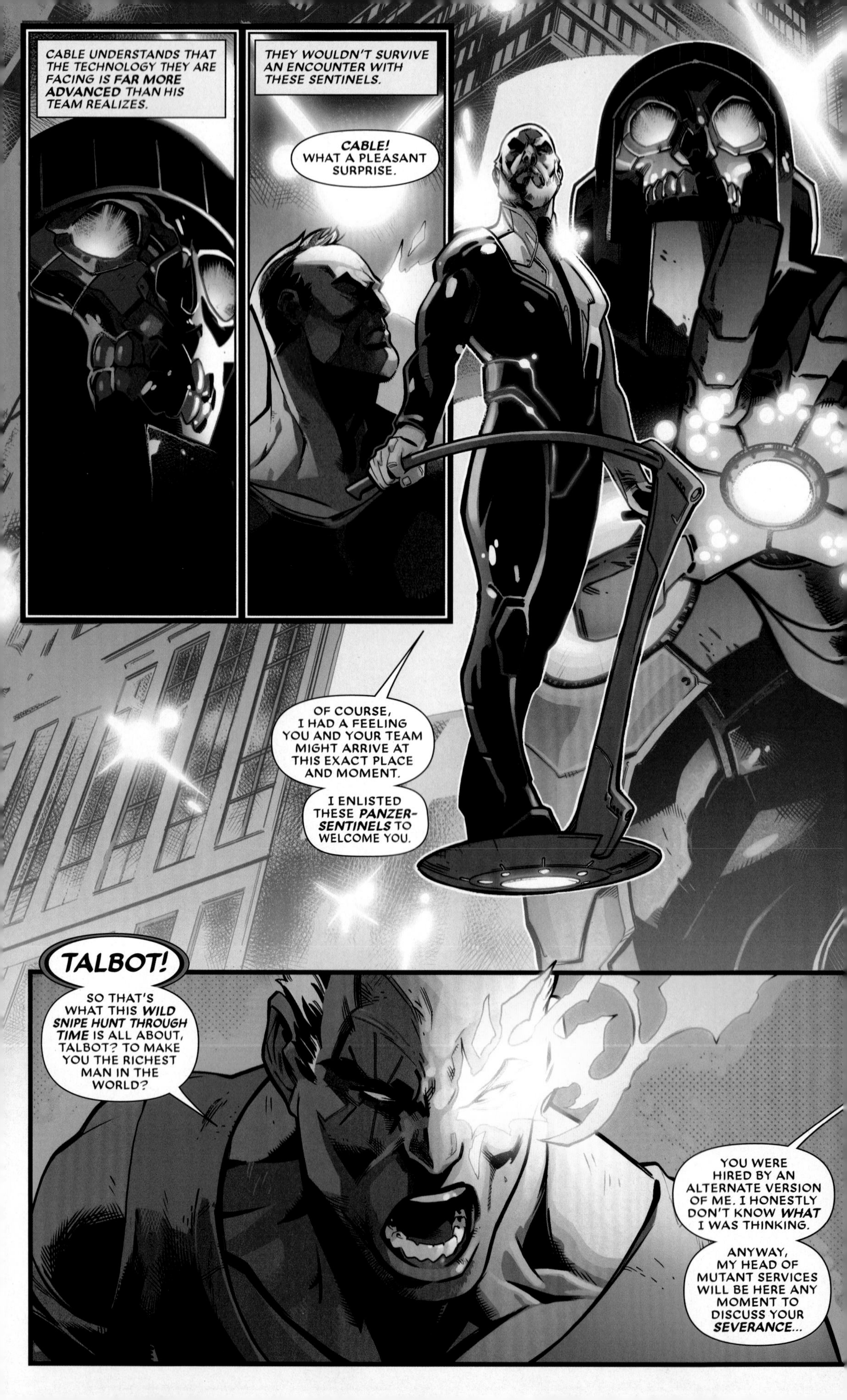
CABLE UNDERSTANDS THAT THE TECHNOLOGY THEY ARE FACING IS FAR MORE ADVANCED THAN HIS TEAM REALIZES.
THEY WOULDN'T SURVIVE AN ENCOUNTER WITH THESE SENTINELS.
CABLE! WHAT A PLEASANT SURPRISE.
OF COURSE, I HAD A FEELING YOU AND YOUR TEAM MIGHT ARRIVE AT THIS EXACT PLACE AND MOMENT.
I ENLISTED THESE PANZER-SENTINELS TO WELCOME YOU.
TALBOT!
SO THAT'S WHAT THIS WILD SNIPE HUNT THROUGH TIME IS ALL ABOUT, TALBOT? TO MAKE YOU THE RICHEST MAN IN THE WORLD?
YOU WERE HIRED BY AN ALTERNATE VERSION OF ME. I HONESTLY DON'T KNOW WHAT I WAS THINKING.
ANYWAY, MY HEAD OF MUTANT SERVICES WILL BE HERE ANY MOMENT TO DISCUSS YOUR SEVERANCE...

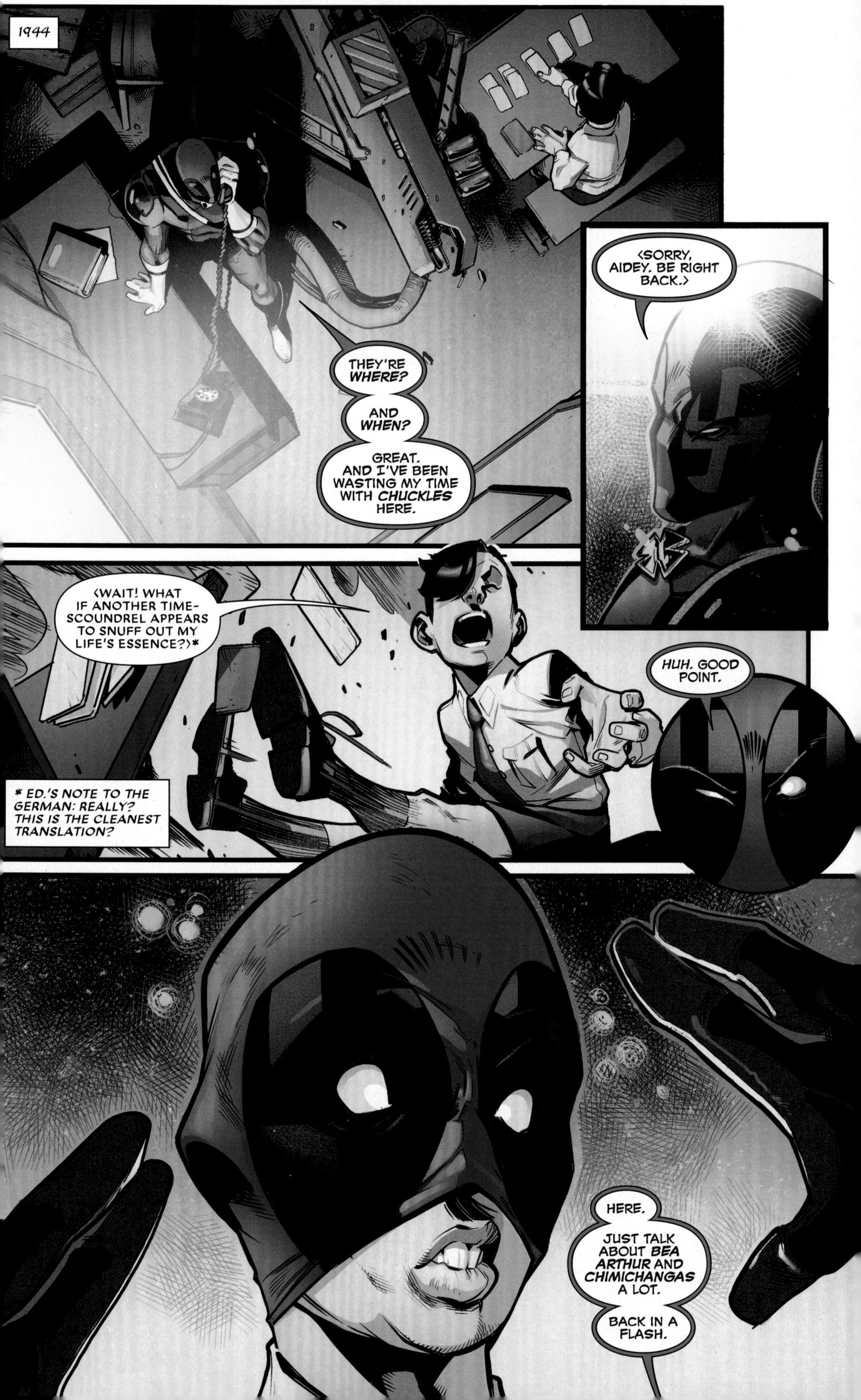
1944
THEY'RE *WHERE?*
AND *WHEN?*
GREAT. AND I'VE BEEN WASTING MY TIME WITH *CHUCKLES* HERE.
‹SORRY, AIDEY. BE RIGHT BACK.›
‹WAIT! WHAT IF ANOTHER TIME-SCOUNDREL APPEARS TO SNUFF OUT MY LIFE'S ESSENCE?›*
HUH. GOOD POINT.
* ED.'S NOTE TO THE GERMAN: REALLY? THIS IS THE CLEANEST TRANSLATION?
HERE.
JUST TALK ABOUT *BEA ARTHUR* AND *CHIMICHANGAS* A LOT.
BACK IN A FLASH.

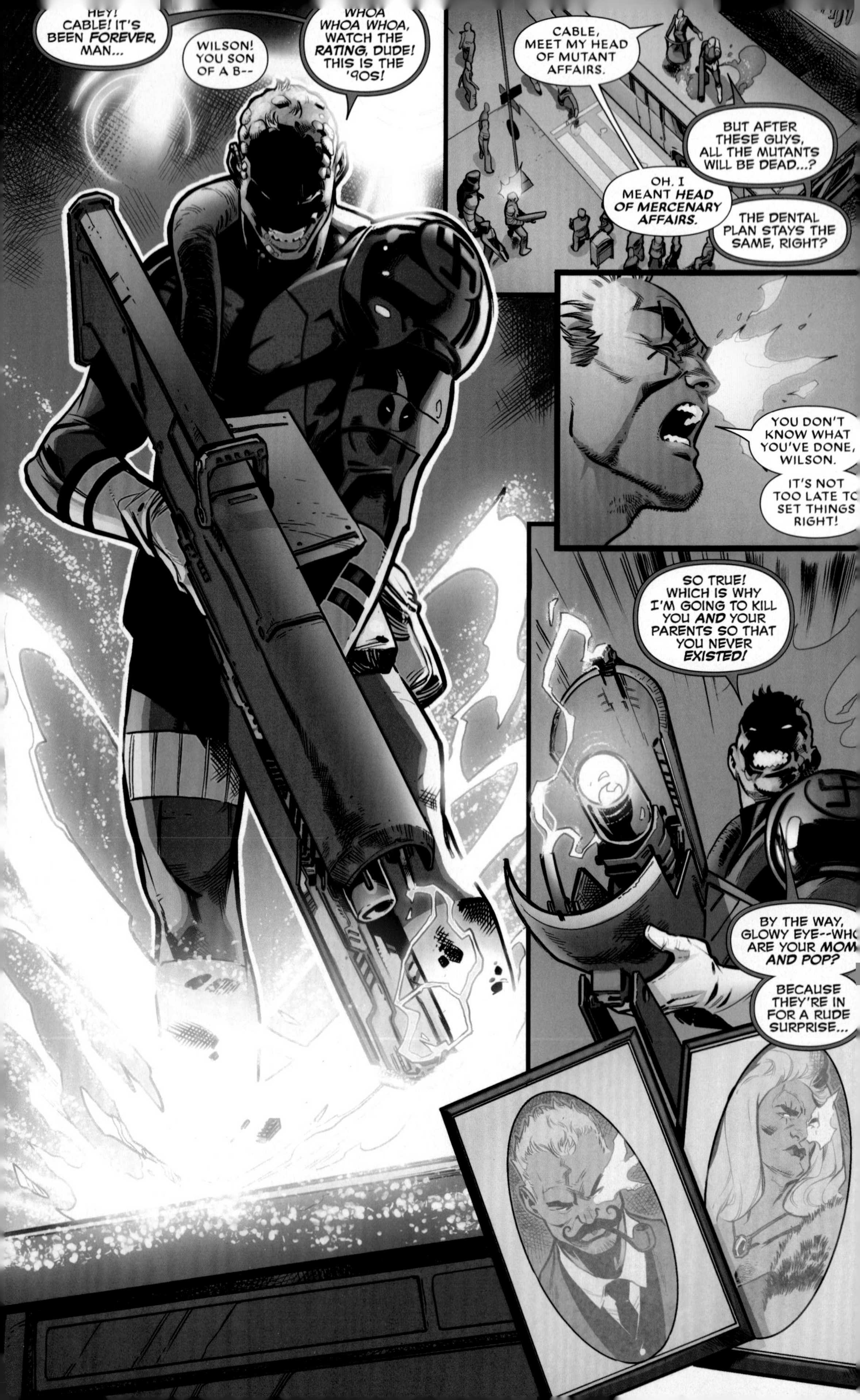
HEY! CABLE! IT'S BEEN FOREVER, MAN...
WILSON! YOU SON OF A B--
WHOA WHOA WHOA, WATCH THE RATING, DUDE! THIS IS THE '90S!
CABLE, MEET MY HEAD OF MUTANT AFFAIRS.
BUT AFTER THESE GUYS, ALL THE MUTANTS WILL BE DEAD...?
OH, I MEANT HEAD OF MERCENARY AFFAIRS.
THE DENTAL PLAN STAYS THE SAME, RIGHT?
YOU DON'T KNOW WHAT YOU'VE DONE, WILSON.
IT'S NOT TOO LATE TO SET THINGS RIGHT!
SO TRUE! WHICH IS WHY I'M GOING TO KILL YOU AND YOUR PARENTS SO THAT YOU NEVER EXISTED!
BY THE WAY, GLOWY EYE--WHO ARE YOUR MOM AND POP?
BECAUSE THEY'RE IN FOR A RUDE SURPRISE...

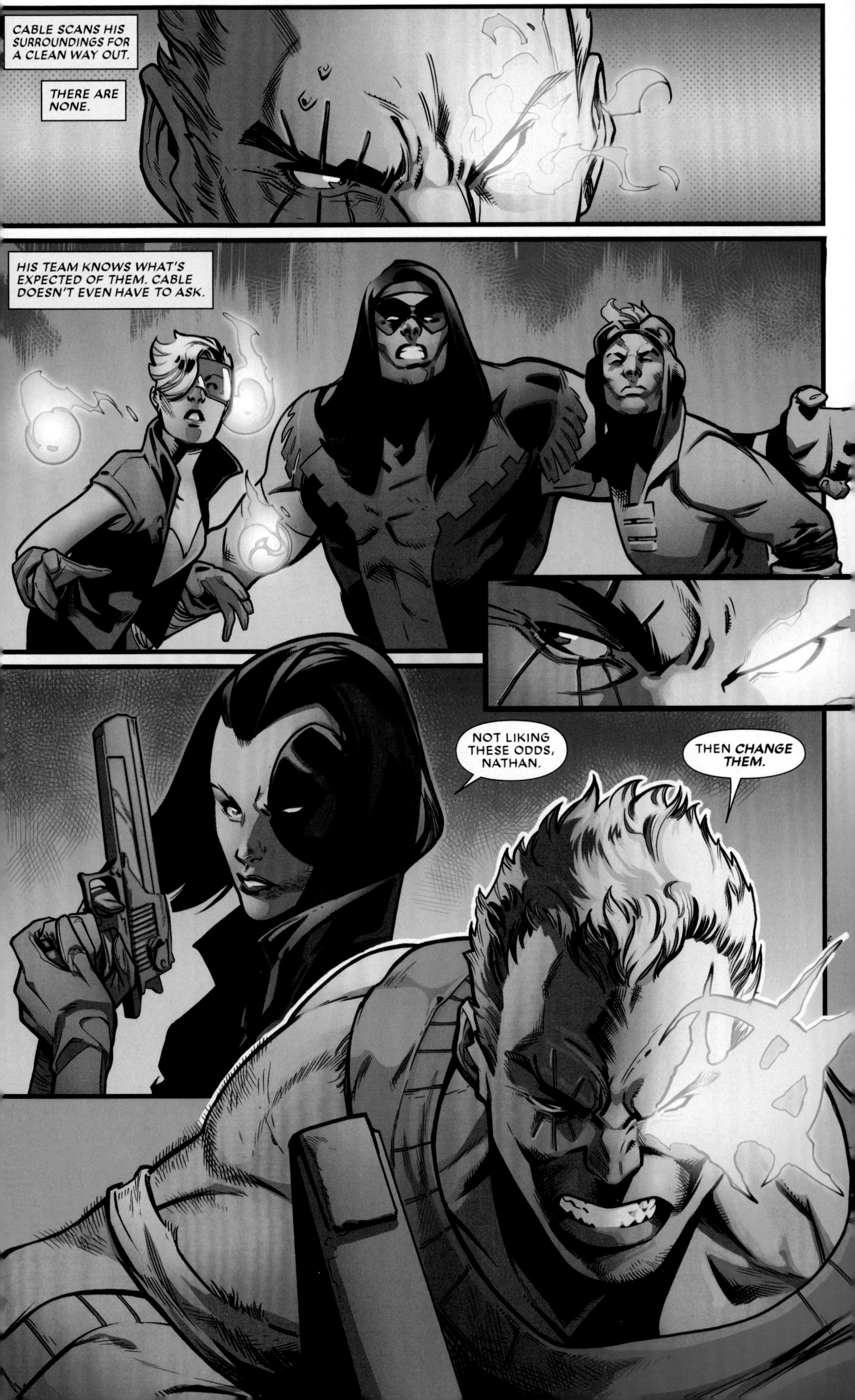
CABLE SCANS HIS SURROUNDINGS FOR A CLEAN WAY OUT.
THERE ARE NONE.
HIS TEAM KNOWS WHAT'S EXPECTED OF THEM. CABLE DOESN'T EVEN HAVE TO ASK.
NOT LIKING THESE ODDS, NATHAN.
THEN *CHANGE* *THEM.*

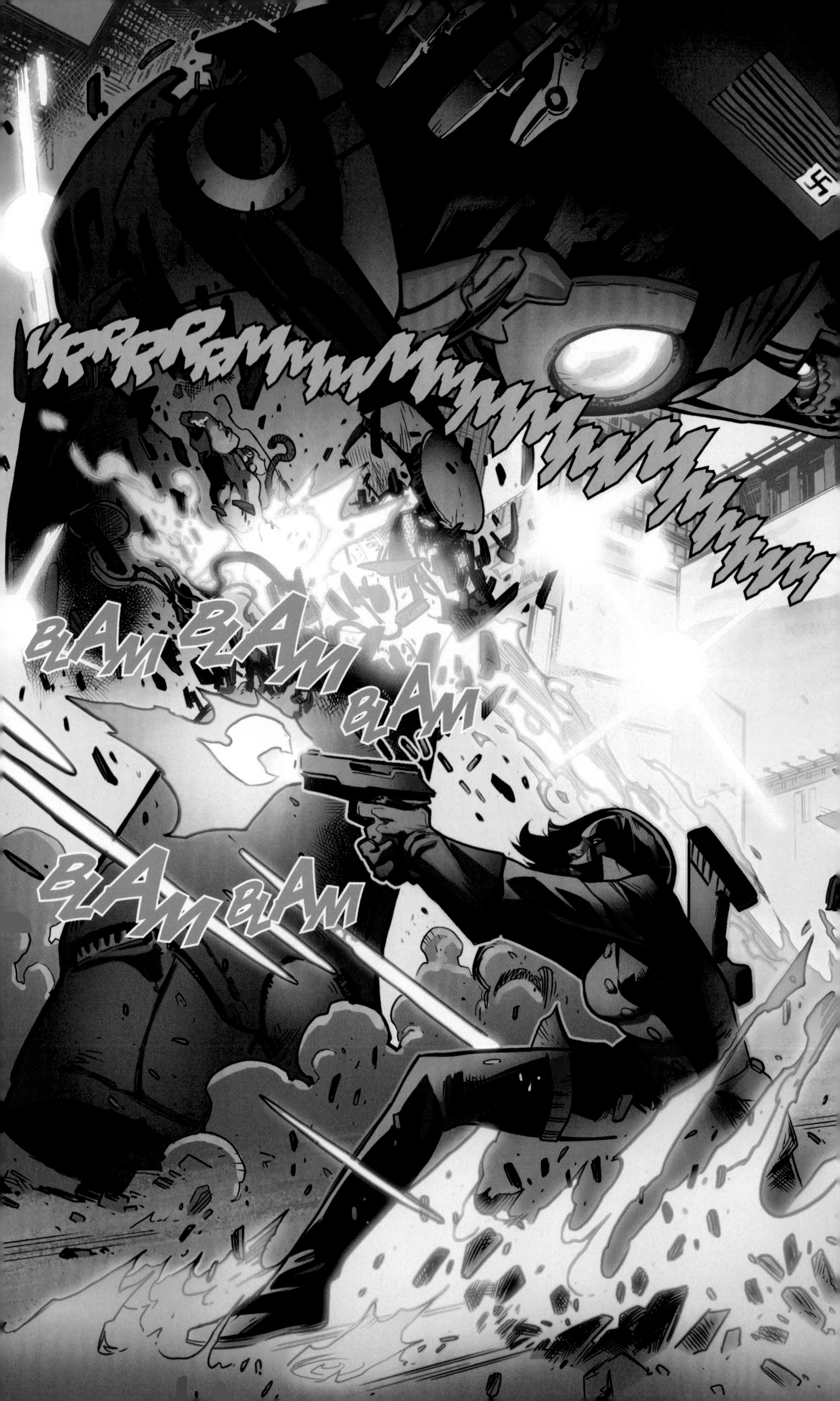
VRRRRAMMMMMMMMMMMMMMM
BLAM BLAM BLAM
BLAM BLAM

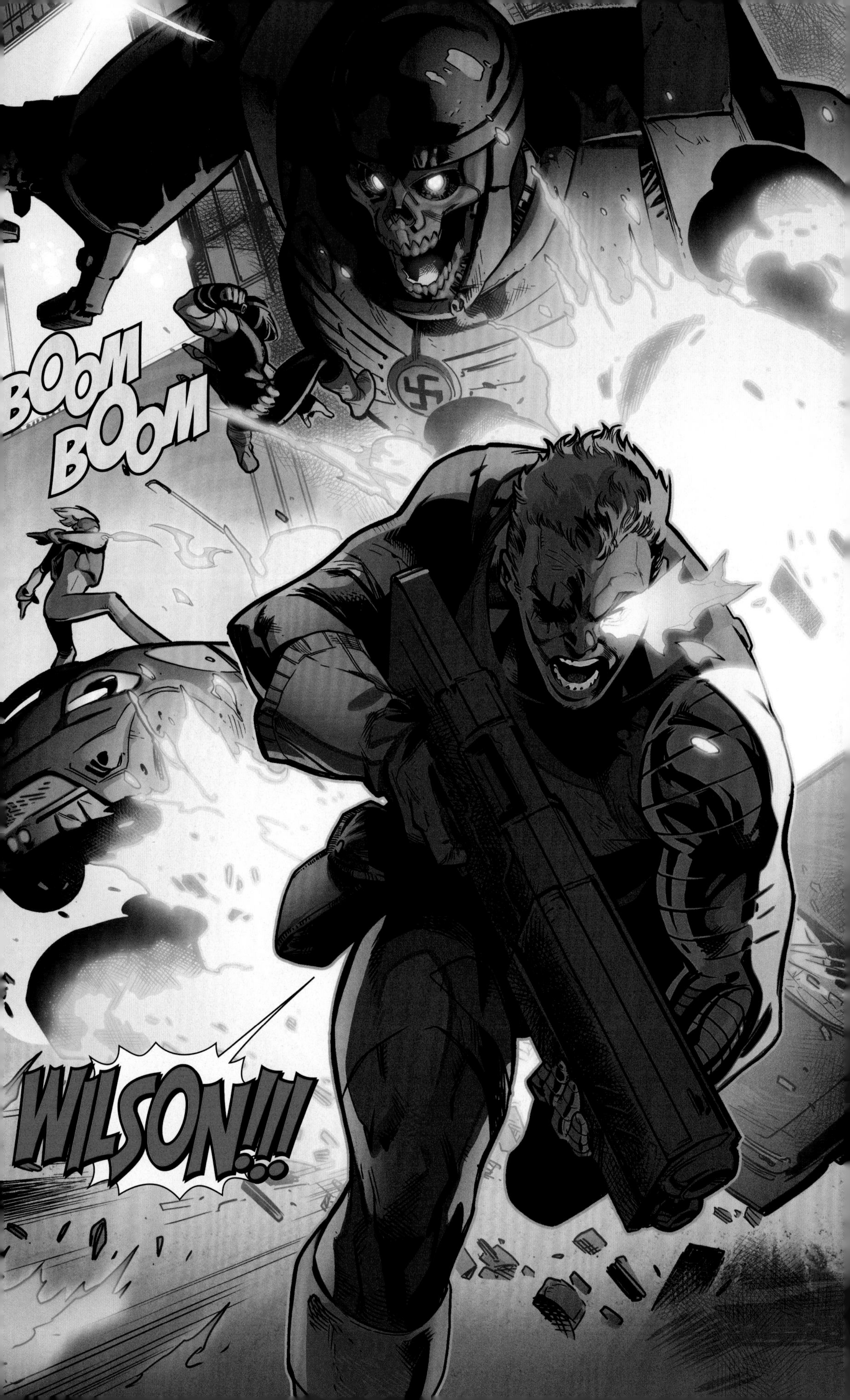
BOOM BOOM
WILSON!!!

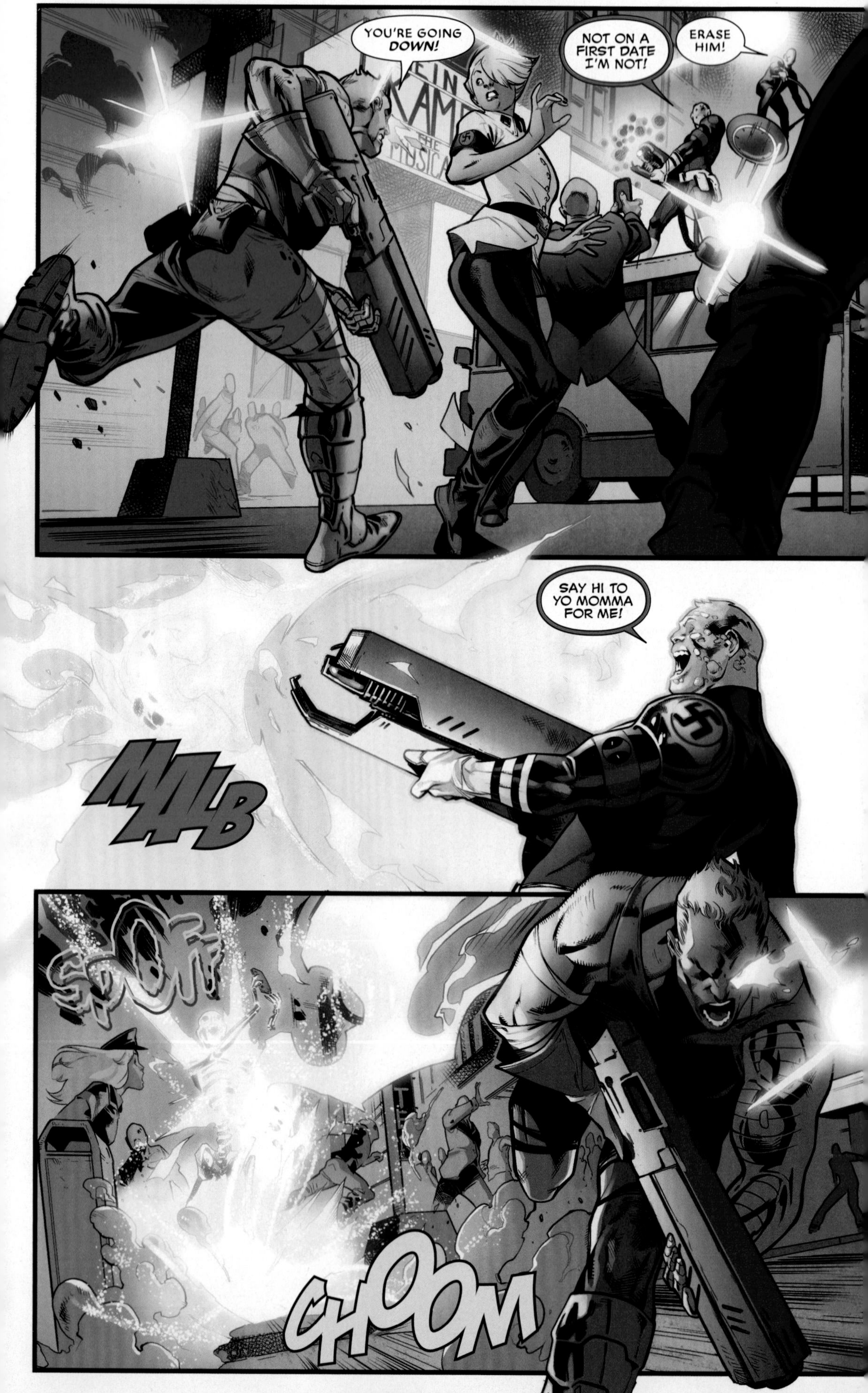
YOU'RE GOING DOWN!
NOT ON A FIRST DATE I'M NOT!
ERASE HIM!
SAY HI TO YO MOMMA FOR ME!
CHOOM

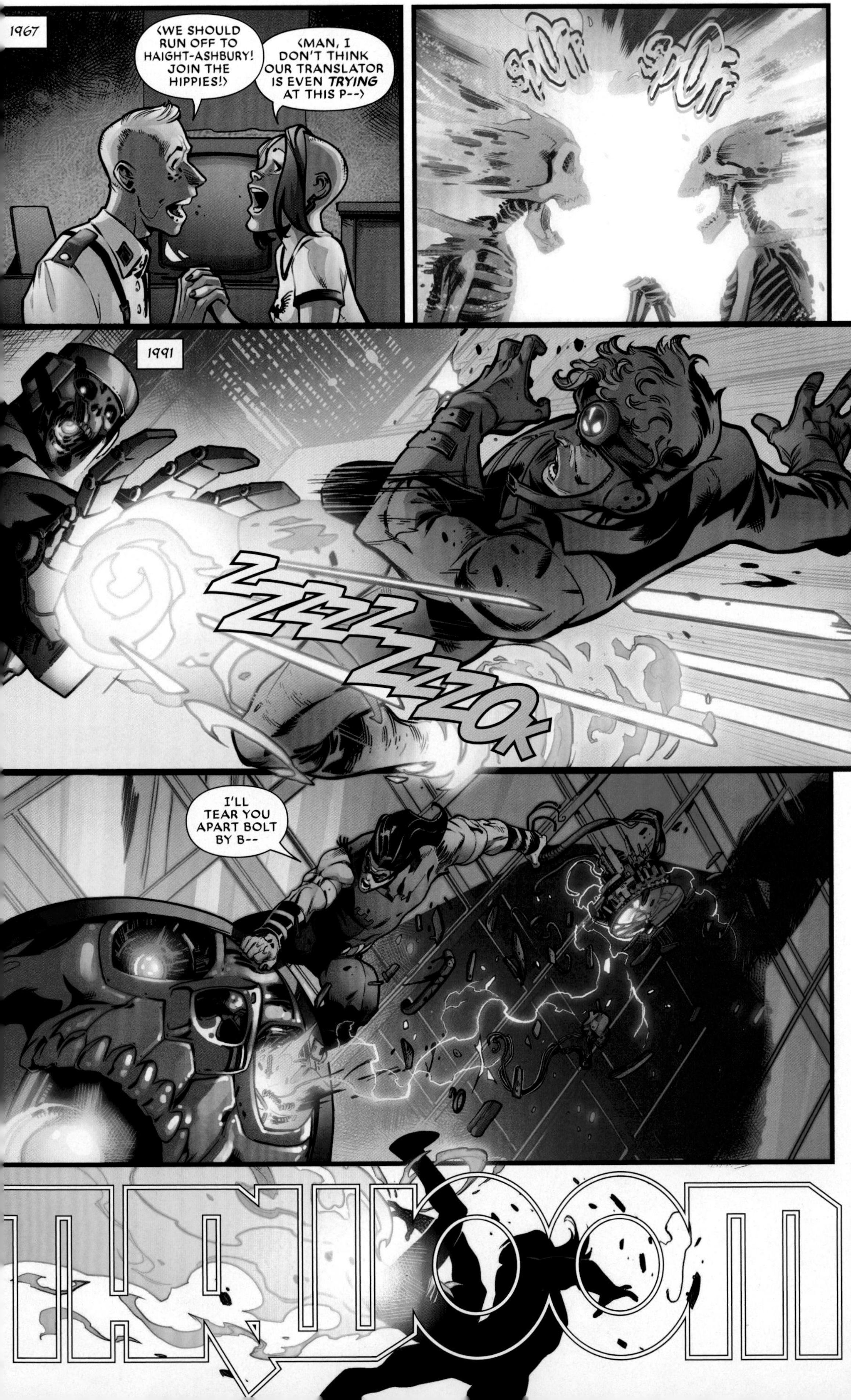
1967
‹WE SHOULD RUN OFF TO HAIGHT-ASHBURY! JOIN THE HIPPIES!›
‹MAN, I DON'T THINK OUR TRANSLATOR IS EVEN *TRYING* AT THIS P--›
1991
I'LL TEAR YOU APART BOLT BY B--
THWOOM

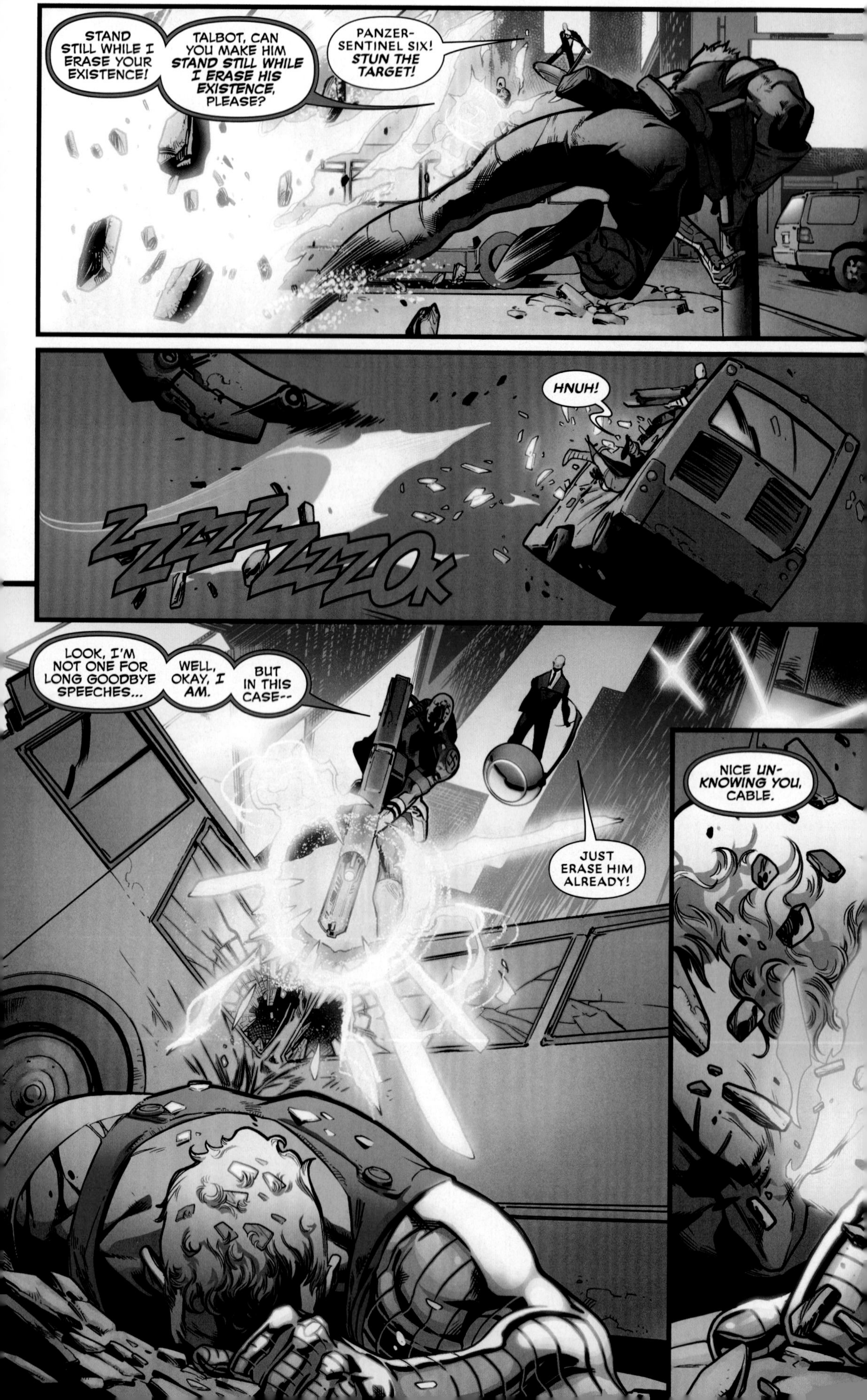
STAND STILL WHILE I ERASE YOUR EXISTENCE!
TALBOT, CAN YOU MAKE HIM STAND STILL WHILE I ERASE HIS EXISTENCE, PLEASE?
PANZER-SENTINEL SIX! STUN THE TARGET!
HNUH!
ZZZZZZZZZZOK
LOOK, I'M NOT ONE FOR LONG GOODBYE SPEECHES...
WELL, OKAY, I AM.
BUT IN THIS CASE--
JUST ERASE HIM ALREADY!
NICE UN-KNOWING YOU, CABLE.

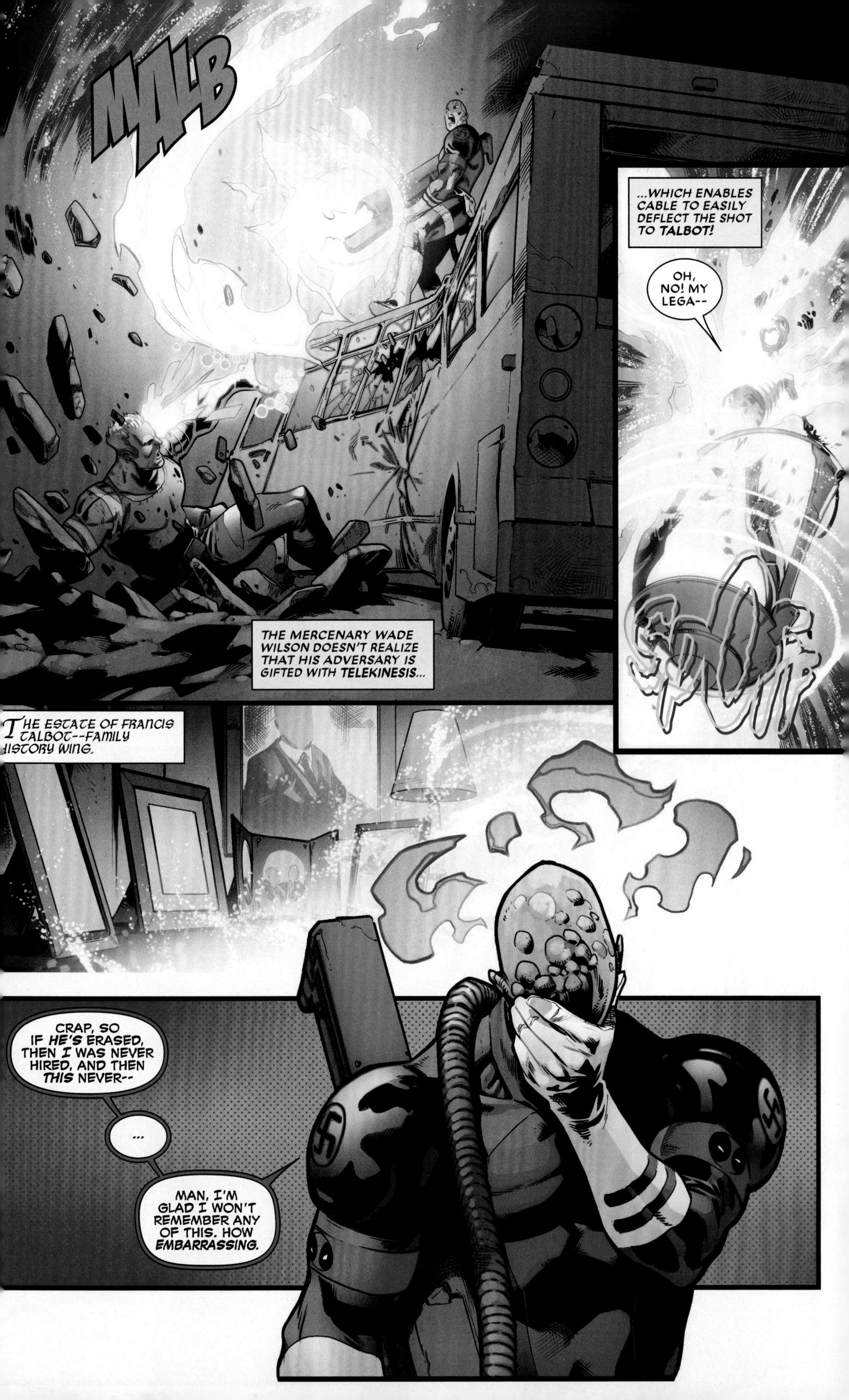
THE MERCENARY WADE WILSON DOESN'T REALIZE THAT HIS ADVERSARY IS GIFTED WITH TELEKINESIS...
...WHICH ENABLES CABLE TO EASILY DEFLECT THE SHOT TO TALBOT!
OH, NO! MY LEGA--
THE ESTATE OF FRANCIS TALBOT--FAMILY HISTORY WING.
CRAP, SO IF HE'S ERASED, THEN I WAS NEVER HIRED, AND THEN THIS NEVER--
...
MAN, I'M GLAD I WON'T REMEMBER ANY OF THIS. HOW EMBARRASSING.

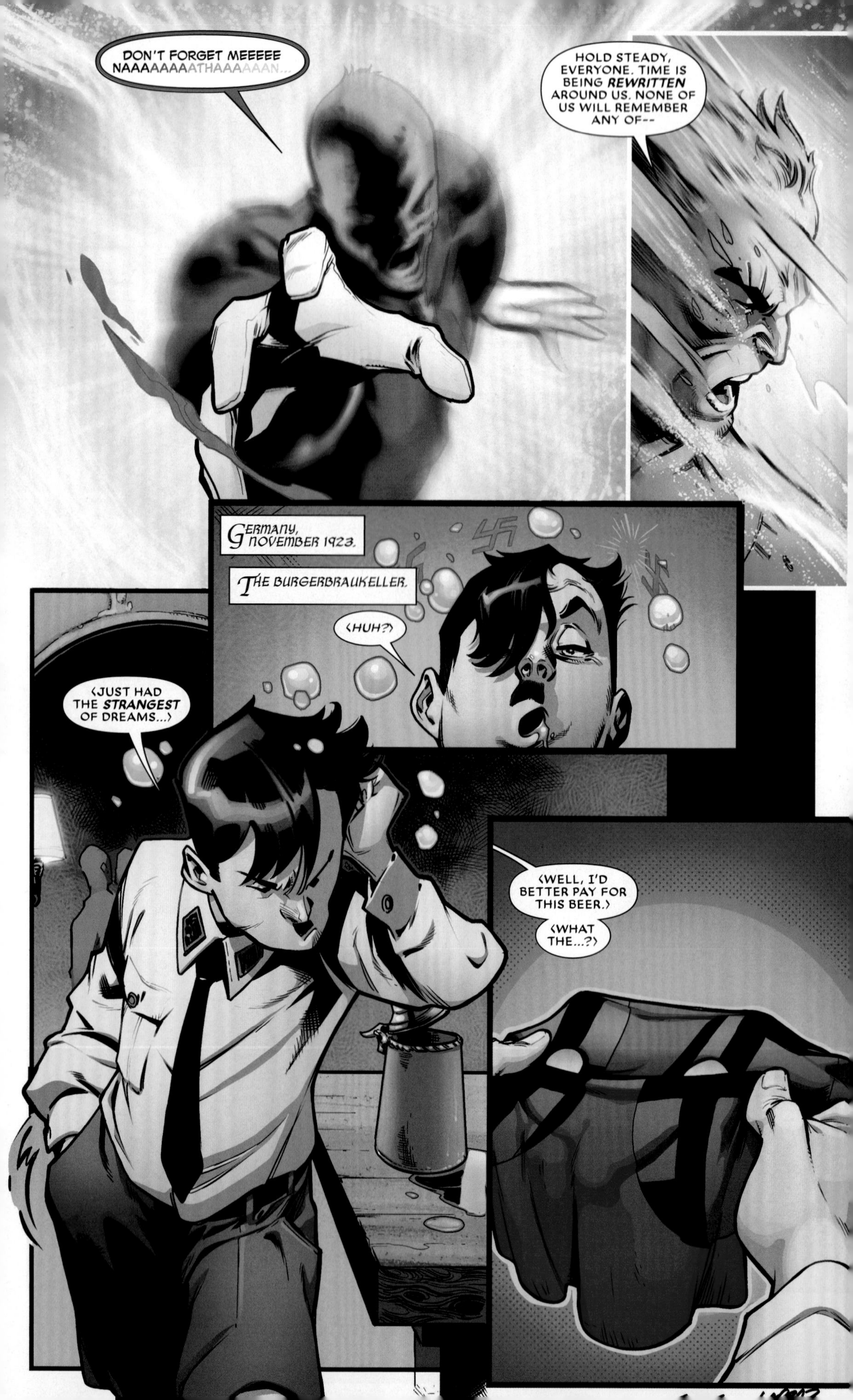
DON'T FORGET MEEEEE NAAAAAAAATHAAAAAAN...
HOLD STEADY, EVERYONE. TIME IS BEING REWRITTEN AROUND US. NONE OF US WILL REMEMBER ANY OF--
GERMANY, NOVEMBER 1923.
THE BURGERBRAUKELLER.
‹HUH?›
‹JUST HAD THE STRANGEST OF DREAMS...›
‹WELL, I'D BETTER PAY FOR THIS BEER.›
‹WHAT THE...?›

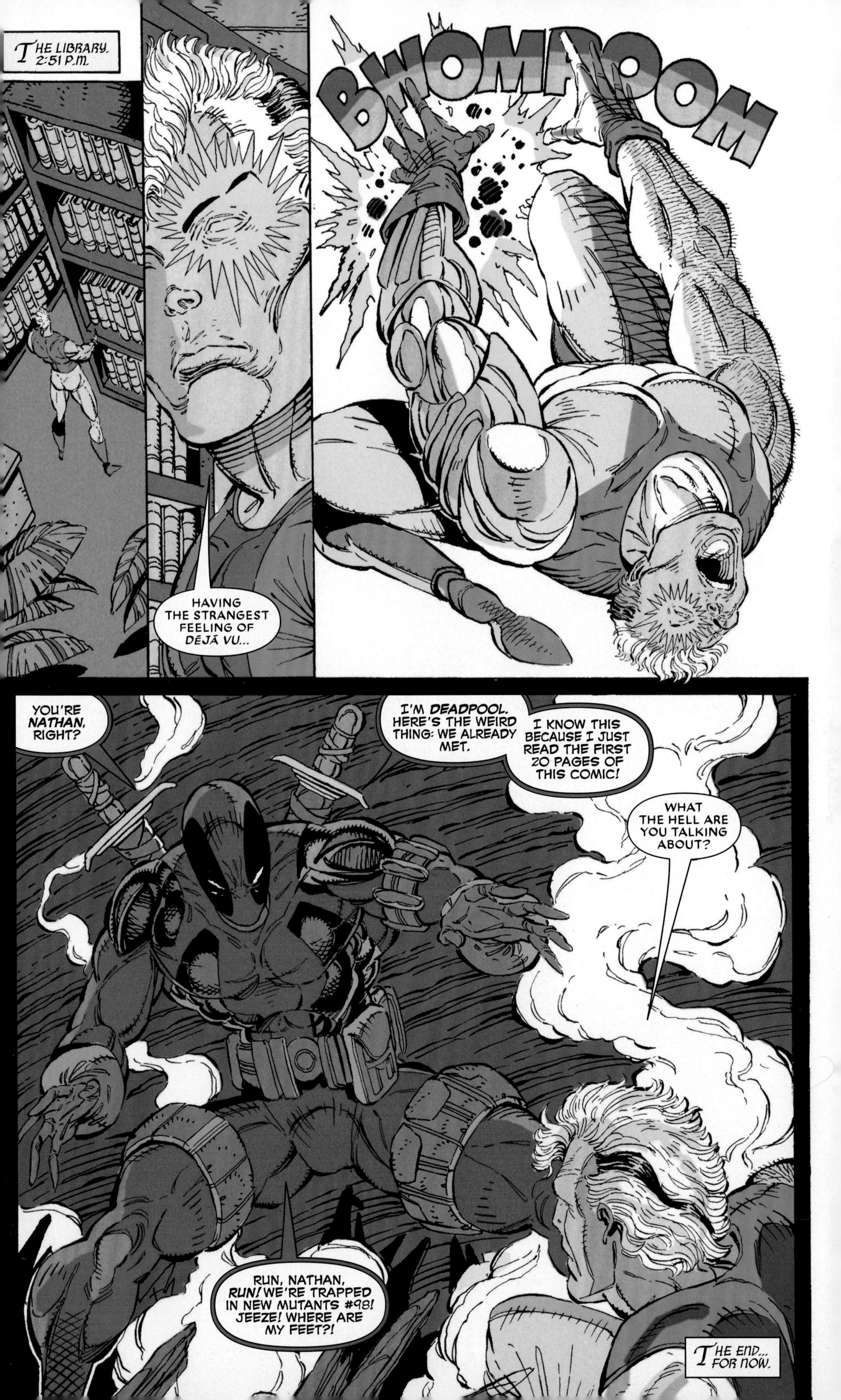
THE LIBRARY. 2:51 P.M.
BWOMPOOM
HAVING THE STRANGEST FEELING OF DÉJÀ VU...
YOU'RE NATHAN, RIGHT?
I'M DEADPOOL. HERE'S THE WEIRD THING: WE ALREADY MET.
I KNOW THIS BECAUSE I JUST READ THE FIRST 20 PAGES OF THIS COMIC!
WHAT THE HELL ARE YOU TALKING ABOUT?
RUN, NATHAN, RUN! WE'RE TRAPPED IN NEW MUTANTS #98! JEEZE! WHERE ARE MY FEET?!
THE END... FOR NOW.

DEADPOOL VS. X-FORCE

Sensing a disturbance in the timestream, time-traveling mutant soldier Cable discovered that billionaire Francis Talbot had hired a mercenary to go back in time to save his grandson from dying in Operation Desert Storm. Instead, the mercenary, a madman named Deadpool (a.k.a. Wade Wilson) had gone back to the Revolutionary War and begun changing American History. Cable gathered a team of Warpath, Boom Boom, Domino, and Cannonball to go back and stop him. No sooner had they engaged him when Deadpool leapt into the timestream again. Boom-Boom and Cannonball stayed in 1777 to try to fix the mess he'd made, while Cable and the others followed Deadpool...into a trap he'd set for them during the Battle of Gettysburg in the Civil War.

Q: Did you...did you really just summarize the entire issue?
A: This is the recap page, isn't that what it's for?

Q: Don't recaps usually come at the beginning of the book?
A: We're innovators.

Q: Deadpool and X-Force have both been around since the 90s...why don't they know each other?
A: Ah, because this story actually takes place BEFORE New Mutants #98, which means it's before Deadpool ever encountered Cable and his crew! Technically, that also means it takes place before X-Force existed, they were still Cable & the New Mutants...but come on. This is X-Force in spirit, am I right?

Q: What about Shatterstar and Feral?
A: Oh, look who's an X-Force expert all of a sudden. They...both had hair appointments when Cable called.

Q: Why does Deadpool not have yellow word balloons?
A: Because when he first appeared in the 90s, his balloons were not yellow, they were white with red strokes around the outside, just like we did here. Eventually, the stroke changed to yellow, then the whole balloons became yellow. A little treat for all the lettering geeks out there!

#1 RECAP PAGE

PREVIOUSLY IN

THE MEDDLESOME MERCENARY DEADPOOL HAS BEEN CUT LOOSE IN THE TIMESTREAM, LAUNCHING HIMSELF BACK INTO THE ANNALS OF AMERICAN HISTORY. TIME-TRAVELING MUTANT SOLDIER CABLE HAS PUT TOGETHER A SQUAD OF MUTANTS TO STOP DEADPOOL BEFORE HE REWRITES THE PAST ACCORDING TO SOME SECRET PLAN. 'POOL'S FIRST STOP WAS THE AMERICAN REVOLUTION, WHERE HE MADE THE COLONISTS' VICTORIES EASIER. HE THEN LEAPT FORWARD TO THE AMERICAN CIVIL WAR. LEAVING CANNONBALL AND BOOM-BOOM IN 1777 TASKED WITH MINIMIZING THE DAMAGE, CABLE TOOK WARPATH AND DOMINO AFTER THE MAD MERCENARY...ONLY TO DISCOVER HIS TAMPERING HAD ALREADY BEGUN TO WORK—THE UNION SOLDIERS WERE USING ANACHRONISTICALLY ADVANCED WEAPONRY. WITH HIS SQUAD BATTLING THE CHANGES IN THE TIMESTREAM IN TWO CENTURIES, CABLE TOOK DEADPOOL ON DIRECTLY, LEAPING WITH HIM THROUGH THE TIMESTREAM...ONLY TO FIND HIMSELF IN EARLY 20TH CENTURY CHINA, ENSLAVED BY A COLLAR GIVEN TO DEADPOOL BY HIS "EMPLOYER".

Q: SO, THAT'S THE WHOLE STORY OF THIS ISSUE?
A: AND LAST ISSUE, YEAH. THE WHOLE STORY SO FAR.

Q: BUT...WHY?
A: IT'S A RECAP PAGE.

Q: BUT WHAT'S TO STOP PEOPLE FROM JUST READING THAT AND SKIPPING THE ISSUE?
A: IDEALLY, A STORY IS ABOUT MORE THAN PLOT SPOILERS. THERE'S, YOU KNOW, ARTISTRY IN THE TELLING OF THE TALE.

Q: HOW DOES DEADPOOL KNOW HE IS IN A COMIC BOOK?
A: HE'S VERY SELF-AWARE. IN MANY WAYS THAT MAKES HIM MORE SANE THAN MOST CHARACTERS, RIGHT?

Q: IF THE TIMESTREAM HAS ALREADY BEEN CHANGED IN CIVIL WAR TIMES, THEN NOTHING THEY DO BACK IN REVOLUTIONARY TIMES IS GOING TO MATTER ANYMORE, RIGHT?
A: YOU'RE NEGLECTING THE FACT THAT EARTH-616 IS A UNIVERSE WHERE EVEN THOUGH IT FEELS CONSISTENT TO THOSE WITHIN IT (EXCEPT DEADPOOL) REALITY IS ACTUALLY SUBJECT TO THE WHIMS OF THE MINDS OF POWERFUL ENTITIES LIVING IN EARTH-1218. THOSE ENTITIES, THOSE CREATORS, CAN IMBUE EVENTS IN EARTH-616 WITH A NARRATIVE FORCE THAT CAN BEND AND BREAK THE LAWS OF PROBABILITY AND PHYSICS. THAT CAPACITY CAN AND DOES CREATE, IN REGARD TO TIME-TRAVEL, SOMETHING I LIKE TO CALL "THE OBJECTIVE NOW," A TIME THAT POSSESSES A LEVEL OF "NOW-NESS" THAT CAN OVERRULE ALL OTHER NOWS...AND CAN, IN SOME INSTANCES, BE SPREAD OVER MULTIPLE NOWS, AS HEREIN. THUS, THINGS CAN HAPPEN "MEANWHILE" A HUNDRED YEARS APART, THROUGH THE THREAD OF THE NARRATIVE OBJECTIVE NOW CREATED BY THE CREATOR **AND OBSERVED BY THE READER.**

#2 RECAP PAGE

PREVIOUSLY IN

THE TRUTH STANDS REVEALED! WHEN THE TIME-TRAVELING SOLDIER, CABLE, SENSED A PROBLEM IN THE TIME-STREAM AND CONFRONTED DR. FRANCIS TALBOT ABOUT IT, THE RECLUSIVE BILLIONAIRE ARMS-SELLER CLAIMED TO HAVE HIRED THE MAD MERCENARY DEADPOOL TO GO BACK IN TIME AND SAVE HIS GRANDSON. HE CLAIMED DEADPOOL THEN WENT ROGUE AND BEGAN CHANGING HISTORY OF HIS OWN ACCORD! THE TRUTH IS, DEADPOOL'S BEEN FOLLOWING TALBOT'S PLAN EVERY STEP OF THE WAY—ENSURING THE AMERICANS DOMINATED IN THE REVOLUTIONARY WAR, THE SOUTH PREVAILED IN THE AMERICAN CIVIL WAR, AND THE CONFEDERATES WERE ABLE TO DOMINATE CHINA IN GLOBAL CONFLICT...ALL THE BETTER TO ENHANCE HIS SALES OF WEAPONRY! NOW, WITH CABLE'S ALLIES CANNONBALL, BOOM-BOOM, DOMINO, AND WARPATH SPREAD THROUGHOUT TIME TRYING TO MINIMIZE THE DAMAGE, DEADPOOL HAS ARRIVED IN 1923 GERMANY, WHERE HE FINDS A DRUNKEN ADOLF HITLER!

Q: YOU REALLY DON'T MIND SPOILING THE ISSUE AT THE END OF THE ISSUE?
A: WELL, IT'S NOT A SPOILER, IT'S A RECAP. OR A "REVERSE SPOILER." LIKE DEADPOOL SAYS ON PAGE 1. BUT THE REVERSE OF A SPOILER MEANS IT, LIKE...DOESN'T SPOIL IT. IT'S MORE LIKE...AN EMBELLISHMENT. A LITTLE ADDED FLAIR.

Q: LIKE A SPOILER ON A CAR?
A: ...YEAH, I GUESS. SO, IT'S LESS LIKE A SPOILER, MORE LIKE A SPOILER.

Q: IS THIS JORDAN D. WHITE ANSWERING THESE QUESTIONS, OR DEADPOOL, LIKE IT SAID IN THAT FOOTNOTE?
A: I AM GOING TO LEAVE THAT TO YOU TO ANSWER. I MEAN, THE LOGICAL ANSWER IS THAT DEADPOOL IS A FICTIONAL CHARACTER WHILE JORDAN D. WHITE IS REAL...BUT THEN AGAIN, IN THE QUOTE-UNQUOTE FICTIONAL MARVEL MULTIVERSE THERE EXISTS A WORLD CALLED EARTH-1218, A.K.A. THE REAL WORLD WHERE YOU ARE READING THIS AND ON THAT WORLD IS A JORDAN D. WHITE WHO DOES NOT BELIEVE DEADPOOL IS REAL. AND YET, OVER ON EARTH-616, THERE DEADPOOL IS, AS REAL AS ANYTHING. BOTH BELIEFS CANNOT BE TRUE. BUT WHO IS TO SAY WHICH IS RIGHT?

Q: OK, THAT WAS WEIRD AND CONFUSING. GOT ANY "SPOILERS" FOR NEXT ISSUE?
A: SINCE THIS STORY IS A FLASHBACK STORY, ANY COMIC PUBLISHED AFTER NEW MUTANTS #98 IS TECHNICALLY A SPOILER FOR ISSUE #4. FOR THE MOST UPDATED SPOILERS FOR ISSUE #4, CHECK OUT DEADPOOL #33 AND X-FORCE #8, BOTH ON STAND NOW!

Q: THAT WAS A PRETTY CHEAP PLUG.
A: AND THAT WAS NOT A QUESTION!

#3 RECAP PAGE

PREVIOUSLY IN

SENSING A DISTURBANCE IN THE FABRIC OF TIME ITSELF, TIME-TRAVELING MUTANT SOLDIER CABLE FOLLOWED IT TO ITS SOURCE—BILLIONAIRE FRANCIS TALBOT. TALBOT ADMITTED TO HAVING HIRED MADMAN MERCENARY DEADPOOL TO GO BACK IN TIME AND SAVE HIS GRANDSON, KILLED IN A RECENT WAR. INSTEAD, DEADPOOL WAS JUMPING THROUGH THE GREAT WARS OF US HISTORY AND UPSETTING THEIR OUTCOMES, ALTERING HISTORY. CABLE PUT TOGETHER A TEAM AND WENT AFTER THE FAST-TALKING SOLDIER-FOR-HIRE. SPREAD ACROSS THE TIMELINE, CABLE'S CREW LEARNED THAT TALBOT HAD LIED—DEADPOOL WAS ACTING UNDER HIS DIRECT ORDERS, MAKING A WORLD OF EVERLASTING WAR, MAKING TALBOT EVEN RICHER AND MORE POWERFUL. RETURNING TO THE WAR-TORN AND NAZI-OVERRUN PRESENT FOR A FINAL BATTLE ROYALE, DEADPOOL'S TIME MACHINE GUN, DESIGNED TO WIPE ITS TARGET FROM HISTORY, WAS FIRED ON TALBOT. WITH THE PERSON WHO SET THE ENTIRE INCIDENT IN MOTION WIPED OUT, TIME WAS REWRITTEN SO NONE OF THE EVENTS EVER OCCURRED.

Q: WAIT. SO...THE WHOLE STORY WAS WIPED OUT? IT NEVER HAPPENED?
A: COMPLICATED QUESTION. IT DID HAPPEN, BUT AS A RESULT, IT DIDN'T. BUT IT HAD TO HAPPEN IN ORDER TO NOT HAPPEN, OTHERWISE IT WOULD HAVE HAPPENED.

Q: SO WHAT IS THE POINT OF READING THE STORY IF IT NEVER HAPPENED?
A: AGAIN—IT DID HAPPEN. AND THEN UNHAPPENED. SO, NOW YOU KNOW THE SECRET TRUTH ABOUT THE REASON THERE IS NOT A FRANCIS TALBOT IN ANY OTHER MARVEL COMICS. ALL THE COMIC READERS WHO DIDN'T READ THIS SERIES WILL FOREVER BE WONDERING..."WHY HAVE I NOT READ ABOUT A CHARACTER NAMED FRANCIS TALBOT? WHERE'S FRANCIS TALBOT IN ALL THIS?"

Q: HANG ON...DIDN'T CABLE SAY THAT TALBOT'S INVENTIONS WERE RESPONSIBLE FOR THE TIME TRAVEL DEVICE HE USES? HOW COME HE'S STILL HERE?
A: UH...BECAUSE IF TALBOT DOESN'T INVENT TIME TRAVEL, SOMEONE ELSE DOES. IT'S OUT THERE, RIPE FOR THE INVENTING. THE NEW GUY WAS COOL, THOUGH.

Q: WHY DOES THE LAST PAGE OF THE COMIC LOOK ALL DIFFERENT FROM THE OTHER ONES?
A: BECAUSE IT WAS DRAWN BY A DIFFERENT ARTIST. THAT'S A PAGE WE MADE FROM TWO PAGES OF NEW MUTANTS #98, THE FIRST APPEARANCE OF DEADPOOL. THE ART IS BY ROB LIEFELD AND S. BUCCELLATO. THAT ISSUE WAS WRITTEN BY ROB LIEFELD & FABIAN NICIEZA... BUT WE CHANGED THE DIALOGUE A LITTLE THERE. GET IT? BECAUSE, LIKE, DEADPOOL NOW KNOWS THAT WAS NOT THE FIRST TIME THEY MET, AND HE IS, LIKE, SELF-AWARE? GET IT?

Q: OK, OK, I GET IT.
A: GREAT! THIS HAS BEEN YOUR RECAP OF THE ENTIRE SERIES. WE KNOW YOU HAVE YOUR CHOICE OF COMIC BOOK RECAP PAGES TO ENJOY, SO THANK YOU FOR READING US TODAY.

#4 RECAP PAGE

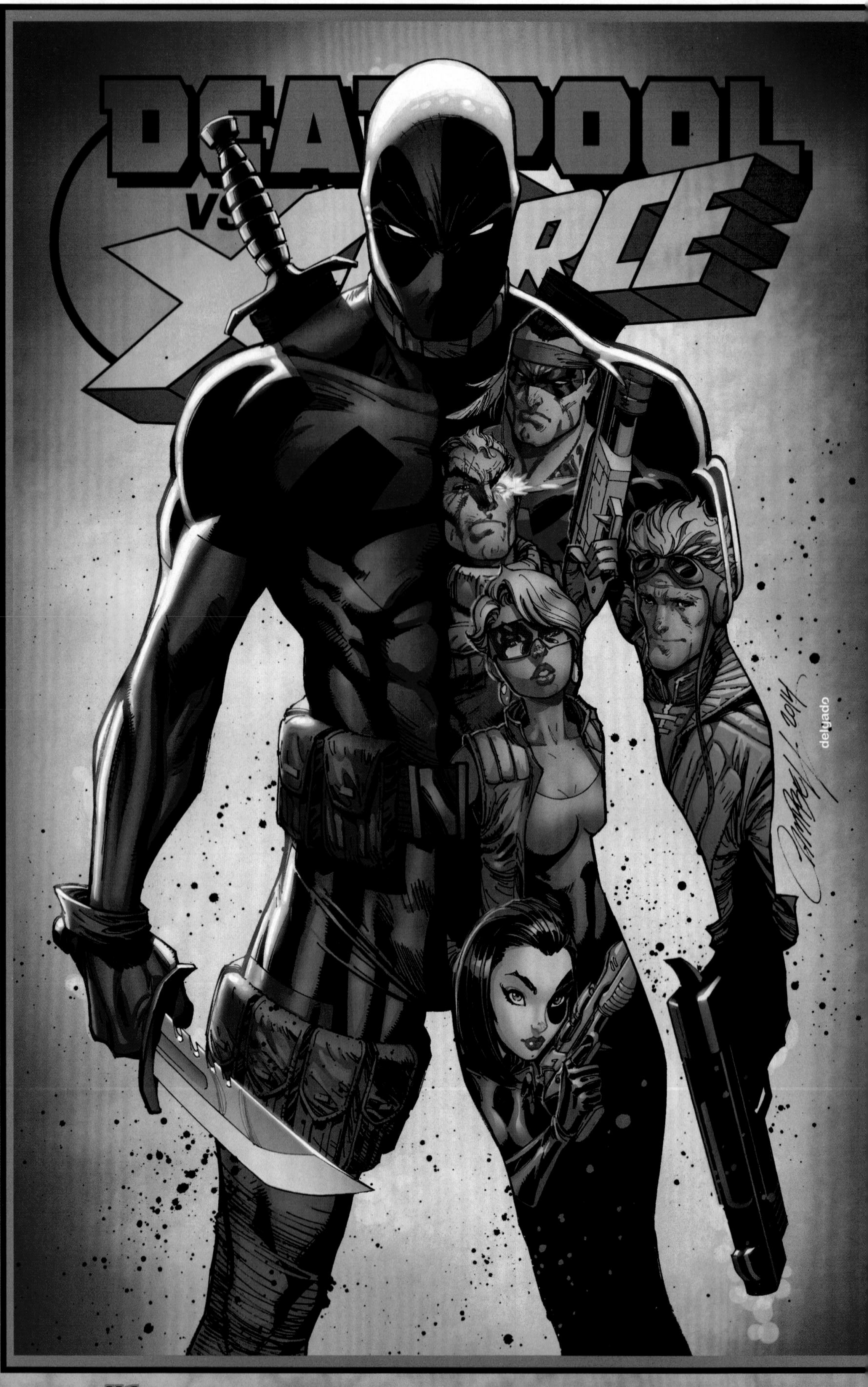
DEADPOOL
VS
X-FORCE
delgado

#1 VARIANT BY J. SCOTT CAMPBELL & EDGAR DELGADO

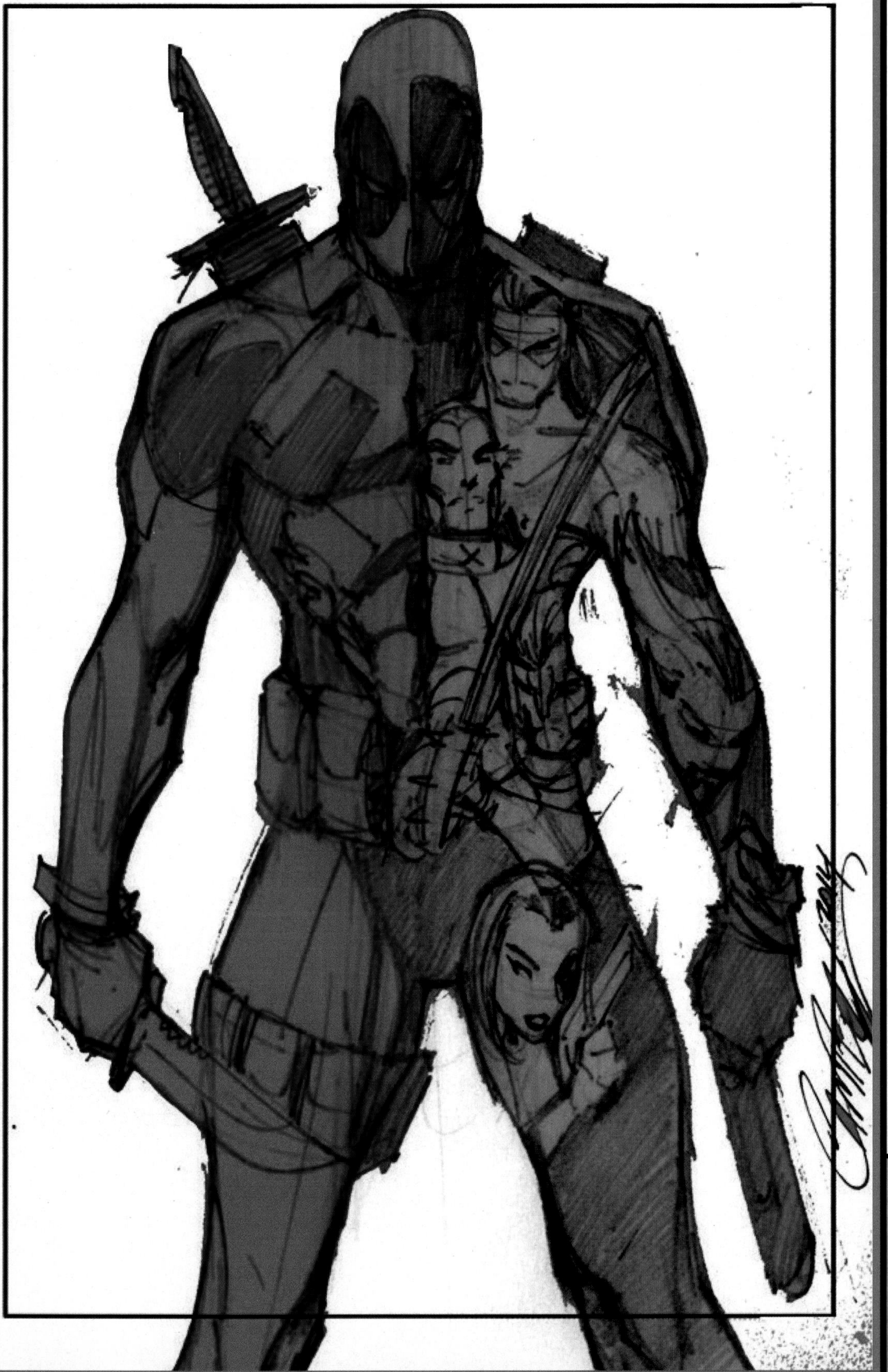

#1 VARIANT SKETCH BY J. SCOTT CAMPBELL

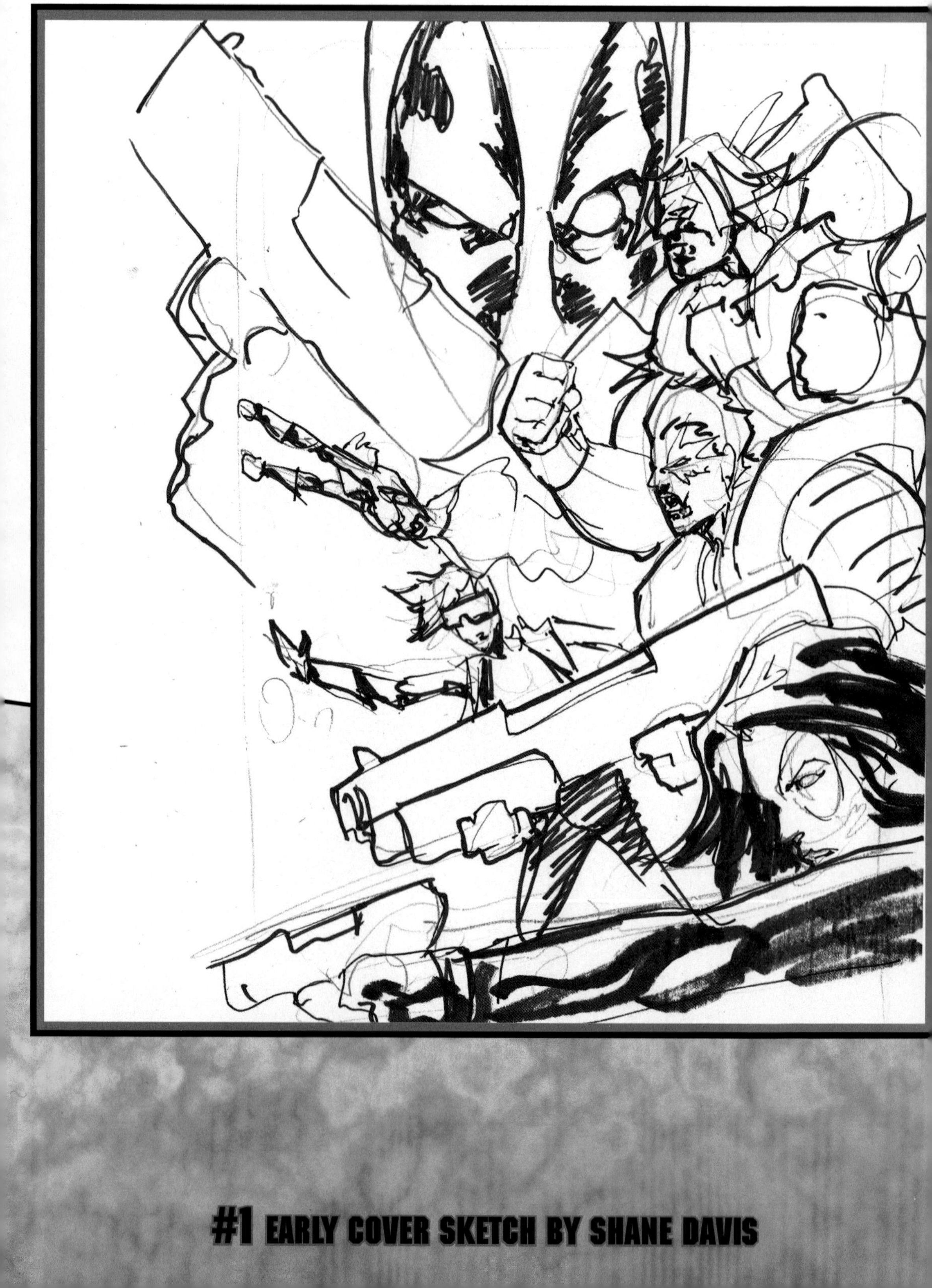

#1 EARLY COVER SKETCH BY SHANE DAVIS

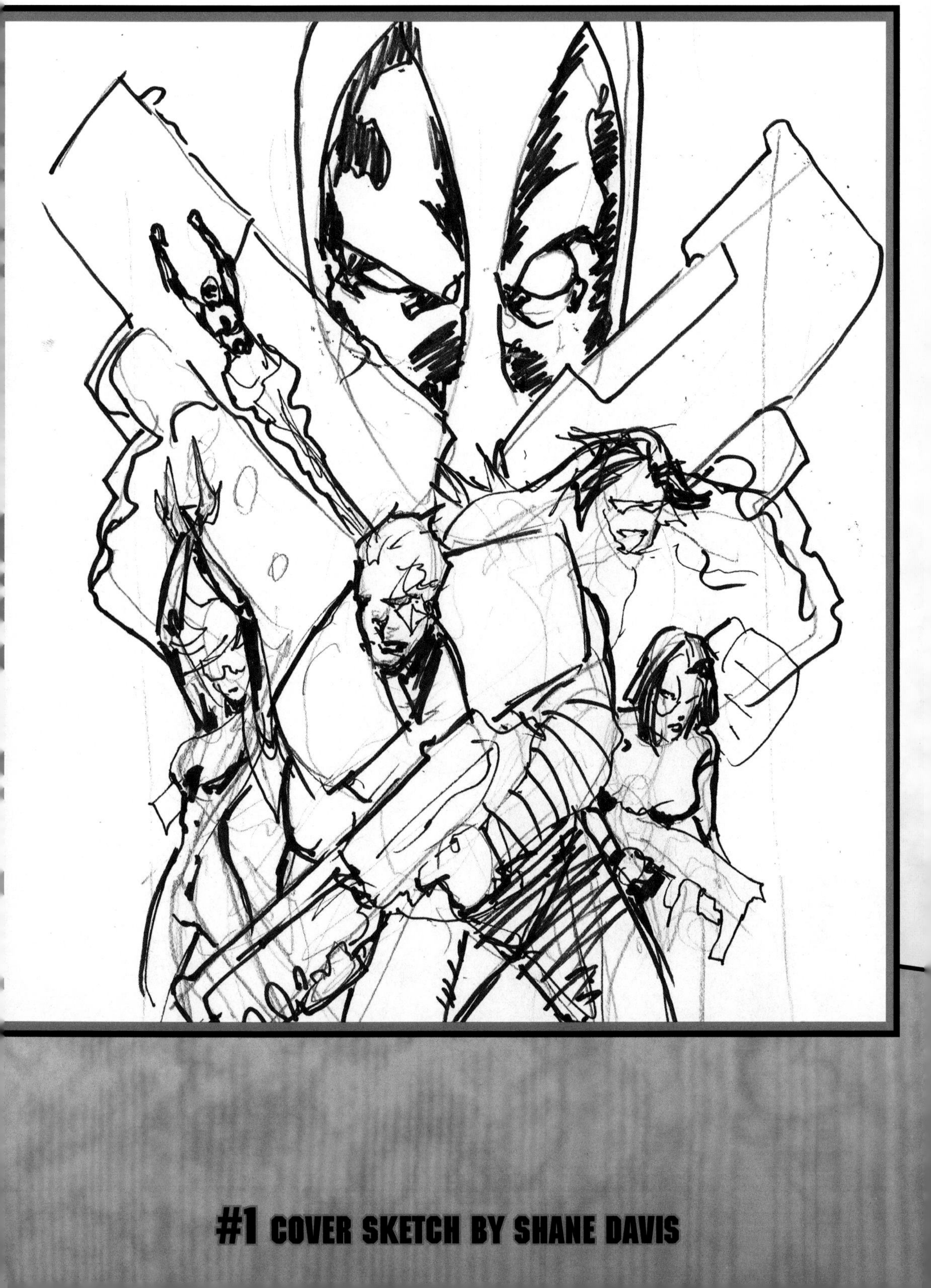

#1 COVER SKETCH BY SHANE DAVIS

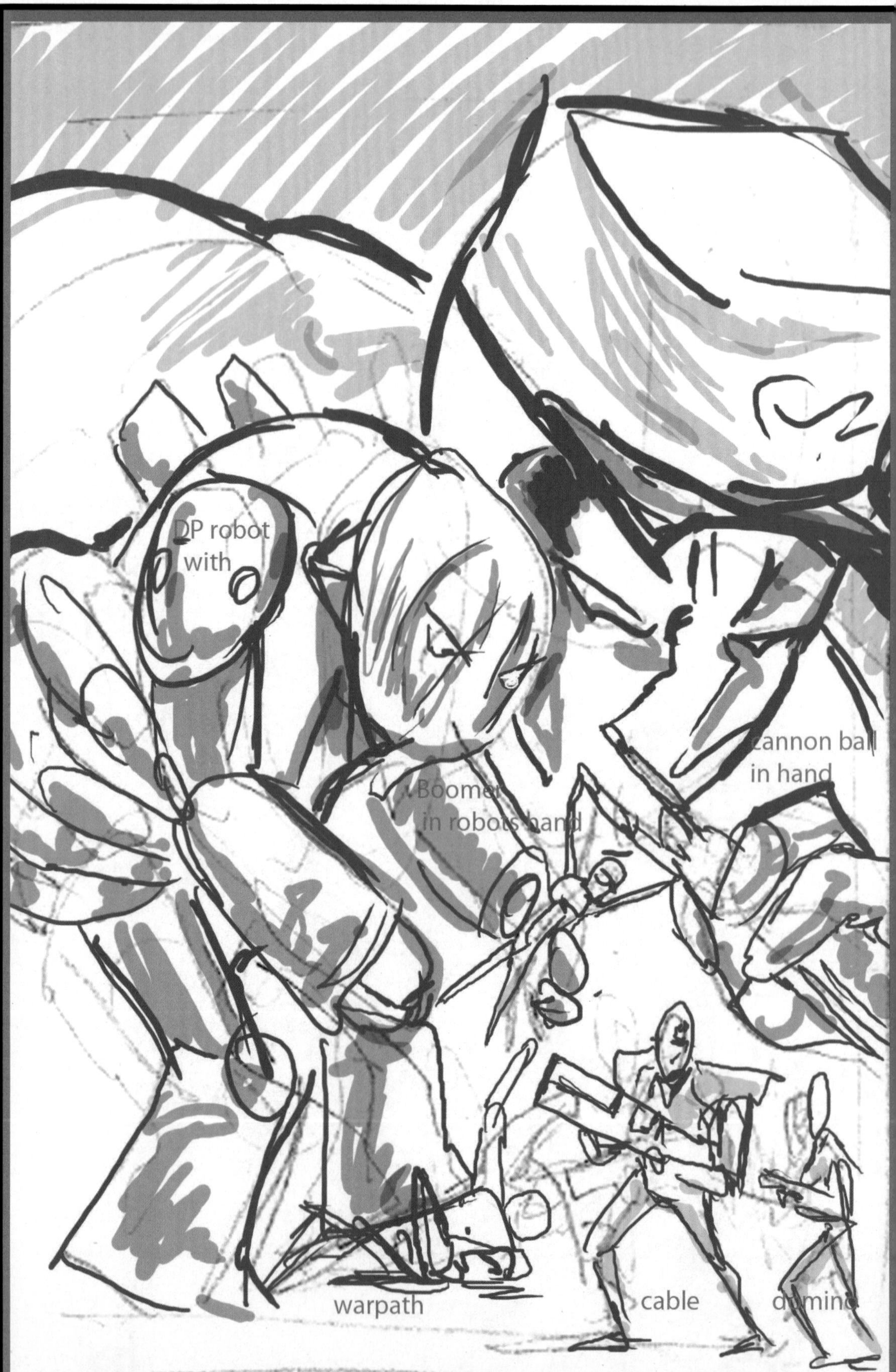
DP robot
with
Boomer
in robots hand
cannon ball
in hand
warpath
cable
domino

#2 COVER SKETCH BY SHANE DAVIS

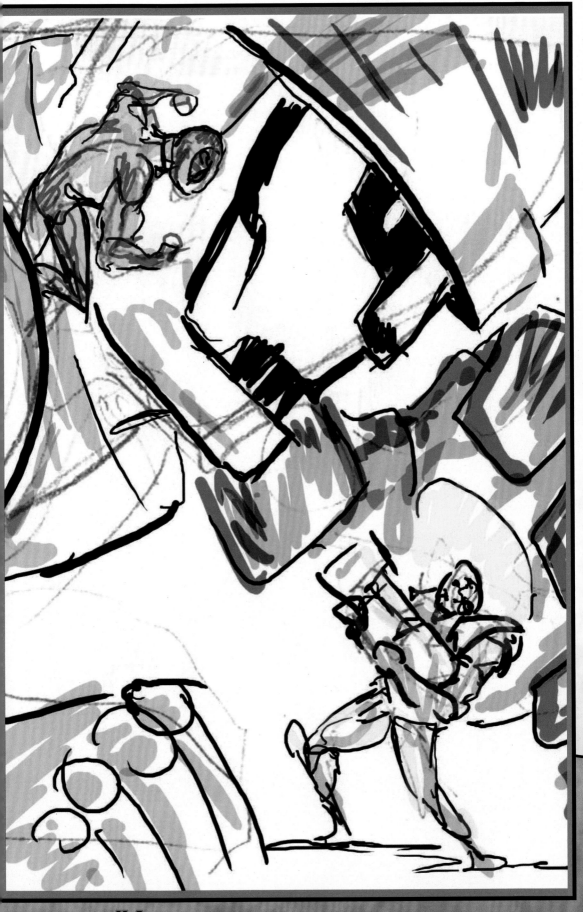

#4 EARLY COVER SKETCH BY SHANE DAVIS

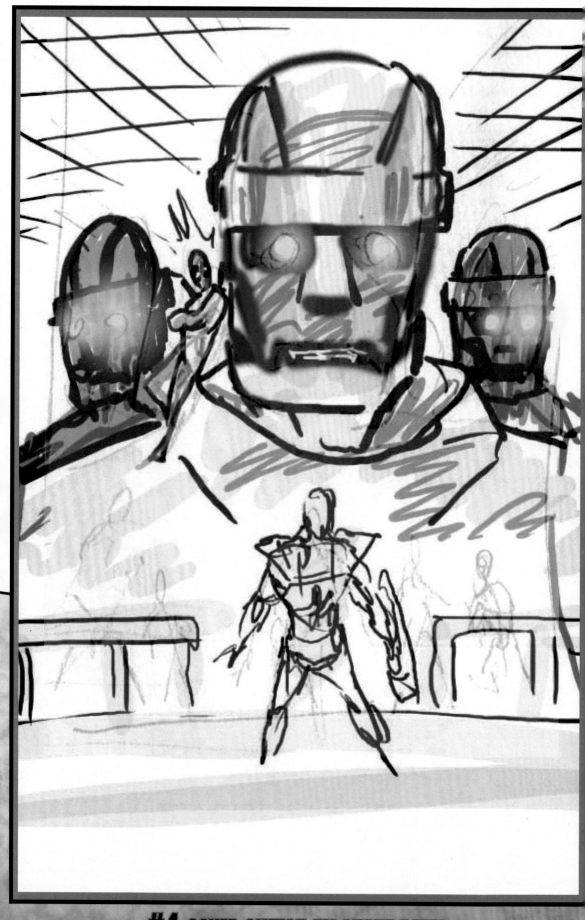

#4 COVER SKETCH BY SHANE DAVIS

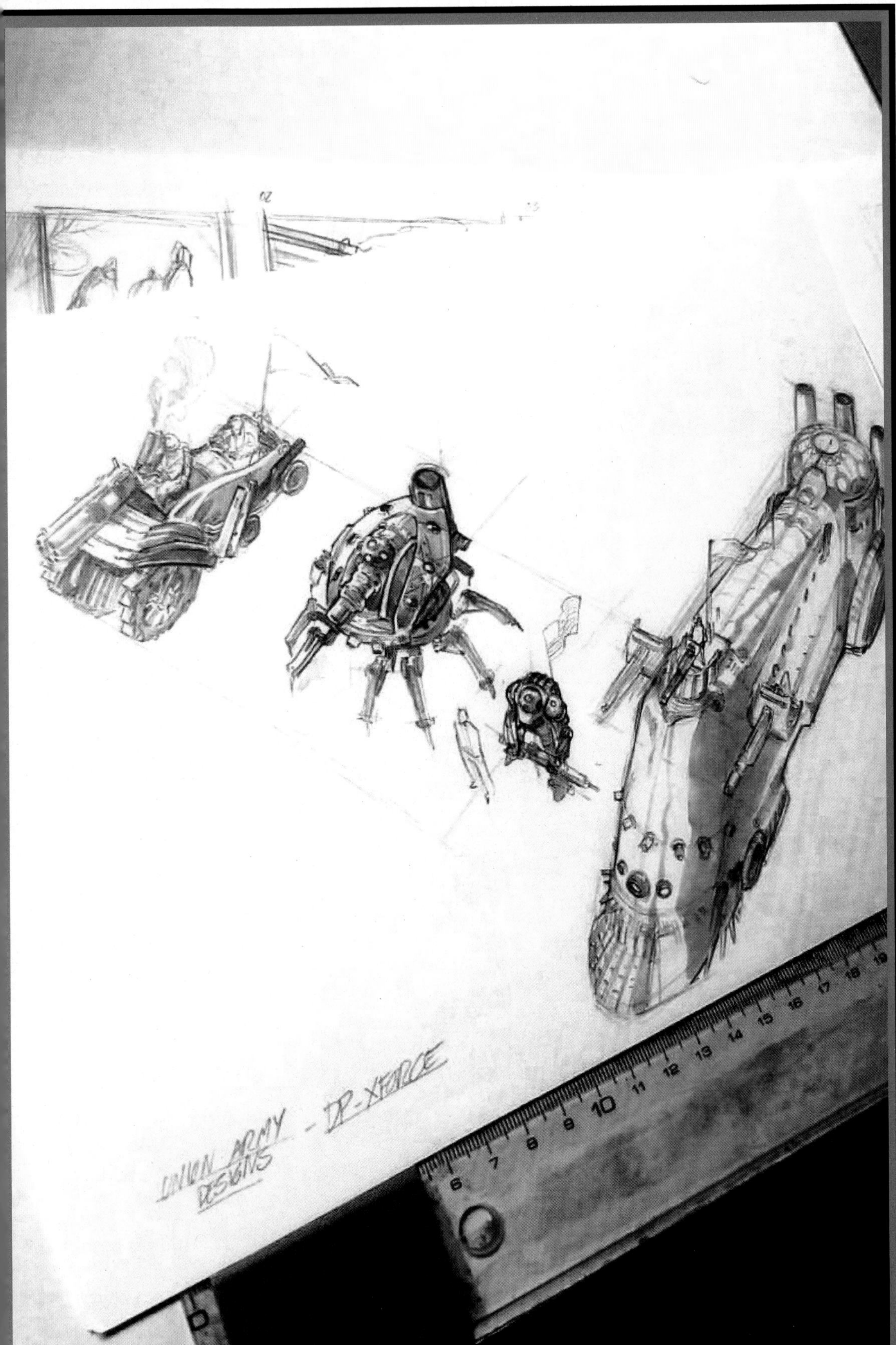
UNION ARMY DESIGNS
- DP-XFORCE

ARMY DESIGNS BY PEPE LARRAZ

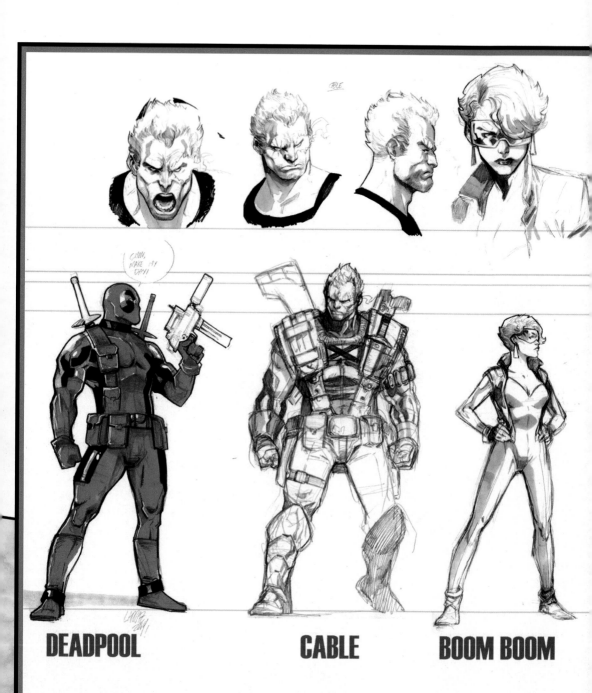

DEADPOOL

CABLE

BOOM BOOM

CHARACTER DESIGNS BY PEPE LARRAZ

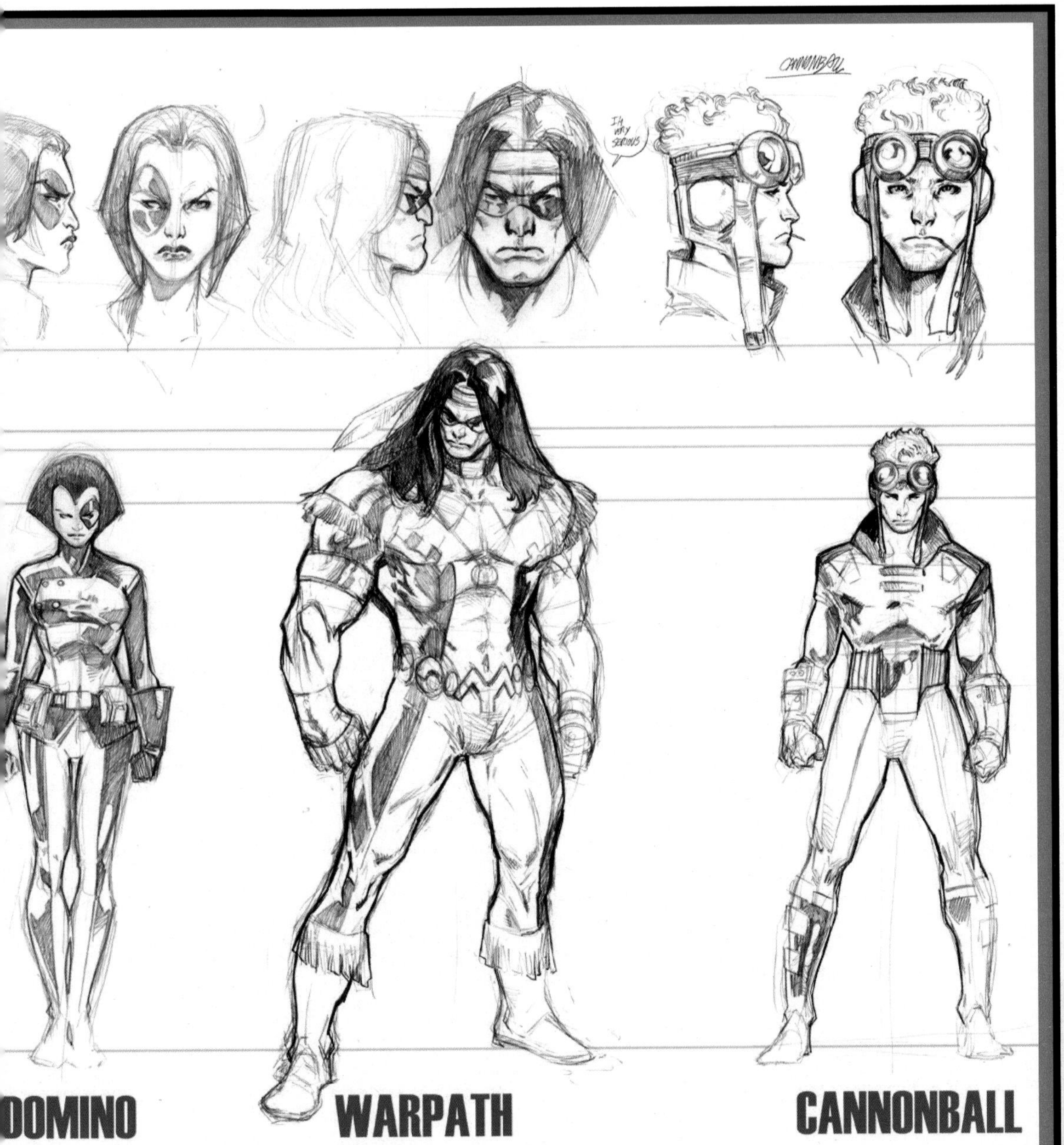
CANNONBALL
I'M VERY SERIOUS
DOMINO
WARPATH
CANNONBALL

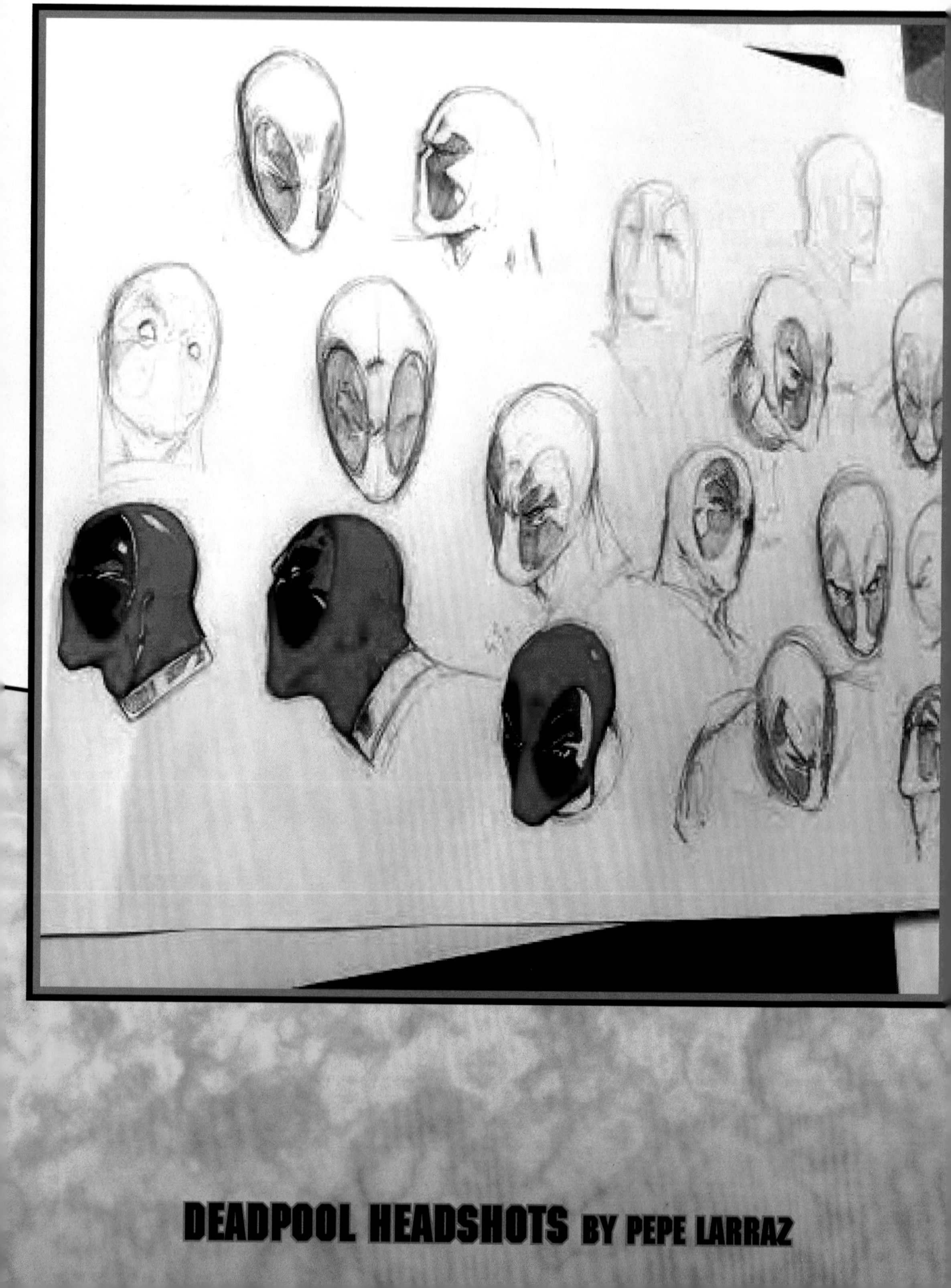

DEADPOOL HEADSHOTS BY PEPE LARRAZ

DEADPOOL VS XFORCE CONCEPTS.
TRIED TO KEEP THE SENTINEL'S FEELING IN HEAD AN PROPORTION
PANZER SENTINEL
NAZIS STATES FLAG!
no offense! it's on the script!
TALBOT'S POWER SUIT
TRON MEETS ARMANI.
5 DEADPOOL NAZI SUIT.
SWASTIKAS (VERY SUBTLE)
IRON CROSS, WHITE BANDS
METAL SHOULDER PADS
WHITE GLOVES AND BELT SIMILAR TO NAZIS UNIFORMS.

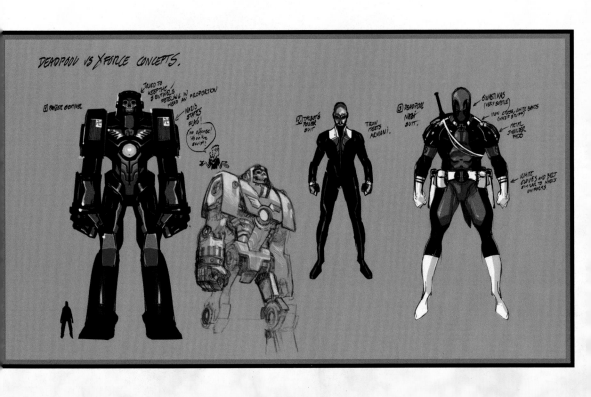

DEADPOOL SKETCHES BY PEPE LARRAZ

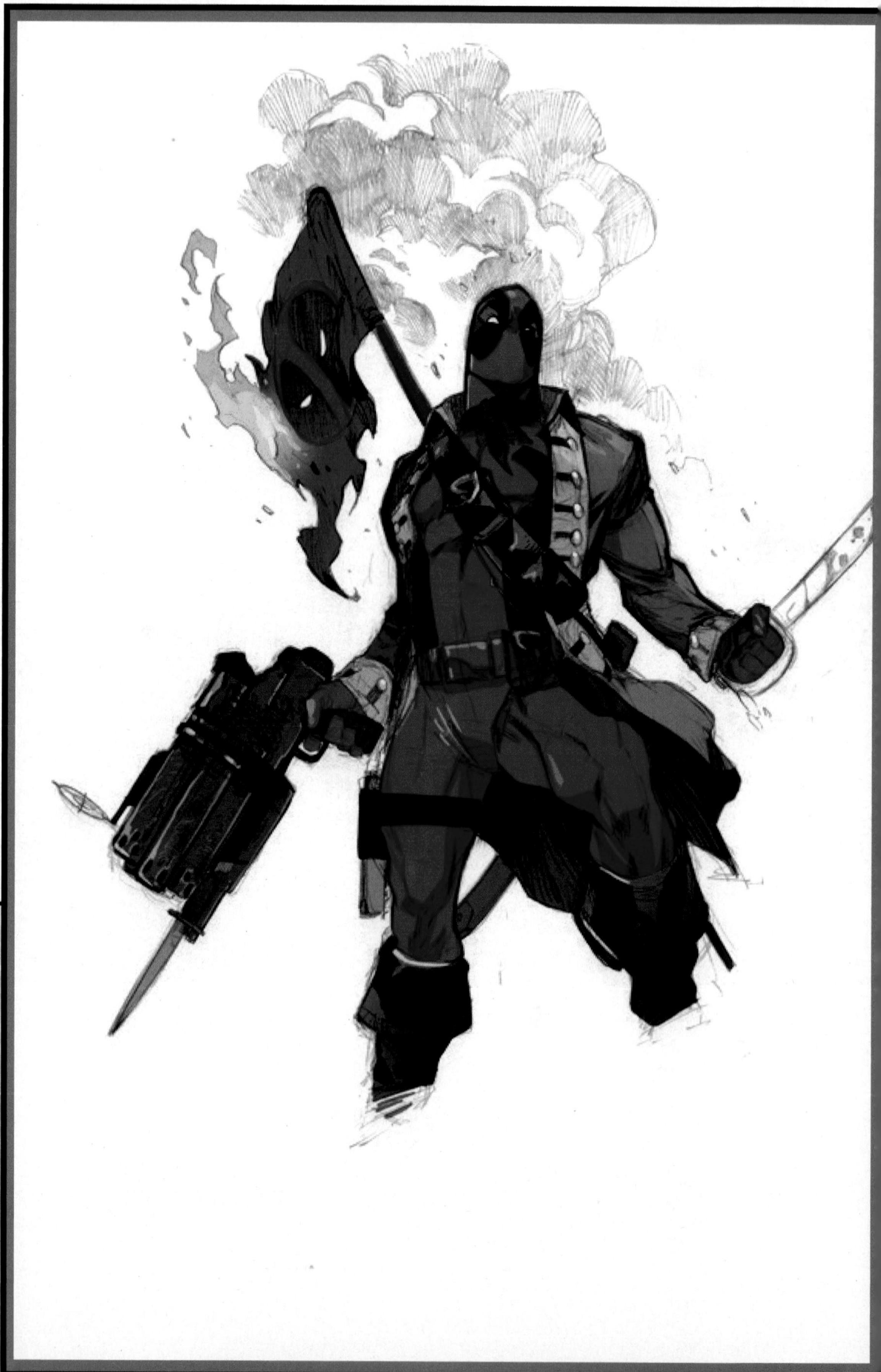

DEADPOOL SKETCH BY PEPE LARRAZ

#1 PAGES 1 & 2 INKS BY PEPE LARRAZ

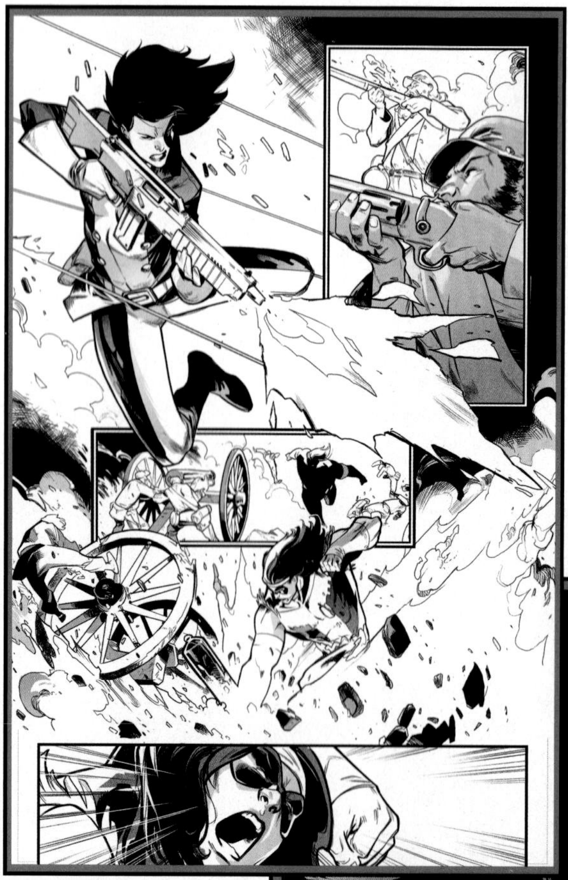

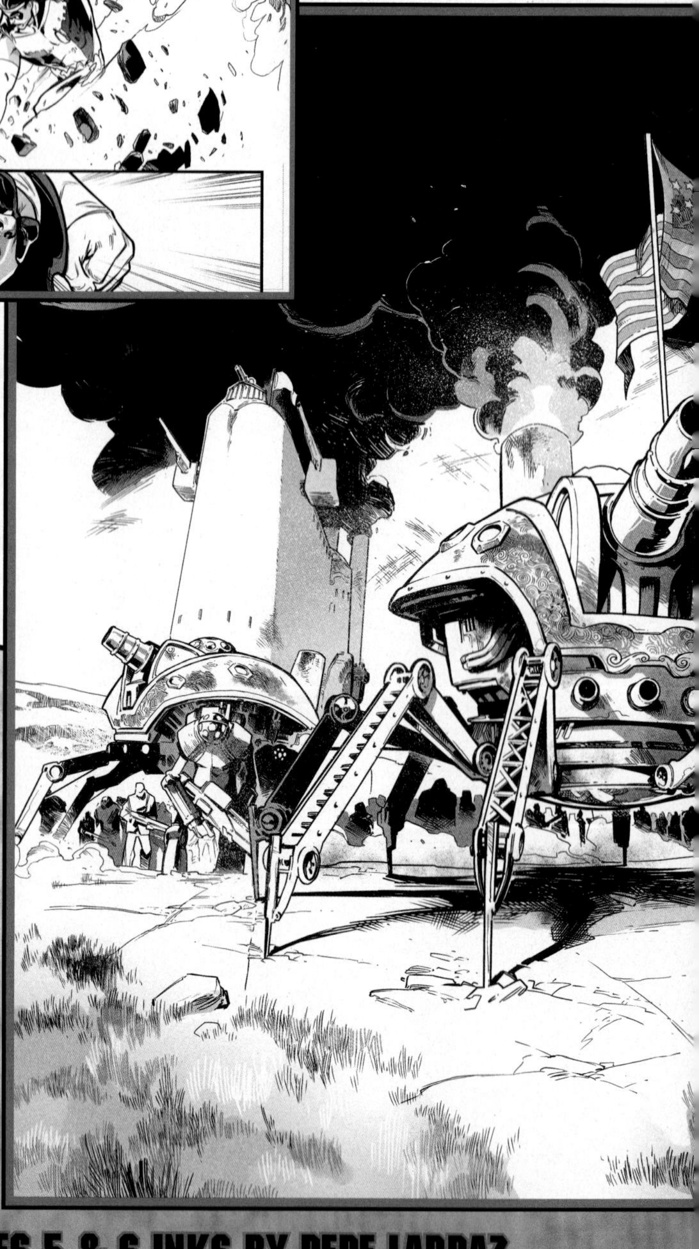

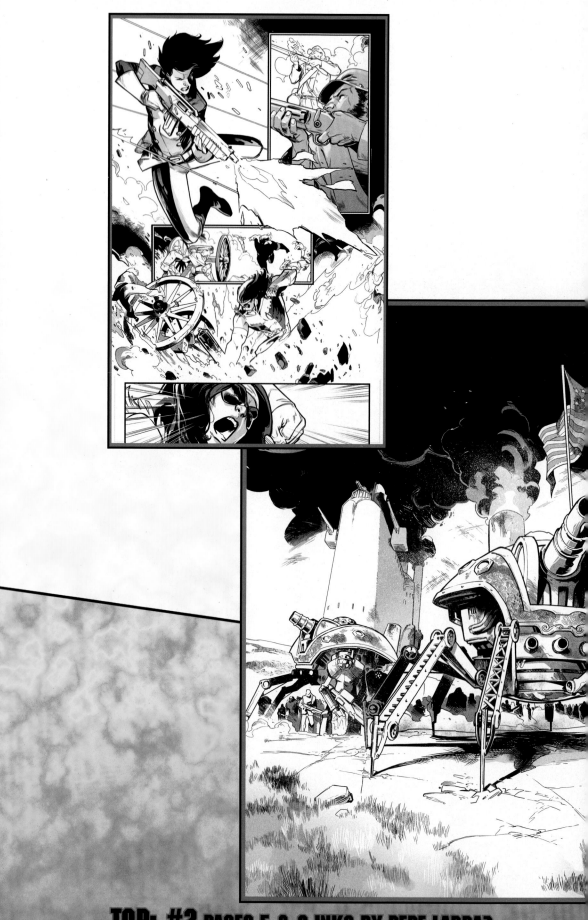

TOP: #2 PAGES 5 & 6 INKS BY PEPE LARRAZ

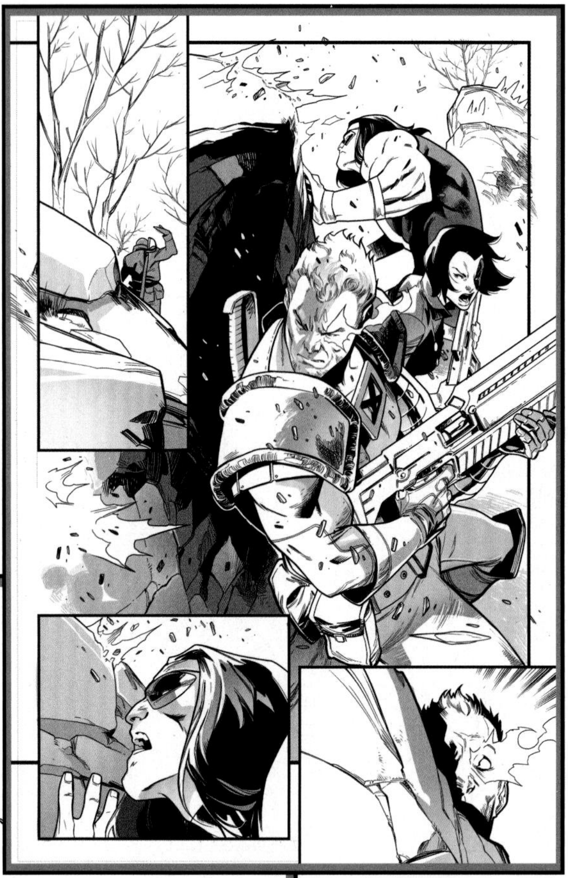

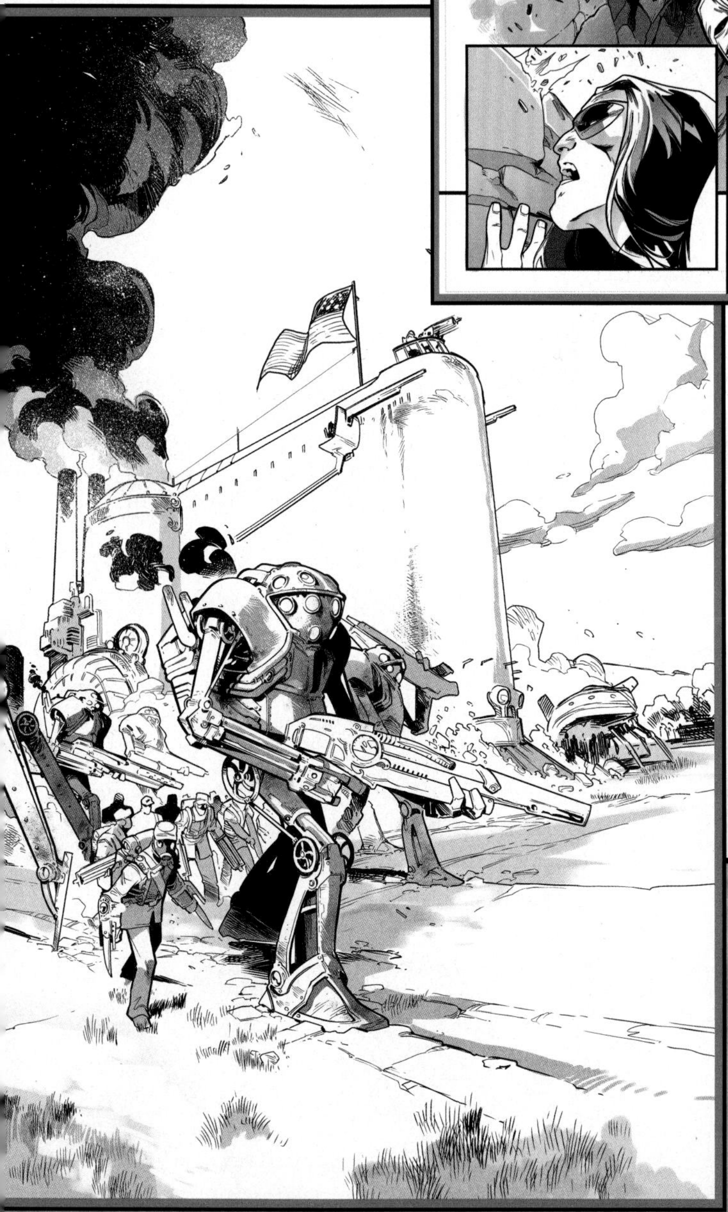

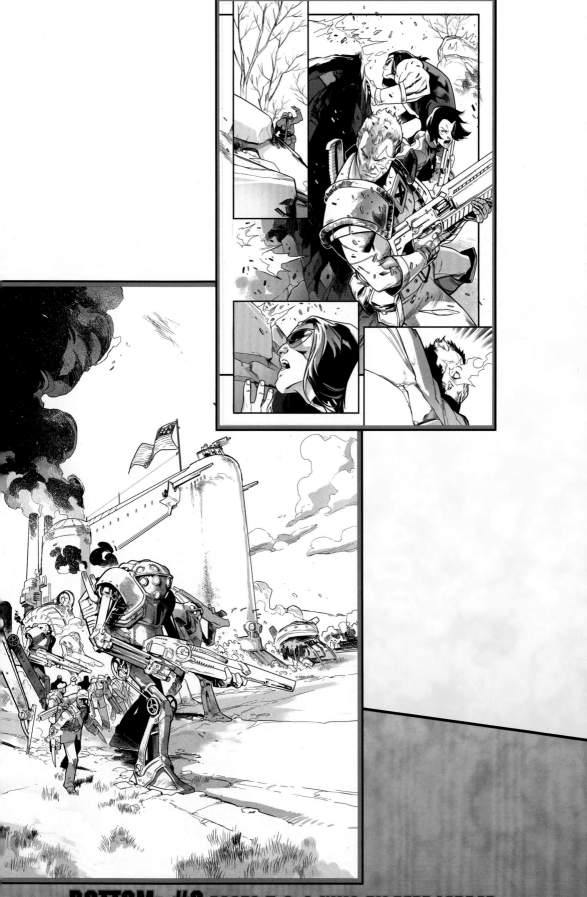

BOTTOM: #2 PAGES 7 & 8 INKS BY PEPE LARRAZ

#2 PAGES 9 & 10 INKS BY PEPE LARRAZ

#4 PAGES 19 & 20 INKS BY PEPE LARRAZ

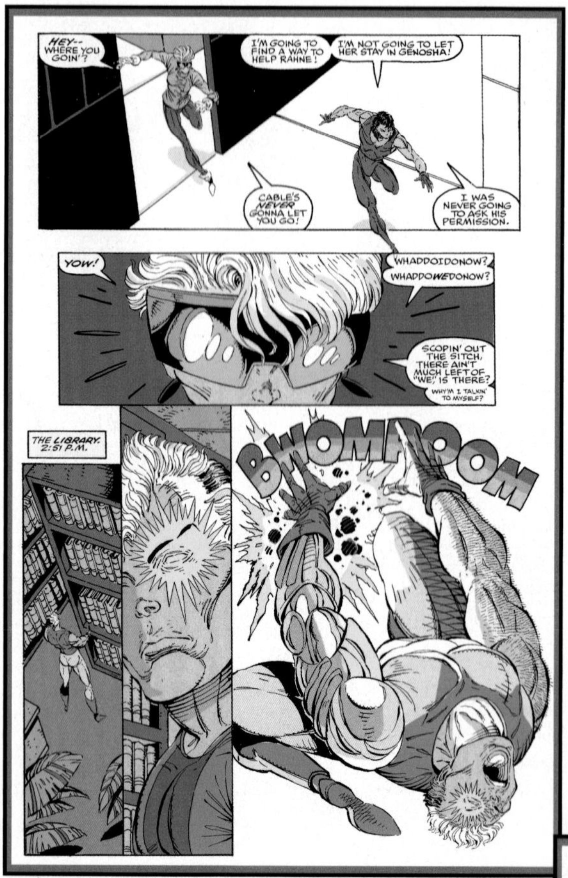
HEY-- WHERE YOU GOIN'?
I'M GOING TO FIND A WAY TO HELP RAHNE!
I'M NOT GOING TO LET HER STAY IN GENOSHA!
CABLE'S NEVER GONNA LET YOU GO!
I WAS NEVER GOING TO ASK HIS PERMISSION.
YOW!
WHADDOIDONOW?
WHADDOWEDONOW?
SCOPIN' OUT THE SITCH, THERE AIN'T MUCH LEFT OF "WE," IS THERE?
WHY'M I TALKIN' TO MYSELF?
THE LIBRARY. 2:51 P.M.
BWOMBOOM

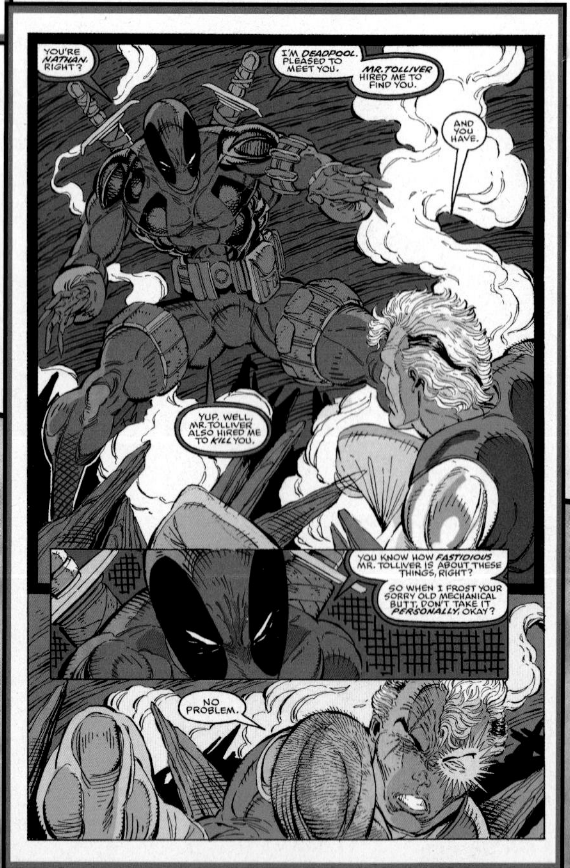
YOU'RE NATHAN, RIGHT?
I'M DEADPOOL. PLEASED TO MEET YOU.
MR. TOLLIVER HIRED ME TO FIND YOU.
AND YOU HAVE.
YUP, WELL, MR. TOLLIVER ALSO HIRED ME TO KILL YOU.
YOU KNOW HOW FASTIDIOUS MR. TOLLIVER IS ABOUT THESE THINGS, RIGHT?
SO WHEN I FROST YOUR SORRY OLD MECHANICAL BUTT, DON'T TAKE IT PERSONALLY, OKAY?
NO PROBLEM.

NEW MUTANTS #98 PAGES 13 & 14 BY ROB LIEFELD & STEVE BUCCELLATO